THE SACRED BOOKS OF THE EAST

F. MAX MULLER (ED.)

LIST OF THE 50 VOLUMES

1. Upanishads.
2. Sacred Laws of Aryas.
3. Texts of Confucianism.
4. Zend-Avesta.
5. Pahlavi Texts.
6. Qur'an.
7. Institutes of Vishnu.
8. Bhagavadgita, & c.
9. Qur'an.
10. (i) Dhammapada.
10. (ii) Sutta-Nipata.
11. Buddhist Suttas.
12. Satapatha-Brahmana.
13. Vinaya Texts.
14. Sacred Laws of Aryas.
15. Upanishads.
16. Texts of Confucianism.
17. Vinaya Texts.
18. Pahlavi Texts.
19. Fo-sho-hing-tsanking.
20. Vinaya Texts.
21. Saddharma Pundarika.
22. Gaina-Sutras.
23. Zend-Avesta.
24. Pahlavi Texts.
25. Laws of Manu.
26. Satapatha-Brahmana.
27. Texts of Confucianism (Li Ki).
28. Texts of Confucianism (Li Ki).
29. Grihya-Sutras.
30 Grihya-Sutras.
31. Zend-Avesta.
32. Vedic Hymns.
33. Minor Law-Books.
34. Vedanta-Sutras.
35. Milinda.
36. Milinda.
37. Pahlavi Texts.
38. Vedanta-Sutras.
39. Texts of Taoism
40. Texts of Taoism
41. Satapatha-Brahmana
42. Atharva-veda.
43. Satapatha-Brahmana.
44. Satapatha-Brahmana.
45. Gaina-Sutras.
46. Vedic Hymns.
47. Pahlavi Texts.
48. Vedanta-Sutras.
49. (i) Buddhakarita.
49. (ii) Mahayana Texts.
50. A General Index

The Sacred Books of the East, Vol. 47

PAHLAVI TEXTS

Edited by

F. MAX MULLER

Translated by

E. W. WEST

PART-V

MARVELS OF ZOROASTRIANISM

GYAN

Published by

GYAN

Gyan Publishing House
5, Ansari Road
Daryaganj, New Delhi-110002
Phone: 011-47034999, 9811692060
E-mail: books@gyanbooks.com

Distribution Network
gyanbooks.com
India, USA, Canada, UK, Australia, France

ISBN : 978-81-212-2937-1 (Set)
ISBN : 978-81-212-2755-1 (PB)
First Published, 1897

2nd Impression 2021

Printed at: Gyan Press, Delhi.

The Sacred Books of the East, Vol. 47

Pahlavi Texts, Part-V
Edited by: F. Max Muller, Translated by: E. W. West

THE

SACRED BOOKS OF THE EAST

TRANSLATED

BY VARIOUS ORIENTAL SCHOLARS

AND EDITED BY

F. MAX MÜLLER

VOL. XLVII

Oxford

AT THE CLARENDON PRESS

1897

PAHLAVI TEXTS

TRANSLATED BY

E. W. WEST

PART V

MARVELS OF ZOROASTRIANISM

Oxford

AT THE CLARENDON PRESS

1897

CONTENTS.

INTRODUCTION.

1. In the summary account of the Spend Nask, given in the eighth book of the Dînka*rd*, chapter XIV, it is stated in § 4 (see S. B. E., vol. xxxvii, p. 32) that many marvels, owing to Zaratû*s*t, are published therein, 'just as there are some which, collected and selected, are noticed by the Dînka*rd* manuscript.' This statement evidently refers to the seventh book of the Dînka*rd*, which contains the legendary history of Zaratû*s*t and his religion, related as a series of marvels extending from the creation to the resurrection of mankind. A much briefer account of some of the same details occurs at the beginning of the fifth book of the Dînka*rd*, and appears to have been abridged from a compilation which was either derived partially from a foreign source, or prepared for the use of foreign proselytes. A third compilation of similar legends is found among the Selections of Zâ*d*-sparam. And a careful translation of these three Pahlavi Texts constitutes the Marvels of Zoroastrianism contained in this volume.

2. As the extent of Dk. VII is about 16,000 Pahlavi words (without allowing for one folio lost), it probably contains about four-fifths of the details included in the Spend Nask, the Pahlavi version of which has been estimated, in S. B. E., vol. xxxvii, p. 469, to extend to 20,500 words. It says very little about Zaratû*s*t's conferences with the sacred beings (mentioned in Dk. VIII, xiv, 5, 6), and gives no description of the other world and the way thither (as reported ibid. 8). But it probably contains many verbatim extracts from other parts of the Pahlavi version of the Spend Nask, which appear, however, to have been previously collected in the Exposition of the Good Religion, an older MS. than the Dînka*rd*, which is quoted as an authority in Dk. VII, i, 2.

3. This seventh book commences with a detailed statement of the descent of the glorious ruling dynasty from the primeval man Gâyômar*d*, through his descendants, the Pê*s*dâ*d*ian and Kayânian rulers, to Kaî-Vi*s*tâsp. Among the individuals, rarely mentioned elsewhere, are the sacred being Hadish (the protector of homesteads in the Visperad), Vâêgere*d* the brother of king Hôshâng, Pâtakhsrôbô king of the Arabs, and Aôshnar the chancellor of Kaî-Ûs. Zaratû*s*t and the three millennial apostles are also mentioned, but the contents of this first chapter are probably derived from the *K*itradâ*d* Nask (see Dk. VII, xiii, 20) and from Yt. XIX, 25–93.

4. Chapter II begins the legendary history of Zaratû*s*t with the descent of his glory, from the presence of Aûha*r*ma*z*d to the house in which Zaratû*s*t's mother was about to be born; and, alarmed at her radiance, the Kavîgs and Karaps, or ruling priests of the district, oblige her father to send her away to another valley, where Pôrûshâspô resided, to whom she was afterwards married; and several legends are related, in which both the archangels and archdemons are active agents, which lead on to the birth of Zaratû*s*t, thirty years before the end of the ninth millennium of the universe, and his complete genealogy is given.

5. Chapter III begins with his laughing at birth, and describes the ill-will of the Karaps, or priests of those times, and their many attempts to destroy him during his childhood, till he openly defied them at the age of seven. At the end of the ninth millennium, when he was thirty years old, as he was bringing Hôm-water out of the fourth effluent of the Dâitî river, he met the archangel Vohûmanô who had come to invite him to a conference with Aûha*r*ma*z*d, about which no details are given.

6. Chapter IV, however, proceeds to mention that, in two years, he returned from his first conference, by order of Aûha*r*ma*z*d, to preach his religion to the Kîgs and Karaps in the presence of their ruler, Aûrvâîtâ-dang the Tûr. They seem to have listened attentively till he advocated Khvêtûkdas, when they demanded his death, and

were supported by the Tûr's brother; but the Tûr's son, who presided, remonstrated with them, and Aûrvâitâ-dang himself protected him, but refused to be converted. Zaratûst was afterwards sent to demand slaves and horses from Vêdvoîst, a rich Karap, who refused them arrogantly; he also went to Parsha*d*-g*a*u in Sagastân and cured his bull with Hôm-water, whereupon Parsha*d*-g*a*u joined him in worship, but not in public. Zaratûst repulsed the demons as in Vd. XIX, 1–4; he is then tempted by a Karap in the form of Spendarma*d*, whom he also repulses. And he is finally sent to the court of Vistâsp, where he is relentlessly opposed by the Kîgs and Karaps who obtained his imprisonment, during which he is saved from starvation by a miracle; then some of the sacred beings arrive to assist him, and Vistâsp is at last converted, twelve years after the coming of the religion when Zaratûst went to his first conference with Aûharmaz*d*.

7. Chapter V refers to the marvels of the last thirty-five years of Zaratûst's life, after Vistâsp's conversion, but says nothing about his own death, except that he departed to the best existence at the age of seventy-seven. It mentions the establishment of ordeals of thirty-three kinds, the victory of Vistâsp over Ar*g*âsp the Khyôn, the useful works and advice of Zaratûst, the compilation of the Avesta, and the birth of Pêshyôtan, the immortal ruler of Kangd*ez*.

8. Chapter VI continues this account of marvels till the death of Vistâsp, which occurred forty-three years later. The legends related are about the presentation of a heavenly chariot to Vistâsp by the soul of an old hero Srîtô who had been killed about 350 years before; and regarding the coming of two high-priests from the southern regions of the earth, ten years after the departure of Zaratûst, to enquire about the religion.

9. Chapter VII relates the marvels occurring after the death of Vistâsp until the end of the sovereignty of Irân; mentioning king Vohûmanô who was a grandson of Vistâsp, the high-priest *S*ênôv who lived throughout the second century of the religion, the devastator Alexander the Great, the four successive high-priests who restore ortho-

doxy in the fifth and sixth centuries of the religion, the apostate Rashn-rêsh of about the same period, king Artakhshatar the founder of the Sâsânian dynasty, his chancellor Tanvasar, Âtû*r*pâ*d*-î Mâ*r*aspendân and his son surnamed Avarethraba*u*, with an anonymous arch-apostate of their time, and then king Khûsrô Anôshêrvân. Finally, it condemns the proceedings of the devastators in later times, whose names are not mentioned.

10. Chapter VIII deals with the ninth and tenth centuries of the religion, which bring the millennium of Zaratû*s*t to a close. After a bitter lamentation over the anarchy in religion and government—in which parts of §§ 34 and 36 are taken from the Var*s*tmânsar commentary on Yas. XXXII in Dk. IX, xxxii, 17, 20—it refers to the arrival of *K*itrô-mêhônŏ, '*him* of the racial home,' a title of Pêshyôtanŏ, son of Vi*s*tâsp, and immortal ruler of Kangd*ez*, who arrives with 150 disciples to restore the religion and destroy the wicked, including the Turkish demons, the Arabs, and the ecclesiastical Shê*d*âspô[1] (Theodosius?). In the thirtieth year before the end of this tenth millennium Aûshê*d*ar, the Developer of Righteousness, is born, and confers with the archangels at the end of the millennium, when the sun stands still for ten days and nights.

11. Chapter IX describes the eleventh millennium, that of Aûshê*d*ar, who produces much prosperity and progress which continue until the fifth century. Then the wizard Mahrkûs appears for seven years, and produces awful winters in four of them, in which most of mankind and animals perish, till he is himself destroyed by the Dâhmân Âf*r*în. Afterwards, Yim's enclosure is opened to replenish the earth with animals and men who then begin to subsist more upon the milk of cattle, which is plentiful; and Ashavahi*s*tô interferes to diminish the slaughter of cattle. At the end of the fifth century two-thirds of the Irânians have become righteous, and in the thirtieth year before the end of this eleventh millennium Aûshê*d*ar-mâh, the Developer

[1] This name can be read Shê*d*âsfa*s* in Byt. III.

of Worship, is born, and confers with the archangels at the end of the millennium, when the sun stands still for twenty days and nights.

12. Chapter X describes the twelfth millennium, that of Aûshê*d*ar-mâh, during which mankind continue to improve, are better supplied, and have fewer wants, while deaths occur only through old age and the executioner. During the last fifty-three years, they leave off eating meat and subsist upon vegetables and milk, for which latter they substitute water for the last three years. But the old tyrant Dahâk breaks loose, and Kerêsâspô has to be roused to smite him. In the thirtieth year before the end of this twelfth millennium Sôshâns, the Triumphant Benefiter, is born; Kaî-Khûsrô and his companions afterwards arrive to assist him, and the sun stands still for thirty days and nights.

13. Chapter XI describes how Sôshâns and his assistants destroy all the evil remaining in the world, during the course of fifty-seven years, while mankind subsist for seventeen years on vegetables, thirty years on water, and ten years on spiritual food. And, at the end of these fifty-seven years, Aharman and the fiend are annihilated, and the renovation for the future existence occurs.

14. Several of the details described in Dk. VII are briefly mentioned in Dk. V, i–iv, where they are introduced by a statement of the siege of Jerusalem by Nebuchadnezzar (*Bûkht-Narsîh*) assisted by Kaî-Lôharâsp, father of Vi*s*tâsp. Excepting this account of the siege, in which the Jews are evidently called 'a congregation or tribe' (*ram*), and some remarks about the same 'tribe' at the end of Chapter IV, all the other details which are mentioned have reference only to Irânians; but they are said to be the sayings of Âtû*r*-farnbag as to the MS. which that tribe call really their Gyêmarâ (Chaps. I, 2, 3; IV, 8), as the name can be most plausibly read. Most of the strictly Irânian details have manifestly been derived from the same sources as were consulted by the writer of Dk. VII, that is, from the Pahlavi versions of the Spend and *K*itradâd Nasks. It would probably be hazardous to suppose that the Jewish compilers of the Gemara could have had access to these

sources, and it might be preferable to assume that Âtûr-farnbag was himself compiling a record of Zoroastrian traditions for the use of some converts from Judaism, to take the place of the Gemara of their former faith.

15. The Zaratûst-nâmak of Zâd-sparam is contained in the latter half (Zs. XII–XXIII) of the first series of his Selections, the former half of which, being a paraphrase of the first half of the Bundahis, has been translated in S. B. E., vol. v, pp. 155–186. In Chapter XII Zâd-sparam relates two of the earliest legends referring to Masda-worship, which he had found in old MSS. The first of these describes the appearance of the archangel Spendarmad, wearing a golden sacred girdle, at the court of king Mânûskîhar, 428 [1] years before the coming of the religion to Zaratûst when he went to his conference with the sacred beings. The other is the legend of the warrior Srîtô, the seventh brother, who was sent by Kaî-Ûs to kill the frontier-settling ox which threatened him, 300 years before the coming of the religion, with future execration by Zaratûst.

16. Chapter XIII refers to the descent of Zaratûst's glory upon his mother at her birth, and the combination of his spiritual and worldly natures; also detailing his genealogy. Chapter XIV describes the attempts of the demons to destroy him before and at his birth, when Vohûmanô entered his reasoning powers and made him laugh with delight and utter one form of the Ahunavair formula. Chapter XV is about the five Karap brothers, with their first cousins the Aûsikhshes, all descended from the demon of Wrath and a sister of king Mânûskîhar; also about the four brothers of Zaratûst who seem to be unmentioned elsewhere.

17. Chapter XVI details the attempts of one of the Karaps to destroy Zaratûst during his infancy, and the means by which he is preserved; it also explains who Râgh and Nôdar were. In Chapter XVII one of the Karaps foretells the future success of Zaratûst. In Chapter XVIII

[1] The MSS. have 528, but this would be twenty-eight years before the accession of Mânûskîhar, see the synopsis in § 55.

his father hears him accused of folly, and takes him to a Karap to be cured. In Chapter XIX the chief Karap comes to the house of Zaratûst's father, and is invited to consecrate the food set before him; but Zaratûst objects and a quarrel ensues, which so much disturbs the Karap that he leaves the house, and drops dead from his horse on the road home. In Chapter XX instances are given of Zaratûst's righteous desires, his compassionate assistance of people fording a river, his liberal disposition, his abandoning worldly desires, his pity for dogs, his wish for a good-looking wife, and his acceptance of progress even from the wicked, during his youth.

18. Chapter XXI relates that, at thirty years of age, on his way to the festival of spring, he saw in a vision all mankind following Mê*d*yômâh, his first cousin, into his presence. He then went on to the bank of the Dâitîh, and crossed its four channels, when he met Vohûmanô who led him to the assembly of the archangels, where he received instruction from Aûharmazd and saw the omniscient wisdom; the archangels also subjected him to various ordeals.

19. Chapter XXII refers to his conferences with the seven archangels, each at a different place, and extending over ten years. In Chapter XXIII, Mê*d*yômâh is converted at the end of these ten years. The next two years are spent on the conversion of Vistâsp, in which Zaratûst is assisted by some of the sacred beings, and the narrative ends by giving the dates of several other conversions, births, and deaths. But after its 300th year the religion is disturbed and the monarchy contested; referring, no doubt, to the effects of Alexander's conquest of Persia.

20. These three narratives appear to be the only connected statements of the Zoroastrian legend that remain extant in Pahlavi, and all three seem to be chiefly derived from the Sâsânian Pahlavi version of the Spend Nask, with some probable additions from the similar version of the *K*itradâ*d* Nask, as may be gathered from the summary accounts of the contents of these Nasks given in Dk. VIII, xiii, 20–xiv, 15, and translated in S. B. E., vol. xxxvii, pp. 31–34. There are, however, allusions to other legends

regarding Zaratûst to be found scattered about in Pahlavi literature, to which we shall return after mentioning the manuscript authorities for the texts translated in this volume.

21. The chief existing authority for the Pahlavi text of the Dînkard, Books III–IX, and the only independent one for Book VII, is the MS. B in Bombay, which has been fully described in S. B. E., vol. xxxvii, pp. xxxiii–xxxvii; it will therefore be sufficient here to give a short statement of the information which was there detailed at full length. This MS., written in 1659, was an unbound quarto volume of 392 folios when it was brought from Irân to Surat in 1783; after which time 70 folios became detached from various parts of the MS., but nearly all these had been discovered more than twenty years ago.

22. The writer of the MS. not only recorded the date of his own work, but also copied two previous colophons of his predecessors, with dates corresponding to A.D. 1516 and 1020, and it appears that there had been an intermediate copy about 1355. The MS. of 1020 had been copied at Bakdâd, possibly from the original MS. of the last editor of the Dînkard, which must have been completed about A.D. 900.

23. For the text of Dk. V we have a second authority, independent of B, in the MS. K43 at Kopenhagen (see S. B. E., vol. xxxvii, pp. xxxvii–viii), written shortly after 1594 and also descended from the MS. of 1020.

24. The Selections of Zâd-sparam are found in some of the old MSS., which also contain the Dâdistân-î Dînîk (see S. B. E., vol. xviii, pp. xv–xvii). Of the two MSS. used for the text of Zâd-sparam's Zaratûst-nâmak, K35 was brought from Irân to Kopenhagen in 1843. It has lost many folios, both at the beginning and end; but, before it was so mutilated, a copy (BK) of it was made, which is now in Bombay and contains a copy of its colophon, the date of which corresponds to A.D. 1592. For the text of Zs. xxii, 4–xxiv, 19, which has been lost from K35, the translator is indebted to this old copy. The other MS. authority T, belonging to Ervad Tehmuras in Bombay

(a copy of which has been used), is dated two generations earlier.

25. Regarding the period of Zâ*d*-sparam's career we are well informed by the date of the third Epistle of Mânû*sk*ihar, corresponding to A.D. 881, at which time Zâ*d*-sparam was probably in the prime of life; but his Selections were certainly compiled as late as A.D. 900, or about the same time as the completion of the Dînka*rd*. So that the Pahlavi texts, from which these three narratives of the Zoroastrian legends have been translated, were no doubt all written about A.D. 900, and the information they contain was nearly all derived from the Pahlavi versions of two of the Nasks.

26. We have reason to believe that the Pahlavi versions of Avesta texts were completed in the fourth century and revised in the sixth, after the downfall of the heretic Mazdak. This may not only be clearly inferred from the traditional account of the compilation and restorations of the Avesta and Zand, preserved in Dk. IV, 21–36, and translated in S. B. E., vol. xxxvii, pp. 412–418; but is also in accordance with the actual condition of the Pahlavi versions of the liturgical Avesta texts. With the exception of a few interpolated passages, the whole of these Pahlavi versions might have been written, or revised, in the time of king Shahpûhar II (A.D. 309–379). And the exceptional passages mention no persons or events of a later date than the reign of king Khûsrô I (A.D. 531–578); being merely references to such persons as Mazdak, the heretic, and certain commentators who lived about that time.

27. If we examine the Zoroastrian legends, translated in this volume, we shall also find it difficult to discover a passage that clearly alludes to any historical personage of later date than Khûsrô I, who is named in Dk. V, iii, 3; VII, vii, 26, although the compiler of the Dînka*rd* had the traditions of 250 years of Arab rule to draw upon for facts, if he had been disposed to continue the statements of the Pahlavi Spend Nask down to his own time. No doubt, these traditions may have intensified his denunciations of

the devastators in Dk. VII, vii, 29–38; viii, 4–9, but, like most Pahlavi writers, he is careful not to mention Muhammadanism. Dk. VII, vii, 33, 34 seem to refer to some particular individual of this later time; but the references to Kaîsar and Khâkân, the Turkish demons with dishevelled hair, the Arab, and She*d*âspô (Theodosius?) of Arûm, may all have been taken from a Pahlavi version revised in the time of Khûsrô I.

28. That the original Pahlavi version was translated from an Avesta text, though many Pahlavi commentaries were intermingled, appears certain. Apart from the numerous quotations from revelation (dênô), which may be safely assumed to have had an Avesta original, there are many passages interspersed with glosses, such as the Pahlavi translators habitually used, as well as numerous sentences beginning with a verb, an Avesta peculiarity which generally disappears in an English translation. Regarding the age of this Avesta text it would be hazardous to speculate without further information than we yet possess.

29. The principal details connected with the Zoroastrian legends which have been noticed in other Pahlavi and Pâzand texts, with references to the passages where they occur, are as follows:—

*G*ôs*û*rvan informed of the future coming of Zaratûst in Bd. IV, 4.
Z.'s genealogy and family in Bd. XXXII, 1–10.
Summary account of Z. and Zoroastrianism, from the creation to the resurrection, in Dk. VIII, xiv, 1–15.
The abode of Z.'s father, when Z. was born, was on the bank of the Dâre*g*a river (Bd. XX, 32; XXIV, 15).
150 demons were prevented from destroying Z., before his birth, by the presence of a fire in his father's house (Sls. X, 4; XII, 11; Sd. XVI, 3).
Detailed account of the birth of Z. in Dk. IX, xxiv, 1–18.
When Z. first saw the archangels, he thought they were archdemons (Ep. I, x, 9).
Omniscient wisdom temporarily conferred upon Z., and what he then saw (Dk. IX, viii, 1–6; Byt. I, 1–5; II, 5–22).
He saw the soul of Davâns tormented in hell, excepting one foot (AV. XXXII, 1–6; Sls. XII, 29; Sd. IV, 3–11).

He also saw a mortal with children and an immortal without any, and preferred the former (Dd. XXXVII, 43).
And he beheld the terrible condition of Keresâsp's soul (Dk. IX, xv, 1–4).
Advice of Aûharmazd to Zaratûst (Sd. XXV, 6–9; LXXXI, 2–16).
The demon Envy (Aresh) converses with Z. in Dk. IX, xxxi, 6–11.
Aharman tempts Z. with the promise of 1000 years dominion, in Mkh. LVII, 24–29.
About Maîdôk-mâh, in Dk. IX, xliv, 19.
Z. coming to preach to king Vistâsp, in Sg. X, 64–68.
Archangels assist Z. in converting Vistâsp, also the war with Argâsp, in Dk. VIII, xi, 2–4.
The war of the religion with Argâsp mentioned in Bd. XII, 33.
The families of Zaratûst, Hvôv, and Vistâsp mentioned in Dk. VIII, xxix, 25.
About Frashôstar and Gâmâsp in Dk. VIII, xxxviii, 68; IX, xlii, 8, 9; xliv, 17, 18.
About Kaî-Vistâsp, Frashôstar, Porûkâst, Gâmâsp, and Hûtôs in Dk. IX, xlv, 3–5.
Brâd-rûkhsh, or Brâdrô-rêsh the Tûr, mentioned as destroying the righteous man, in Dd. LXXII, 8; Sd. IX, 5; Dk. VIII, xxxv, 13; IX, x, 3.
The last millenniums mentioned in Dk. IX, xxxix, 18; xli, 6–8.
Events in the last two millenniums, in Byt. II, 22–III, 62.
The resurrection described in Bd. XXX.

30. Beyond the frequent occurrence of the names of the chief actors in the traditions, there are not many references to the Zoroastrian legends in the extant Avesta. This is owing to the fact that three-fourths of the Avesta texts, including the Nasks specially devoted to these legends, have been lost. The chief references to them that still survive in the Avesta are as follows:—

The passing on of the kingly glory from ruler to ruler, from Haoshyang,ha to Kava-Haosrava, from Zarathustra to Kava-Vîstâspa and the Saoshyant, in Yt. XIX, 25–90.
The terror of the demons on hearing of the birth of Z., in Vd. XIX, 43–47.
Z. mentioned as son of Pourushaspa in Yt. V, 18.
Verethraghna gives Z. strength, health, vigour, and keenness of sight (Yt. XIV, 33).

References to Z.'s conference with Ahura Mazda, and his rejection of the demons, in Yas. XII, 5, 6.

The demons attempt to destroy Z., and to tempt him, but are repelled by recitations, in Vd. XIX, 1–10.

Commentary on the Ahunavair, in Yas. XIX.

Z. converses with Haoma, in Yas. IX, 1–16.

Fate of the soul after death revealed to Z., in Vd. XIX, 26–34.

Z. is taught various spells, in Yt. XIV, 34–38.

He prays that he may convert the queen Hutaosa, in Yt. IX, 26; XVII, 46.

References to the battle with Aregad-aspa, in Yt. V, 109, 113, 116, 117; IX, 30; XVII, 50, 51.

Z.'s reply to Frashaostra regarding the ritual, in Yas. LXXI, 1–11.

There are also other references to Kava-Vîstâspa, Frashaostra, Gâmâspa, Pourukistâ, Maidhyômau, the Haêkadaspas, Spitamas, and Saoshyants. And the Fravashis of all the righteous persons receive homage in Yt. XIII. Of the unbelievers, the Karapans and Kavis are mentioned several times in the Gâthas and Yasts, including the Hôm Yast; and the Usikhsh once in the Gâthas.

31. So far as these references in the Avesta extend, they agree with the Pahlavi versions of the legends, and occasionally state some further particulars. We may, therefore, safely conclude that these Pahlavi versions present a fairly complete view of the Zoroastrian legends current in Sâsânian times. But we have another means of testing this conclusion more fully in the Persian Zartust-nâmah, translated by Eastwick in the Appendix to *The Parsi Religion, as contained in the Zand-Avastá*, by John Wilson, D. D. (Bombay: 1843).

32. This Zartust-nâmah contains 1570 Persian couplets, composed by Zartust Bahrâm Pazdû, apparently at the ancient city of Raî, and finished on August 12, 1278. But Eastwick's English translation was made from a good MS. of this poem, written by Dastûr Barzû Qiyâmu-d-dîn (=Kâmdîn) in 1636, belonging to the Wilson Collection and now in the library of Lord Crawford at Wigan. Zartust Bahrâm relates how a priest of Raî, named Kaî-Kâûs, son of Kaî-Khusrô, showed him an old Pahlavi MS.

narrating the history of Zartust, and offered to interpret it, if he would undertake to paraphrase it, in Persian verse. for the information of others.

33. After mentioning Z.'s grandfather and father, descended from king Frêdûn, a frightful dream of his mother is related, in which she sees herself attacked by wild beasts eager for the destruction of her son, who drives them away. She relates her dream to an astrologer, who prognosticates a wonderful career for the unborn child; but this dream is an addition to the Pahlavi texts.

34. The child is born, and laughs at birth, exciting admiration among the women and dismay among the magicians. Dûrânsarûn, their chief, comes to see the child. and tries to kill him with a dagger; but his hand is withered, and the magicians carry off the child, who is exposed to death from fire, oxen, horses, and wolves, but all in vain, as his mother brings him home safe on each occasion. Another magician, named Bartarûsh, then foretells that Z. cannot be destroyed, and will establish a new religion; and he repeats this to the child's father, naming Gustâsp as his future protector. This narrative corresponds with Dk. VII, iii, 2–31; but then follows the addition that he was confided to the care of an old man, named Barzînkarûs, till he completed his seventh year.

35. Then Dûrânsarûn and Bartarûsh went together to see him, and tried their magic arts upon him in vain (ibid. 32, 33). Afterwards, when Z. was sick, Bartarûsh supplied him with filthy drugs, but he threw them on the ground, which seems to be another version of Zs. XVIII, 5, 6. Then follows a paraphrase of Dk. VII, iii, 34–48, and Zs. XX, 4, 5; XXI, 1–20, 23–27, with some additional remarks about worship and the Avesta being taught to Z. The conferences with the six archangels are more detailed than in Zs. XXII, and more ritualistic in their tendency.

36. When Z. returns to the earth, he is met by the demons and magicians, who oppose him, but are killed or dispersed by the utterance of an Avesta text; in which account we have an extreme condensation of Dk. VII, iv, 36–46, 57–62. He then goes to the court of king Gustâsp,

where he is hospitably received by the king, surrounded by his princes and wise men. With the latter Z. enters into argument, and overcomes them all successively. This is repeated, till all the learned of the realm are vanquished in argument, in the course of three successive days.

37. Then Z. produces the Avesta and Zand, and reads a chapter; but the king hesitates to accept it, until he learns more about it; and Z. retires to his lodgings. In the meantime, the wise men form a conspiracy to ruin Z., by secreting in his lodgings, with the connivance of his doorkeeper, many of the impure things used by sorcerers. The next day, while the king and Z. are examining the Avesta, the wise men denounce Z. as a sorcerer; his lodgings are searched, and the impurities are brought to the king, who becomes angry and commits Z. to prison.

38. Now the king had a magnificent black horse, and when Z. had been a week in prison, this horse fell sick, and was found with its four feet drawn up to its belly. When the king was informed, he summoned his wise men, but they could suggest no remedy; so the king and all his people remained fasting all day and lamenting, and the jailer forgot to take any food to Z. till the evening, when he told Z. about the state of the black horse.

39. Z. requested the jailer to inform the king that he could cure the horse; and the king, on hearing this the next day, releases Z., who undertakes to restore the horse's limbs to their natural state, on receiving four solemn promises, one for the cure of each leg. Three of these promises are that the king, his son Isfendyâr (=Spend-dâ*d*), and the queen, should each undertake to accept his religion and never forsake it; and the fourth promise is that the false accusation of sorcery, made by the wise men, should be investigated.

40. After each promise Z. prays vehemently, and each limb is restored to use. While, on the confession of Z.'s doorkeeper, the wise men are convicted of fraudulent deceit, and are sent to execution. The Persian version is here a highly embellished paraphrase of Dk. VII, iv, 64–70, especially in the horse episode.

41. King Gustâsp next asks Z. to pray for information as to the king's future position in the other world, also that he may become invulnerable, omniscient as to worldly affairs, and immortal; but Z. tells him that he must be satisfied with the first wish for himself, and the remaining three for other persons. The next day, while the king is sitting in court with Z. present, horsemen arrive, who are the archangels Bahman and Ardabahist, with the spirits of the Khûrdâd and Gusâsp fires. They are sent to testify the truth of Z.'s mission, and to urge the king to accept the religion; this he does, and they then depart; when Z. informs the king that his four wishes will be granted, as he will soon see. For some of these details see Dk. VII, iv, 74–82.

42. Zartust then performs the Darun ceremony, having provided wine, perfume, milk, and a pomegranate. After reciting prayers from the Avesta, he gives the wine to the king to drink, who then falls into a trance and sees his own future position in heaven, and those of others. His son Peshôtan receives the milk which makes him immortal. The perfume, or incense, is given to *G*âmâsp who obtains knowledge of all events till the resurrection. And Isfendyâr, the warlike son of Gustâsp, eats one grain of the pomegranate and becomes invulnerable. The Pahlavi versions are silent about the king's four wishes and their fulfilment, except such hints as may be conveyed in Dk. VII, iv, 84–86. Afterwards, Z. reads the Avesta to the king and comments upon it; concluding with praises of the creator.

43. To this narrative Zartust Bahrâm adds a further episode of Z. asking for immortality, at the time when he went with Bahman to confer with the creator. His request is refused, but the creator gives him a drop of liquid to drink, like honey, and he sees everything in both worlds, as in a vision. When he wakes up, he relates what he saw in heaven and hell; and also describes a tree with seven branches of gold, silver, copper, brass, lead, steel, and mixed iron, respectively, overshadowing the world. The creator explains that these seven branches represent seven

powerful personages who arise in successive ages of the world. The golden branch is Z. himself, the silver is Gustâsp, the copper is an Askânian king, the brass is Ardashîr the Sâsânian, the lead is king Bahrâm (Gôr), the steel is Nôshêrvân who destroys the heretic Mazdak, and the mixed iron is the malicious monarch who upsets the true faith. Then follow many details of the lamentable evils which then occur; and when the Hazârahs[1] appear, the condition of Irân becomes still worse. as described in Byt. II, III, until the arrival of king Bahrâm the Hamâvand from India, and Peshôtan from Kangdiz, who restore the Irânian monarchy and religion.

44. This additional narrative is evidently a paraphrase of the Pahlavi Bahman Yast, translated in S. B. E., vol. v, pp. 191–235; and that Pahlavi text appears to be merely an enlarged edition of Fargard VII of the Sûdkar Nask, of which a short summary is given in Dk. IX, viii.

45. From the foregoing epitome of the Persian Zartustnâmah, it will be evident that its author's information was a combination of the statements still surviving in Dk. VII and Zs. XII–XXIII, so far as they suited his fancy and convenience. Many statements are omitted. others either condensed, or greatly elaborated; but very few novelties can be detected, excepting such as are clearly due to the writer's own imagination. Whether any small residuum of these novelties can be attributed to other sources than the Persian writer's fancy, must remain doubtful until some older authority for such details is discovered.

46. With regard to Z.'s vision of heaven and hell, which is mentioned in Zartust Bahrâm's final episode, his immediate informant was certainly Byt. II, 11–13; but the original authority was the Spend Nask, as summarized in Dk. VIII, xiv, 7, 8, although Dk. VII omits this incident, and Zs. XXI, 21, 22 merely mentions the bodily appearance of the omniscient wisdom, without referring to Z.'s vision. The details of the conferences with the six archangels,

[1] Those specially belonging to the latter millenniums, probably meaning the people who were expected to make most of the last two centuries intolerably wicked.

which are summarized in Dk. VIII, xiv, 9, as having existed in the Spend Nask, are also omitted in Dk. VII, though briefly stated in Zs. XXII.

47. It is worthy of notice that Z. was first sent to offer his religion to the Kîgs and Karaps and their sovereign, Aûrvâîtâ-dang the Tûr (see Dk. VII, iv, 2–20), who seem to have received his doctrines favourably, excepting his advocacy of Khvêtûk-das[1], which led to their rejection of his proposal. He was next sent to the Karap Vêdvôîst (ibid. 21–28), whom Aûharmazd had hitherto befriended; but this Ḳarap was rejected for illiberality and arrogance. Z. then went to Parshad-tôrâ in Sagâstân (ibid. 31–35), taking some Hôm-water with him, to cure an infirm bull belonging to this chieftain, as soon as the latter had accepted the religion in public; the chieftain assented to the religion, though only privately, but this was sufficient to obtain the cure of his bull. It was only after these three trials that the conversion of king Vistâsp was attempted.

48. There is some difficulty in understanding the exact difference between the primeval religion and that taught by Zaratûst. When Dk. VII, i, 9–11 speaks of Aûharmazd talking with Masyê and Masyâôî; or Hadish tells them of Aûharmazd, the archangels, and the Ahunavaîr (ibid. 12, 13); or the sacred beings are said to have taught them the primitive arts (ibid. 14); or we are told of the existence of demons in the times of Hôshâng and Tâkhmôrup (ibid. 18, 19); or of Ashavahistô in the time of king Pâtakhsrôbô (ibid. 34); it may be urged that the mention of these beings in connection with the men of those times is no proof that their existence was known then. Because it only shows that the old writers, being satisfied that these beings existed in their own time and were immortal, only logically assumed that they must have existed in former times. The really weak point in their argument being the assumption of the existence of such beings in their own time.

49. Safer conclusions may be formed by noticing the

[1] For the meaning of this term, as defined by the texts which use it, see S. B. E., vol. xviii, pp. 389–430.

dogmas that Zaratûst most strongly advocates and reprobates. When he goes to his first conference (Dk. VII, iii, 56–62) he goes in search of righteousness. When he went to Aûrvâîtâ-dang, as mentioned above, he advocated the praise of righteousness, scorn of the demons, and the observance of ceremonies; but it was only his scorn of the demons, which took the form of Khvêtûk-das, that the Karaps really rejected. In Dk. VII, iv, 14, he says, 'worldly righteousness is the whole worship of the demons, and the end of the Ma*zd*a-worship of Z.' Though the Hôm plant was sacred before Z.'s birth (ibid. ii, 22–47), the Hôm-water (ibid. iv, 29–35) seems to have been a distinctive token of Z.'s religion; also chanting the Ahunavair (ibid. iv, 38, 41, 42, 56, 61) and the Avesta in general (ibid. 63). The perverted religion and demonizing of the Kîgs and Karaps appear to have been the worst faults he had to find with them (ibid. 64, 67). And the archangels tell Vi*s*tâsp that the world requires the good religion which proceeds through Z.'s recitation, so he should chant the Ahunavair and Ashem-vohû, and not worship the demons (ibid. 79, 80). Again, when Dûrâsrôb and Brâ*d*rôk-rêsh partake of food with Pôrûshâspô and Zaratûst (ibid. iii, 34, 38), the latter does not object to the form of worship proposed, but to the person selected to conduct it; and he then proclaims his own reverence for the righteous and the poor.

50. From these statements we may conclude that the old writers, who have handed down these legends from ancient times, were of opinion that Zaratûst was not so much the founder of a totally new religion, as he was a reformer who retained as much of the prior religion as was not seriously objectionable. While strongly insisting upon the necessity of reverencing all good spirits, he strictly prohibited all propitiation of evil spirits. His law was to resist and destroy all that is evil and injurious to man, and to respect and honour all that is good and beneficial to him. According to the legends, he seems to have found little gross idolatry, in the form of image-worship, to reprobate. From the times of the idol-worship encouraged by Dahâk in Bâpêl (Dk. VII, iv, 72), and of the destruction of the

celebrated idol-temple on the shore of Lake *Kêk*ast by Kaî-Khûsrôî (ibid. i, 39; Mkh. ii, 95), we find nothing in the legends about this form of idolatry, till 'the oppressiveness of infidelity and idol-worship,' shortly after the downfall of the Sâsânians, is lamented (Dk. VII, viii, 6). Demon-worship (ibid. iii, 35; iv, 30; vii, 17, 36, 37; viii, 7, 34), although a term sometimes applied to idolatry, seems to be often used in its literal sense of 'worship of evil spirits,' one form of which is described by Zaratû*s*t (ibid. iv, 47–53).

51. Another interesting study, for which these Zoroastrian legends supply materials, is the traditional chronology which they contain; and how far it will be found, upon examination, to harmonize with the system stated in Bd. XXXIV, or to explain the manifest inaccuracies of that system. The matter is rather complicated, but the Zoroastrian system can be connected with the European system of chronology with some degree of probability.

52. The epoch of Zoroastrian chronology is 'the coming of the religion,' but it has long been doubtful whether this event was the birth of Zaratû*s*t, or his going to conference with the sacred beings, or the acceptance of the religion by Vi*s*tâsp. Any doubt, however, as to the meaning of the phrase, has now been removed by the statement in Dk. VII, viii, 51, that the first century of the religion is that from the time when Zaratû*s*t came forth to his conference, which event happened when he was thirty years old (ibid. iii, 51, 60, 62). It is also stated, in Bd. XXXIV, 7, that Vi*s*tâsp reigned thirty years before the coming of the religion, that is, before Zaratû*s*t went to his conference. From these data it is evident that the traditional Zoroastrian chronology makes the birth of Zaratû*s*t coincide with the accession of Vi*s*tâsp.

53. The nearest date to these events, which is well defined in both the Zoroastrian and European systems of chronology, is that of the death of Alexander, near midsummer in B.C. 323, which Bd. XXXIV, 7, 8, places 272 years after the coming of the religion, that is, after the thirtieth year of Vi*s*tâsp's reign. And if this were the first

year of the religion, the death of Alexander must have occurred in its 273rd year, according to the Bundahis.

54. But this has to be reconciled with the statement in Zs. XXIII, 12, that, after its 300th year, 'the religion is disturbed and the monarchy is contested;' which statement is expressed more definitely by AV. I, 2-6, when it asserts that the religion remained in purity for 300 years, but then Alexander came to Irân and destroyed the monarchy. If these statements be accepted literally, they imply that Alexander invaded Irân either in the 300th year of the religion, or shortly after that date, but certainly not before it. We cannot place Alexander's invasion of Irân itself at a later date than the battle of Gaugamela (B.C. 331); and if this were the 300th year of the religion, the death of Alexander (B.C. 323) must have occurred in its 308th, instead of its 273rd year, and the coming of the religion would have to be put back thirty-five years. This may be done with some plausibility by assuming an omission of thirty-five years between the reigns of Hûmâî and Dârâî, where the Bundahis passes from traditional to historical personages. Alexander's invasion must also have been a good and sufficient reason for the dissolution of the hundred-discipledom, or priestly college, established by *S*ênô, which lasted only till the 300th year, as Zs. XXIII, 11 informs us.

55. If we now adopt the abbreviations A.R. for '*anno religionis*' and B.R. for '*before the religion*,' we are prepared to compile the following synopsis of Zoroastrian Chronology according to the millennial system of the Bundahis, extended to the end of time, but dealing only with traditional matters, combined with the European dates of the same events, deduced from the synchronism of A.R. 300 with B.C. 331, as stated above in § 54:—

B.R. 9000, B.C. 9630. Beginning of the first millennium of Time; and formation of the Fravashis, or primary ideas of the good creations, which remain insensible and motionless for 3000 years (Bd. I, 8; XXXIV, 1).

" 6000, B.C. 6630. Beginning of the fourth millennium, when the spiritual body of Zaratûst is framed together, and remains 3000 years with the archangels (Dk. VII, ii, 15, 16), while the primeval man and ox exist undisturbed in the world, because the evil spirit is confounded and powerless (Bd. I, 20, 22; III, 1, 3, 5; XXXIV, 1).

B. R. 3000, B. C. 3630. Beginning of the seventh millennium, when the evil spirit rushes into the creation on new-year's day, destroys the primeval ox, and distresses Gâyômar*d*, the primeval man (Bd. I, 20; III, 10–20, 24–27; XXXIV, 2). Z. appears to remain with the archangels for 2969 years longer.

„ 2970, B. C. 3600. Gâyômar*d* passes away (Bd. III, 21–23; XXXIV, 2).

„ 2930, B. C. 3560. Masyê and Masyâôî had grown up (Bd. XV, 2; XXXIV, 3).

„ 2787, B. C. 3417. Accession of Hôshâng (Bd. XXXIV, 3).

„ 2747, B. C. 3377. Accession of Tâkhmôrup (ibid. 4).

„ 2717, B. C. 3347. Accession of Yim (ibid.).

„ 2000, B. C. 2630. Beginning of the eighth millennium. Accession of Dahâk (ibid. 4, 5).

„ 1000, B. C. 1630. Beginning of the ninth millennium. Accession of Frê*d*ûn (ibid. 5, 6).

„ 500, B. C. 1130. Accession of Mânû*sk*îhar (ibid. 6).

„ 428, B. C. 1058. Spenda*r*ma*d* comes to Mânû*sk*îhar at the time of Frâsiy*âv*'s irrigation works (Zs. XII, 3–6). The MSS. have B. R. 528, but to bring this date into the reign of Mânû*sk*îhar would be inconsistent with the millennial arrangement; while to assume a clerical error of one century is a probable explanation, as it makes the date more consistent with the allusion to Frâsiy*âv*, whose irrigation works, mentioned in Bd. XX, 34; XXI, 6, must have been carried out in the latter part of Mânû*sk*îhar's reign.

„ 380, B. C. 1010. Accession of Aûzôbô (Bd. XXXIV, 6).

„ 375, B. C. 1005. Accession of Kai-Kobâ*d* (ibid. 6, 7).

„ 360, B. C. 990. Accession of Kaî-Ûs (ibid. 7).

„ 300, B. C. 930. Zaratû*s*t first mentioned by the ox that Srîtô killed (Zs. XII, 7–20).

„ 210, B. C. 840. Accession of Kaî-Khûsrôî (Bd. XXXIV, 7).

„ 150, B. C. 780. Accession of Kaî-Loharâsp (ibid.).

„ 45, B. C. 675. The Glory descends from heaven at the birth of Dûk*d*ak (Zs. XIII, 1).

„ 30, B. C. 660. Accession of Kaî-Vi*s*tâsp (Bd. XXXIV, 7). Vohûmanô and Ashavahi*s*tô descend into the world with a stem of Hôm (Dk. VII, ii, 24). Zaratû*s*t is born (ibid. v 1).

B. R. 23, B. C. 653. Z. is seven years old when two Karaps visit his father, and Dûrâsrôbô dies (Dk. VII, iii, 32, 34, 45).

„ 15, B. C. 645. Z. is fifteen years old when he and his four brothers ask for their shares of the family property (Zs. XX, 1).

„ 10, B. C. 640. Z. leaves home at the age of twenty (ibid. 7).

A. R. 1, B. C. 630. Beginning of the tenth millennium. Z. goes forth to his conference with the sacred beings on the 45th day of the 31st year of Vi*s*tâsp's reign (Dk. VII, iii, 51–62; viii, 51; Zs. XXI, 1–4).

„ 3, B. C. 628. Z. returns from his first conference in two years, and preaches to Aûrvâîtâ-dang and the Karaps without success (Dk. VII, iv, 2–20).

„ 11, B. C. 620. After his seventh conference, in the tenth year he goes to Vi*s*tâsp; Mê*d*yômâh is also converted (ibid. 1, 65; Zs. XXI, 3; XXIII, 1, 2, 8).

„ 13, B. C. 618. Twelve years after Z. went to conference, Vi*s*tâsp accepts the religion, though hindered for two years by the Karaps (Dk. VII, v, 1; Zs. XXIII, 5, 7).

„ 20, B. C. 611. A Kavîg, son of Kûndah, is converted (Zs. XXIII, 8).

„ 30, B. C. 601. Defeat of Ar*g*âsp and his Khyons (ibid.).

„ 40, B. C. 591. Vohûnêm is born (ibid.). About this time the Avesta is written by *G*âmâsp from the teaching of Z. (Dk. IV, 21; V, iii, 4; VII, v, 11).

„ 48, B. C. 583. Z. passes away, or is killed, aged seventy-seven years and forty days, on the 41st day of the year (Dk. V, iii, 2; VII, v, 1; Zs. XXIII, 9).

„ 58, B. C. 573. Arrival of the religion is known in all regions (Dk. VII, vi, 12).

„ 63, B. C. 568. Frashô*s*tar passes away (Zs. XXIII, 10).

„ 64, B. C. 567. *G*âmâsp passes away (ibid.).

„ 73, B. C. 558. Hangâûrûsh, son of *G*âmâsp, passes away (ibid.).

„ 80, B. C. 551. Asmôk-khanvatô passes away, and Akht the wizard is killed (ibid.).

„ 91, B. C. 540. Accession of Vohûman, son of Spend-dâ*d* (Bd. XXXIV, 7, 8).

„ 100, B. C. 531. *S*ênô is born (Dk. VII, vii, 6).

„ 200, B. C. 431. *S*ênô passes away (ibid.; Zs. XXIII, 11).

„ 203, B. C. 428. Accession of Hûmâî (Bd. XXXIV, 8).

[Here ends the fragment of the old millennial system preserved in the Bundahi*s* which omits thirty-five years in this place, as explained in § 54, with the effect of postponing the end of the millennium. It then proceeds to finish the chronology in its own fashion; mentioning only three historical names, which are here added; the thirty-five omitted years being also inserted.]

A. R. 268, B. C. 363. Accession of Dârâî (ibid.).

„ 280, B. C. 351. Accession of Dârâî, descendant of Dârâî (ibid.).

„ 294, B. C. 337. Accession of Alexander[1] (ibid.).

„ 300, B. C. 331. Invasion by Alexander. *S*ênô's hundred-discipledom ends, the religion is disturbed, and the monarchy contested (Zs. XXIII, 11, 12; AV. I, 2–6).

„ 308, B. C. 323. Death of Alexander (Bd. XXXIV, 8).

„ 400, B. C. 231. Benightedness arises (Dk. VII, vii, 9).

„ 440–560, B. C. 191–71[2]. Orthodoxy is still upheld by four successive high-priests (Dk. VII, vii, 8–10).

„ 800–950, A. D. 170–320. The ninth and tenth centuries are represented as very evil and miserable (ibid. viii, 2–45, 61).

„ 971, A. D. 341, Aûshê*d*ar is born (ibid. 55–57).

„ 1001, A. D. 371. Beginning of the eleventh millennium, when the sun stands still for ten days, and Aûshê*d*ar is thirty years old and confers with the sacred beings (ibid. 58–60).

„ 1400–1500, A. D. 770–870. In this century the wizard Mahrkûs produces seven awful winters successively, in which most of mankind and animals perish, including himself (ibid. ix, 3).

„ 1971, A. D. 1341. Aûshê*d*ar-mâh is born (ibid. 18–20).

„ 2001, A. D. 1371. Beginning of the twelfth millennium, when the sun stands still for twenty days, and Aûshê*d*ar-mâh is thirty years old and confers with the sacred beings (ibid. 21–23).

„ 2971, A. D. 2341. Sôshâns is born (ibid. x, 15–18).

„ 3001, A. D. 2371. Beginning of the preparation for the Renovation, when the sun stands still for thirty days, and Sôshâns is thirty years old (ibid. 19); but another passage (ibid. xi, 2) implies that this is the date of his birth.

„ 3028, A. D. 2398. The renovation of the universe occurs at the end of the fifty-seventh year of Sôshâns (ibid. 4, 7).

---

[1] He became king of Macedon B. C. 336, and of Persia in 331.

[2] The erroneous dates in the Bundahi*s* chronology (see § 57) alter this period to B. C. 156–36.

56. We must suppose that the millennial chronology, which the Bundahi*s* discontinues in the middle of the tenth millennium. was originally completed to the end of Time, as attempted in this synopsis, in accordance with the statements in Byt. and Dk. But the allusions to future events and denunciations of coming evils were, no doubt, of a mythological or general character, such as those still surviving in Dk. VII, vii, 29–32; viii, 40, 41, 44–46, 48–60; ix–xi. Whenever we meet with seemingly prophetic descriptions and denunciations, which clearly allude to historical events, such as those in Dk. VII, vii, 3–28; viii, 2, 10, 23, 32–36, 42, 43, 47, 61, they must, of course, be treated as interpolations of a later date than the events themselves. And there are several passages that may belong to either class.

57. It has been already shown, in § 54, that the death of Alexander, which the Bundahi*s* places in A. R. 273, must have occurred in A. R. 308 according to other traditional records. If this error of thirty-five years stood alone, it might be considered accidental; but when we find that the Bundahi*s* supplies only 284 years for the A*s*kânians, to fill up the whole interval of 548 years between Alexander and Ardashîr, son of Pâpak, we must conclude that these two errors were intended for the purpose which they both fulfil, that of postponing the end of the tenth millennium. On the other hand, the Sâsânians who ruled for 425 years, are allowed 460 years in the Bundahi*s*, which just counterbalances the thirty-five years omitted after the time of Hûmâî. This third error may be considered unintentional, as it probably arose from counting the year of each succession twice over, first in the reign of the deceased king, and again in that of his successor.

58. The extent to which the Bundahi*s* chronology is distorted, by these three errors, will be better understood on inspection of the following tabular statement than from any description of the results, merely observing that the year of the religion (A. R.) is given according to Bundahi*s* dates in the first column, and according to real dates in the second. Several intermediate events have been inserted,

for the sake of illustration, and each of their Bundahis dates includes its proper proportion of the errors [1]:—

Bd. date.	Real date.		Real date.	Bd. date.
A. R. 265,	A. R. 300.	Invasion by Alexander . .	B. C. 331,	B. C. 331.
" 273,	" 308.	Death of Alexander . . .	" 323,	" 323.
" 321,	" 400.	Real date of A. R. 400 . .	" 231,	" 275.
" 400,	" 553.	Bd. date of A. R. 400 . . .	" 78,	" 196.
" 528,	" 800.	Real date of A. R. 800 . .	A. D. 170,	" 68.
" 557,	" 856.	Accession of Ardashîr . .	" 226,	" 39.
" 605,	" 900.	Real date of A. R. 900 . .	" 270,	A. D. 10.
" 647,	" 939.	Accession of Shahpûhar II .	" 309,	" 52.
" 713,	" 1000.	Real date of A. R. 1000 . .	" 370,	" 118.
" 786,	" 1068.	Accession of Yaz*d*akar*d* II .	" 438,	" 191.
" 800,	" 1081.	Bd. date of A. R. 800 . .	" 451,	" 205.
" 841,	" 1118.	Accession of Kavâ*d* . . .	" 488,	" 246.
" 884,	" 1158.	Execution of the Mazdakites	" 528,	" 289.
" 887,	" 1161.	Accession of Khûsrô I . .	" 531,	" 292.
" 900,	" 1173.	Bd. date of A. R. 900 . . .	" 543,	" 305.
" 951,	" 1220.	Accession of Khûsrô II . .	" 590,	" 356.
" 1000,	" 1265.	Bd. date of A. R. 1000 . .	" 635,	" 405.
" 1017,	" 1281.	Death of Yaz*d*akar*d* III . .	" 651,	" 422.

59. The object of preparing this statement has been to ascertain the reason for the intentional errors in the Bundahis chronology, and the probable period at which they were introduced. It has been mentioned, in § 57, that the effect of both the errors, which are not accidental, has been to postpone the end of the tenth millennium, but they also postpone the dates of some other events which are mentioned in the Zoroastrian legends.

60. Thus, we are told in Dk. VII, vii, 9, that benightedness arises after A.R. 400, which is postponed by the errors from B. C. 231 to 78, but both of these times seem to have been equally unpropitious to the Zoroastrians. Then we learn (ibid. 10, 11) that in the fifth and sixth centuries, say A.R. 440–560, orthodoxy is still upheld by four successive high-priests. This period is postponed by the errors from B. C. 191–71 to 156–36 (see p. xxxi, n. 2), and Zoroastrianism was probably flourishing the whole time. So far, no reason for the alterations can be discovered, as the vague description of events, supplied by the old writer, appears to be

[1] The basis of calculation is the real date of each event and real century, but the Bd. date of each Bd. century. The only Bd. data are 284 years from the death of Alexander to the accession of Ardashîr, and 460 years from the latter to the death of Yaz*d*akar*d* III, as stated in § 57.

just as applicable to the original periods as to the altered ones.

61. We are further informed (Dk. VII, viii, 2–45) that much evil and misery occur in the ninth and tenth centuries (A.R. 800–1000), at all events until the birth of Aûshê*d*ar (ibid. 55–57) in A.R. 971; and such events as war, invasion, fall of monarchy, oppression, persecution, infidelity, and apostasy are mentioned. Aûshê*d*ar confers with the archangels in A.R. 1001 (ibid. 58–60), and the evils afterwards pass away till A.R. 1400–1500 (ibid. ix, 3), when frightful winters occur. The evil period A.R. 800–971 was originally A.D. 170–341, or from the middle of the reign of Vologeses III to the middle of that of Shahpûhar II. But the Bundahi*s* postpones this period to A.D. 451–608, or from the time of the Armenian revolt in the reign of Ya*zd*akar*d* II, to that of the first total defeat of a Persian army by the Arabs near Dhû-Qâr in the reign of Khûsrô II. The evil times were probably expected to continue till the end of the millennium, or later, as in the case of Zaratû*s*t himself; for Aûshê*d*ar does not go to his conference till A.R. 1001, and might not be expected to begin to preach till A.R. 1011. These dates, originally A.D. 371–381, comprising the remainder of the reign of Shahpûhar II, would be altered by Bd. to A.D. 636–645, a period which includes the last two great battles with the Arabs, that decided the downfall of the Sâsânian dynasty, though king Ya*zd*akar*d* III lived some six years longer as a fugitive[1].

62. It is hardly possible that king Ardashîr (A.D. 226–241) and his chancellor Tanvasar, when collecting and revising their sacred books, would have compiled the original traditional system of chronology, however general might have been the terms in which the evils were described by the records they possessed, because it would have been a voluntary confession that they had no power to remedy

---

[1] The authorities consulted, for Persian historical facts and dates, have been Nöldeke, *Aufsätze zur persischen Geschichte;* and A. von Gutschmid, *Geschichte Irans und seiner Nachbarländer von Alexander dem Grossen bis zum Untergang der Arsaciden:* edited by Nöldeke.

the evils of their own time. But if they found the system in an ancient document, they might have been quite willing to admit that evils existed, owing to their enemies, which would have become much worse if they had not been mitigated by their own exertions. In fact, an old document prophesying evil which actually occurred at the time specified, could be used as evidence of the truth of their religion, and would therefore be carefully preserved. And it is quite certain that, if they had altered the chronology of an old document which foretold the time of the downfall of the monarchy, they could not have correctly guessed that time before the downfall occurred. For these reasons we must conclude that the original system of chronology, handed down by the Bundahi*s*, was neither compiled nor altered in the time of Ardashîr.

63. For the long reign of Shahpûhar II (A.D. 309-379) the original tradition predicted not only a continuation of evil times, but also the birth and education of a new apostle, Aûshê*d*ar, for the next millennium, who was expected to put an end to evil for about four centuries. His birth was to take place in A. D. 341, and his conference was to commence in 371. These dates are so well defined that, if we could discover any important religious teacher to whom they could refer, we might be justified in believing that the original chronology was compiled in his time. Unfortunately, we know very little of the internal history of Persia during this reign; there was war with the Romans in 337-350 and 358-363, and on the eastern frontiers in the intervening period; also a persecution of the Christians, beginning about 339; all of which fairly represent the predicted evils.

64. Regarding the priesthood and religious history of the reign, we have only the traditions handed down in Pahlavi texts to guide us. In these we are told that Âtû*r*pâ*d*, son of Mâ*r*aspend (Dk. VII, vii, 19), was born in the steel period (Dk. IX, viii, 4), and lived in the reign of king Shahpûhar II, son of Aûhar*m*a*z*d (AV. p. 145 n), being high-priest over the religion (Dd. XXXVII, 36). He also collected and preserved the Nasks (Dk. VIII, i, 22),

and, after he had proved his orthodoxy by ordeal (Sg. X, 70, 71), the king proclaimed his intention of not allowing any more heterodoxy (Dk. IV, 27 [1]). In his old age he obtained a son, after devout prayer, and named him Zaratûst (Pandnâmak, 1); but this son also bore the Avesta title of Avarethrabau (Dk. VII, vii, 20, 21; VIII, xiii, 18), who is called the son of Râstare-vaghent in Yt. XIII, 106, showing that this latter Avesta title was adopted by Âtûrpâd himself. Finally, we meet with another Âtûrpâd, son of Zaratûst, described in Peshotan's Dk. III, cxxxvii, 2, as high-priest in the reign of Yazdakard I (A.D. 399–420), son of Shahpûhar, and also mentioned in Pahl. Yas. p. 120, ll. 14, 15 Sp. (translated in Dk. VIII, i, 7 n).

65. We have here, evidently, three successive high-priests, father, son, and grandson, and all celebrated men. The father had been employed in collecting and revising, or probably translating, some of the sacred books, and then, after a religious discussion, submitted himself to the ordeal of melted metal, as a test of his orthodoxy. The king was convinced, and his proclamation meant persecution of the heterodox, such as was commenced about A.D. 339, as regards the Christians. So that we may safely assume that Âtûrpâd's ordeal took place shortly before this date, and probably shortly after 337, when the Roman war commenced. As we must also certainly assume that the original chronology could not have come into existence at a much later date than 341, when so remarkable an event as the birth of a new apostle was fixed by it to occur, we have to consider who this apostle could have been; and whether it may not have been intended to identify him with Âtûrpâd's own son.

66. In the first place, is such a suspicion consistent with known dates? To represent Aûshêdar, according to the original chronology, the son must have been born A.D. 341 (§ 63); and we may suppose that the time of Aûshêdar's conference (371) would represent the time of Âtûrpâd's

[1] See S. B. E., vol. xxxvii, p. 415.

death, when his son succeeded him in the high-priesthood. If Âtûr*p*â*d* were aged eighty-one at his death, he would have been fifty-one at the birth of his son, or approaching old age; and he would have been born in 290, or nineteen years before the king. His grandson may have been born in 365, when his father Zaratû*s*t was twenty-four, and may have succeeded that father in the high-priesthood about 400, the second year of king Ya*zd*aka*rd* I. As all these dates are reasonably consistent with the few facts that are known, there seems to be no impossibility in the hypothesis that the original chronology of Aûshê*d*ar's birth may have had some connection with the date of the birth of Âtû*r*pâ*d*'s son. The dates assumed, with regard to these three high-priests, which may be slightly varied, are as follows:—

Âtû*r*pâ*d*,	born 290,	high-priest 320,	died 371.
Zaratû*s*t,	„ 341,	„ 371,	„ 400.
Âtû*r*pâ*d*,	„ 365,	„ 400,	„ 420, or later.

67. On the other hand, we must recollect that the time of the birth of Aûshê*d*ar was not an isolated date which could be varied at pleasure, to suit any circumstances that might arise; but it was intimately connected with the dates of birth of three other apostles, which were each placed at the same distance from the ends of three other millenniums. It would perhaps be more difficult to suit a new millennial system of chronology, to the accidental year of a particular child's birth, than to have the child born in a particular year of an old system already existing. And, if so, it may be safer to assume that Âtû*r*pâ*d*, knowing the year of the expected birth, took measures to secure the fulfilment of the prophecy, so far as the birth was concerned. If the child did not turn out so capable of regenerating the world as had been expected, that was a matter for posterity to explain. Under such circumstances of merely seeming fulfilment of a single particular, fraudulently obtained, the original prediction might be of any age.

68. It does not appear that the priestly councillors assembled by Khûsrô I (Byt. I, 7), made any alteration in

the original chronology, although they slightly revised the Pahlavi Vendidad. In fact, the priests, who must have been long expecting the end of Zaratûst's millennium, were probably looking forward for the approaching downfall of the Sâsânian monarchy, which might readily be understood, as the surest sign of the termination of this period, from such statements as those in Dk. VII, viii, 1, 2. At any rate, the alterations in the chronology, for the purpose of postponing the end of the tenth millennium till A. D. 635, would not have been made till some time after the termination of the monarchy in 651, but probably long before the compilation of the Bundahis about 900. The effects of these alterations upon the dates of the evil ninth and tenth centuries, and upon those of the birth, conference, and preaching of Aûshêdar, have been already stated in § 61. And their object has evidently been to adapt the old predictions as much as possible to real events; for which purpose also, the predictions themselves have probably been often made more definite than they were originally.

69. It follows, from the foregoing investigation, that the original chronology must have existed A.D. 341, and, in fact, we have found no sufficient reason for supposing that it was compiled as late as Sâsânian times. While the alterations, we find in the Bundahis, could have hardly been made till after 651.

70. Regarding the age in which Zaratûst lived, the dates stated in the synopsis of traditional chronology (§ 55), are B.C. 660–583, while the reign of Vistâsp, which extends to the fabulous length of 120 years, or 660–540, evidently represents a short dynasty, including Hystaspes and his next four forefathers, if we accept the traditional identification of Vistâsp with the father of Darius I. But the names of those four forefathers, which are known on the unimpeachable authority of the Behistûn inscription of Darius himself, render it almost impossible to accept this traditional identification, as they differ totally from those of the forefathers of Vistâsp in the Avesta. The two dynasties are as follows:—

Behistûn :	Hakhâmanis	Avesta :	Kavi Kavâta
	*K*aispis		Kava Usa
	Ariyârâmna		Kava Husrava
	Arshâma		Aurva*d*aspa
	Vistâspa		Kava Vistâspa[1].

Unless it can be shown that these two series of names have the same meaning in two different languages, there seems little chance of proving the identity of the two dynasties. We may, however, quote the instances of the high-priest Âtûrpâ*d*=Âtare-pâta and his son Zaratûst=Zarathustra being called Râstare-vaghent and Avarethrabau, respectively, in the Avesta (see § 64); but these latter names seem more like titles than translations.

71. The date of Zoroaster and his religion has formerly been fully discussed by Windischmann[2] and others, and the question has been lately re-examined by Williams Jackson[3]. He divides the ancient statements, that have been made on the subject, into three classes: those which declare that Zaratûst lived before B.C. 6000, those which associate his name with Ninus and Semiramis, and the native tradition which, as we have seen, places his life in the period B.C. 660–583. Singularly enough, the oldest writers, those who lived only two to four centuries after the traditional period of the lifetime of Zaratûst, are those who report that he lived some 6000 years before that period. Pliny the Elder (Nat. Hist. XXX, 2) quotes Eudoxus (B.C. 368) as stating that Zaratûst existed 6000 years before the death of Plato, that is, B.C. 6347, which is also confirmed by Aristotle. And he quotes Hermippus (about B.C. 250) as placing him 5000 years before the Trojan war, that is, B.C. 6184. A third mode of describing this period

[1] These were the reigning sovereigns, but the last two are descended from a collateral branch, and their actual pedigree is as follows:—Kavi Kavâta, Kavi Aipivanghu, Kavi Pisanangh, Manus, Uzava, Aurva*d*aspa, Kava Vistâspa (Bd. XXXI, 28, 29).

[2] *Zoroastrische Studien*, von Fr. Windischmann, edited by Spiegel, 1863; pp. 121–165, 260–313.

[3] *On the date of Zoroaster*, by A. V. Williams Jackson; Journal of American Oriental Society, vol. xvii, pp. 1–22.

seems to have been used by Xanthus of Lydia (B.C. 500–450)[1] who stated that Zaratûst lived 6000 years before Xerxes, as quoted by Diogenes Laertius, that is, B.C. 6485.

72. Three or four other classical writers mention similar statements, and Jackson points out that these extravagant dates are probably owing to the European writers misunderstanding Persian statements with reference to the pre-existence of Zaratûst's Fravashi. It will, in fact, be seen from the synopsis (§ 55) that the traditional account is that the spiritual body of Zaratûst was framed together as early as the beginning of the fourth millennium, which occurred B.C. 6630, and this may be accepted as a close approximation to the three dates, B.C. 6347, 6184, and 6485, indicated by the ancient writers, considering that their statements are made in even thousands of years.

73. Pliny also mentions, on the authority of other writers who are not named, that another Zoroaster, a Proconnesian, lived a little before the time of Osthanes who accompanied Xerxes to Greece (B.C. 480). And, so far as time is concerned, this Zoroaster might have been the traditional Zaratûst who died 103 years before this journey of Osthanes.

74. The old statements about Zoroaster or Oxyartes, the Magian king of Bactria in the time of Ninus and Semiramis, can hardly refer to the traditional Zaratûst who is never represented as a king, although the supreme Zarathustra of the Avesta was apparently a ruling priest. The time in which this Bactrian lived is also very uncertain, for though Semiramis has recently been placed about B.C. 800, her position in Albîrûnî's tables is certainly 1200 years earlier.

75. It seems, therefore, that the ancient statements, regarding the date of Zaratûst, reported by Pliny and corroborated by a few other classical writers, can be fully explained from the traditional system of chronology used in Pahlavi texts, by identifying the classical Zoroaster of the seventh millennium B.C. with the traditional Zaratûst

[1] There are some doubts as to the correctness of these dates.

in his ante-natal spiritual state, after he had ceased to be a mere Fravashi, or primary idea, and had become an intelligent, moving, and personal existence, but still a spirit. While the later Zoroaster of Pliny, who flourished before the fifth century B.C., must have lived about the same time as the same traditional Zaratûst after he came into the worldly existence, and may reasonably be identified with him, although Pliny had little information to give about him.

76. It will be noticed that this explanation depends entirely upon the peculiarly artificial system of the traditional chronology, in which the whole of time is assumed to consist of twelve millenniums devoted to different purposes; and if this particular system had not been in use at the time the statements, quoted by Pliny and Diogenes Laertius, were made, those statements could not have been explained as referring to the same individual. But if they do not refer to the same individual, we have only the options of rejecting all the statements, or believing an impossible date to be literally correct; neither of which decisions would be altogether satisfactory to a judicious mind. The only reasonable conclusion seems to be that the chronology based upon the twelve millenniums was in use in the fifth century B.C., about which time the earliest quoted statement seems to have been made.

77. It will also be observed that this millennial chronology is inextricably associated with the idea of the primeval existence of all good creations in the state of Fravashis. These are described as spiritual existences who remained three millenniums unthinking, unmoving, and intangible (Bd. I, 8); and the next three millenniums they still remained undisturbed by evil. mankind being represented, for that period, by Gâyômar*d* in the world (Bd. XXXIV, 1) and by the spiritual form of Zaratûst in heaven (Dk. VII, ii, 15), while the animals were symbolized by the primeval ox for the same period. Six millenniums, which are half the duration of time, were thus appropriated to Fravashis, spiritual and embodied, probably before the birth of Plato, if we may rely upon classical statements; and it must have

been before this date that the series of millenniums was arranged for all future history, till Time was expected to merge once more into Eternity at the renovation of the universe.

78. As we have seen that Zoroastrian tradition is very consistent in fixing the date of Zaratûst's activity about the end of the seventh century B.C., it may be asked, why have Avesta scholars so strongly insisted upon its greater antiquity? They may have had several reasons, but three, at least, were important. First, they had the classical statements which, as we have seen (§ 71), generally placed Zaratûst as far back as the seventh millennium B.C., on the testimony of persons who lived from two to four centuries after the traditional date of Zaratûst's death. No one, of course, could believe in the literal accuracy of the number of millenniums, which referred, as we have seen, to an imaginary period of spiritual existence, but this number was considered merely as an exaggeration which might be reduced to any amount that seemed reasonable. At the same time, this evidence for antiquity was quite sufficient, in the second place, to discredit the traditional date, of which these old authorities seemed ignorant, though it was a period then comparatively recent. And, if this discredit had not been sufficient to shake the faith of Avesta scholars in the traditional date of Zaratûst, they still had a third reason for their scepticism, when they discovered that the language of the Avesta was not merely a sister of Sanskrit, but that a large portion of it was sister to the oldest Sanskrit with which they were acquainted, and which appeared to them certainly older than the time of Gautama Buddha, who lived about one generation later than the traditional Zaratûst.

79. How far Avesta scholars were justified in their conclusions must be left for future ages to determine; at present we have no really historical information about the origin of Zoroastrianism, and must still consider it as decidedly prehistoric; though, it may be admitted that the Parsi calendar, as used in Persia, so far agrees with tradition, that it still bears witness to its own original institution in

the reign of Darius Hystaspes, as will be seen from the following details.

80. The Parsi year consists of twelve months, each consisting of thirty days, with five additional days added at the end of the year, and the total number of 365 days never varies, so that, whenever a leap-year occurs in our calendar, the beginning of the Parsi year retreats one day in the Christian calendar. In this manner, the total number of days which the beginning of the Parsi year has retreated, since the institution of their calendar, records the number of leap-years which would have occurred in the same period of Christian years, if the regular leap-years had existed the whole time; and four times the number of leap-years would be the total number of years. But as leap-years have not been used the whole time, we have to calculate from astronomical data.

81. In the first place, we want to know at what season the Parsi year originally began, and we learn this from Bd. XXV, 7, 20, where we are told that the winter of the rectified year ends with the five extra days, and the spring begins with the first month; which means that the rectified year begins with the vernal equinox. We also have to observe that, retreating at the rate of one day every four years, the beginning of the year retreats all round the year in 1460 years; and we know from general history that the period, with which we have to deal, is much more than 1460 years and less than 2920. Then we have to ascertain the exact length of the tropical year, which astronomers say is 365·2422 days, with an infinitesimal decrement, quite inappreciable in the period we have in view.

82. We may calculate back from any vernal equinox which occurs not too far from noon, say that of March 22, 1865, when the beginning of the Parsi year, according to Persian reckoning, had retreated to August 24, 1864, or 210 days, in addition to a previous retreat of a whole year of 365 days, or altogether 575 days since the establishment of the calendar. So that the difference between the Parsi year of 365 days and the correct tropical year of 365·2422 days had then accumulated to a total of 575 days. Divid-

ing the accumulated error of 575 days by the annual increment of 0·2422 of a day, we obtain a quotient of 2374 years, including A.D. 1865, as the time in which this error had accumulated, and this carries us back to B.C. 510 as an approximate date of the establishment of the Parsi calendar, with the first day of the year coinciding with the vernal equinox.

83. This date is, however, liable to some modifications for errors of observation on the part of the ancient astronomers, one of which errors, being constantly in one direction, must be taken into account. These old observers were not aware of the effect of refraction, which always makes the night seem somewhat shorter than it is in reality; and this would lead them to antedate the vernal equinox by rather more than a day; so that they would observe an apparent equinox in B.C. 505 on the same day in the Parsi year as that on which the real equinox occurred in B.C. 510. The most probable date of the establishment of the Parsi calendar is therefore B.C. 505, with a margin of four to eight years in either direction for *accidental* errors of observation.

84. A few years before this period we know, from the cuneiform inscriptions of Behistûn, that Darius Hystaspes used an older calendar, when recording his early victories over insurgents, which consolidated his empire. It was a time when he was introducing many reforms in the government, and, being a believer in Auramazdâ, his most influential advisers would probably be Zoroastrian priests. If they thought it necessary to reform the old calendar, the adoption of strictly Zoroastrian names for the new months and days in the Parsi calendar would be fully explained.

85. But, besides this ordinary civil calendar, in which new-year's day was constantly retreating, the Persians had a rectified calendar for religious purposes, which intercalated an extra month from time to time, for the purpose of bringing new-year's day forward again to the vernal equinox, and restoring the festivals to their proper seasons. It is this calendar which is used in Bd. XXV, and its days

and months are distinguished by the epithet vehî*k*akîg (veh + î*k* + ak + îg), 'belonging to what is really good,' or vehî*k*ak, 'belonging to the really good,' which, in this connection, may be best expressed by the word 'rectified.'

86. This intercalation is described by Albîrûnî in various passages[1] which inform us that, after the new-year's day had retreated more than a month from the vernal equinox, the king would order the priests to arrange for the solemn proclamation of an extra month to be intercalated, between the last month of the year and the five extra days, by merely moving those five days from the end of the twelfth month to the end of the first month of the next year. The effect of this was to put an extra month into the earlier year which, beginning with the first month, would also end with the first month augmented by the five extra days as the usual termination of the year. All following years would begin with the second month, and end with the first month and the five extra days, until the second intercalation, when a year of thirteen months and five days would be again obtained, by merely moving the five extra days to the end of the second month which would thus become the last month of the year, while the third month would begin the year until the third intercalation. By these means, any number of intercalations could be made without any additional month being named, and the position of the five extra days always indicated the end of the rectified year, and that the rectified first month, which followed them, was to become the last month of the preceding year at the next rectification, or intercalation.

87. If the Parsi calendar, as used in Persia, were established B.C. 505, as we have calculated, it ought to have been rectified by an intercalation of one month about each of the following years:—B.C. 381, 257, 133, 10, A.D. 115, 239, 363, 487, 610. Albîrûnî (p. 121), however, has recorded only one intercalation of two months in the time of Yaz*d*akar*d* I (A.D. 399–420), son of Shahpûhar, when the

[1] Sachau's Albîrûnî's *Chronology of Ancient Nations*, pp. 12, 13, 38, 53–56, 121, 184, 185, 220, 221.

five extra days were removed to the end of the original eighth month Âbân, where they remained until Albîrûnî's own time (Alb. p. 56), about A.D. 1000. The reason for intercalating two months at once, was because the time for the seventh intercalation (A.D. 363) was already long past; so the eighth was added three or four score years in advance, being due in 487.

88. All that Albîrûnî says about this double intercalation is quite in accordance with the original establishment of the calendar by Darius Hystaspes, and would render any date more than thirty-seven years later than his reign impossible[1]. With regard to the earlier intercalations (which must have occurred to account for the movement of the five extra days) that of A.D. 115 was neither in the reign of Vologeses I, nor in that of Vologeses III, one of whom must have been the A*s*kânian renovator of the Avesta. That of A.D. 239, if carried out punctually, would have been at the extreme end of the reign of Ardashîr; but the intercalations seem to have been usually delayed, as in the case of that of 363 which was delayed for thirty to fifty years, although it ought to have been carried out under the direction of one of those ultra-orthodox high-priests, Âtû*r*pâ*d* son of Mâ*r*aspend, or his son Zaratû*s*t, in the reign of Shahpûhar II.

89. It is worthy of notice that the names of both the days and months, which have come down to us in this calendar of Darius, include the names of the six Ameshaspe*n*tas, which, according to Darmesteter's hypothesis, were not invented till the time of Vologeses I, in the first century A.D. We have positive evidence that the calendar of twelve months of thirty days each, with five extra days to complete the year, must have been established in the time of Darius. This fact being recorded mechanically by the extent of the retreat of the Persian Parsis' new-year's day down to the present time, and by the number of months intercalated in their religious calendar down to the fifth

[1] If the calendar had been established thirty-eight years after the death of Darius, the seventh intercalation would not have been due till one year after the death of Yaz*d*aka*r*d I.

century A.D., being known from the position of the five extra days in the rectified calendar. We have no evidence of any change of names having been made in this calendar at any time; and only positive and indisputable evidence could be admitted, because reformers of calendars are hardly ever satisfied with mere change of names, and the calendar itself is a permanent witness that no alteration can have been made in any other particular, since the time of Darius.

90. Darmesteter's theory of a late origin for the Avesta having been mentioned, it may be allowable to add, that the likelihood of this theory does not increase upon closer examination. It is a brilliant hypothesis, very carefully prepared to meet ordinary criticism; but it does not appear to convince Avesta scholars in general, for want of sufficient evidence, as it is very necessary to distinguish carefully between possibilities and probabilities; the former being not admissible as evidence, unless corroborated by positive facts. Its chief use has been in checking the tendency to exaggerate the age of the Avesta, but it seems itself to be an exaggeration in the opposite direction, a returning swing of the ever-restless pendulum of judgment. On the other hand, the traditional age of the religion cannot be fairly considered as exaggerated, for the chief difficulty in accepting it as sufficiently old, is that the nearer our researches penetrate to that time the less real light we obtain.

E. W. West.

April, 1897.

ABBREVIATIONS USED IN THIS VOLUME.

A.D. for Anno Domini; Alb. for Albîrûnî's Chronology of Ancient Nations, translated by Sachau; A.R. for Anno Religionis; Ar. for Arabic; AV. for the Book of Ar*d*â-Vîrâf; Av. for Avesta; B for Bombay MS. of Dînka*rd*, brought from Irân in 1783; B.C. for Before Christ; Bd. for Bundahi*s* (S. B. E. v, 1–151), and Band (volume); Beh. for Behistûn inscription; BK for an old copy of K35, made when this MS. was more complete than it is now; B.R. for Before the Religion; Byt. for Bahman Ya*s*t (S. B. E. v, 189–235); Chald. for Chaldee; Chap. for chapter; Chaps. for chapters; Dd. for Dâ*d*istân-î Dînîk (S. B. E. xviii, 1–276); Dk. for Dînka*rd* (S. B. E. xxxvii, 1–397, 406–418, and this volume); ed. for editor or edition; Ep. for Epistles of Mânû*s*k*î*har (S. B. E. xviii, 277–366); Études irân. for Études irâniennes; Farh. Oîm for Farhang-i Oîm-aêvak; gen. for genitive case; Gesch. der Sas. for Geschichte der Perser und Araber zur Zeit der Sâsâniden; Gf. for the Tale of Gô*s*t-î Fryânô; Heb. for Hebrew; Ibid. for ibidem; Ind. vers. for Indian version; J. for Jâmâsp's old MS.; K for University Library at Kopenhagen; L for India Office Library at London; l. for line; ll. for lines; Mkh. for Mainyô-i Khira*d* (S.B.E. xxiv, 1–113); MS. for manuscript; MSS. for manuscripts; n. for footnote; nom. for nominative case; p. for page; Pahl. for Pahlavi; Pers. for Persian; pp. for pages; Pt. for Peshotan's old MS.; S. B. E. for Sacred Books of the East; Sd. for Sad-dar (S. B. E. xxiv, 253–361); Sg. for *S*ikand-gumânîk Vigâr (S. B. E. xxiv, 115–251); Sls. for Shâyast-lâ-shâyast (S. B. E. v, 237–406); Sp. for Spiegel's edition; T for Tehmuras's MS. of Dd., Zs., &c.; Vd. for Vendidad, ed. Geldner; Vig. for Vigîrka*rd*-î Dînîk; Visp. for Visperad, ed. Geldner; vol. for volume; Westerg. Frag. for Westergaard's Fragments; Yas. for Yasna, ed. Geldner; Yt. for Ya*s*t, ed. Geldner; YZ. for Geiger's Yâtkâr-i Zarîrân; Z. for Zaratû*s*t; Zs. for Selections of Zâ*d*-sparam, first series.

MARVELS OF ZOROASTRIANISM

AS STATED IN

THE SEVENTH AND FIFTH BOOKS

OF THE

DÎNKA*RD*

AND IN THE

SELECTIONS OF ZÂ*D*-SPARAM

CHAPTERS XII–XXIV.

OBSERVATIONS.

1. For all divisions into chapters and sections the translator is chiefly responsible, as the stops found in the manuscripts are not used systematically.

2. Italics are used for any English words which are not expressed, or fully understood, in the original text, but are added to complete the sense of the translation.

3. Italics occurring in Oriental words, or names, represent certain peculiar Oriental letters (see the 'Transliteration of Oriental Alphabets' at the end of this volume), or certain abbreviated modes of writing Pahlavi letters. Italic *a*, *â*, *b*, *d*, *e*, *ê*, *h*, *i*, *î*, *kh*, *l*. *p*, *r*, *sh*, *u*, *v*, *zd* indicate no change of pronunciation; but *g* should be sounded like j, *hv* like wh, *k* like ch in 'church,' *s* like sh, and Avesta *z* like French j.

4. In the translation words in parentheses are merely explanatory of those that precede them, and often translate Pahlavi glosses in the original text.

5. For the meaning of the abbreviations, used in the notes, see the explanatory list after the Introduction.

6. The manuscripts used for the Dînka*rd* are :—

B (written A. D. 1659), the only independent authority for Book VII; it was brought from Irân to Surat in 1783, and one folio, at the end of Chap. iv, appears to be missing.

K 43 (written A. D. 1594 and later), No. 43 in the University Library at Kopenhagen, which contains another independent authority for Book V in its later portion.

7. The manuscripts used for the Selections of Zâ*d*-sparam are :—

K 35 (probably written A. D. 1572), No. 35 in the same library, which was brought from Irân by Prof. Westergaard in 1843, along with No. 43.

T, a copy of a MS. about fifty years older, belonging to Ervad Tehmuras Dinshawji Ankalesaria of Bombay.

MARVELS OF ZOROASTRIANISM.

DÎNKA*RD*.—BOOK VII.

CHAPTER I.

1. *For* the gratification *of* the creator Aûha*r*ma*zd*, even through the complete superiority of the Ma*zd*a-worshipping religion, adorned by omniscience, in the world.

2. The seventh *book* is about the marvellousness of the greatest reminder of the Ma*zd*a-worshipping religion, Zaratû*s*t[1] of the Spîtâmas; also of the mindfulness of that illustrious *one* by Aûha*r*ma*zd*, and *of* his religion, arisen through the word of Aûha*r*ma*zd*, being blessed among those of the region of king Vi*s*tâsp; from the Exposition of the Good Religion[2].

3. But, before that, *there* is purposely written whatever *was* the progress of the character and effect of the good religion and its first acceptor in the spiritual and worldly *existences*; and, after that,

[1] Nearly always spelt Zaratûkhsht in the MS., the counterpart of the Persian form Zaratuhsht or Zaraduhsht.

[2] This Nikêzô-î Vêh-dênô was evidently the name of an older book, from which the Dinka*r*d quotes much of its information on religious matters.

the prophets, apostles, *and* upholders in the period as far as Zaratûst, *whose* guardian spirit is reverenced, and their religion, which is this, due to the utterance and splendour with which they have been blessed with prophecy among mankind [1].

4. According to the Mazda-worshipping religion *and* the Exposition of the Good Religion, it is the nature *of* Aûharmazd's disposition and his knowledge as to the complete obtainment of the first creature, the archangel Vohûmanô, and the first progress spiritually among the archangels *and* the other sacred beings of the spiritual *and worldly existences*, and materially in Gâyômard, the first man, through concurrent *and* complete acceptance from the creator Aûharmazd, and the needful atonement in his own period through meditation, and the smiting thereby of the fiend of that period and the opposition thereof, by thinking of the creator's teaching, *that constitute* the whole *of* that first utterance [2] of the religion of Aûharmazd.

5. According to the declaration of the good religion about the production of existence, which is the praise of him who *was* the causer of existence and creator, the beneficent spirit, the first craving among mankind *was* this, that 'we be happy and *be* the creation of Aûharmazd;' and the last, as regards the preservation of a remedy for mankind, is *this*, *that* 'the best is this, that the formation of lives *be* perfect now, though rendered sickly by him; and the spiritual existences of mankind *be so* now, though the destroyer *has* come to the creatures.' 6. *For*

[1] This preliminary matter occupies the whole of Chap. I.

[2] The Yathâ-ahû-vairyô, or most sacred religious formula of the Parsis.

human beings of the lineage of Gâyômar*d* this is the one thing good, when they shall perform their duty and good works; and one's work is to smite one's own opposing fiend; an instance presentable to *any* of the lineage, that it is important *for* every one of you to smite his own opposing fiend, is the freedom from molestation which occurs thereby, and the non-contamination of the creatures by the destroyer; and it is that effect which the creator *of* creation *has* produced for it.

7. And this, too, is declared by the good religion, that through a true-spoken statement Gâyômar*d* attained to the good spiritual lordship [1] of the archangels (that is, *he was* fit for the supreme heaven [2]). 8. And after Gâyômar*d*, at various periods until the ever-favouring [3] Zaratû*s*t of the Spîtâmas, *whose* guardian spirit is reverenced; much also *was* his acquaintance with knowledge, and *his* work *was* the preservation of the mankind of that time in which he came into notice; moreover he became requisite for conference with the creator: and because of *their* superior carrying on of destiny [4], by command of the

---

[1] Reading hû-ahûîh, Av. hvanghevi. This section is one of the numerous quotations from the Pahlavi version of a lost Avesta text. When we are furnished with a complete Pahl.-Av. vocabulary, it will be possible to recover much of the original Avesta of such quotations, with some degree of certainty.

[2] Pahl. garô*d*mânîg. Such glosses and comments, inserted by the Pahlavi translator, are always marked as parenthetical.

[3] Pahl. hamâî-bâhar; it might be read hamâî-bîdâr, 'ever vigilant.'

[4] Reading vakhsh (=Pers. bakhsh), which is usually expressed by its Zvâri*s* equivalent ga*d*â (traditionally gadman), and this means both 'destiny' and 'the star, or glory, of destiny' (Av. hvarenô, Pers. khura). Here the first letter of vakhsh is omitted, and this error converts the word into khayâ, the Zvâri*s* of *g*ân, 'life.'

creator, *it is* declared in the good religion, *that* the combined titles of prophet (vakhshvar), acceptor, *and* promoter *are* enumerated of them.

9. As Gâyômar*d* passed away, *it*[1] *came* to Masyê and Masyâôî[2], the second of worldly beings who *were* the progeny of Gâyômar*d* the first; *and it is* declared, by the word of Aûha*r*ma*zd*, that he spoke to them, when they had been produced by him, thus: 'You are the men I produce, you are the parents of the parents of all embodied existence; and so do you men not worship the demons, for the possession of complete mindfulness is the best *thing* produced by me for you, so that you *may* fully observe duty and ordinances with complete mindfulness.' 10. And the bountifulness of Aûha*r*ma*zd was* extolled by them, and they went on with their own duty; they also performed the will of the creator, enjoyed the advantage of the many duties of the world, *and* practised next-of-kin marriage for procreation, union, and the complete progress of the creations in the world, which are the best good works of mankind. 11. The creator showed them the sowing of corn, as declared in the words of Aûha*r*ma*zd* thus: 'This is thine, *O* Masyê! which is an ox; thine, too, is this corn; and thine those other appliances; henceforth thou shouldst know *them* well.'

This must have also occurred twice in a previous copy of the MS. in § 28, where the word is written *g*ân, 'life,' in the MS. B. In S. B. E., vol. xxxvii, Dk. VIII, xiii, 20, vakhsh has been erroneously translated 'word.'

[1] The glorious destiny. §§ 9 and 10 have been previously translated in S. B. E., vol. xviii, pp. 411, 412.

[2] Literally 'man and woman' who grew up as plants from the earth fertilized by Gâyômar*d*, the prototype of the human race; see Bd. XV, 1–5.

12. This, too, is declared by the good religion, that Aûharmazd spoke to Hadish [1], one of the sacred beings thoroughly worthy through righteousness, thus: '*O* Hadish, who *art* thoroughly worthy through righteousness! thou shouldst proceed to Masyê and Masyâôî, thou shouldst procure thy [2] corn *and* bread from Masyê and Masyâôî, *and* shouldst bless theirs thus: "This corn comes up owing to you, *and*, as it came unto you from Aûharmazd and the archangels, may the corn extend from you unto your descendants without disturbance from the demons;" *and* two Ahunavairs [3] are to be recited for the staying away *of* the demon and fiend.' 13. And Hadish, the thoroughly worthy through righteousness, went to Masyê and Masyâôî, and he procured his corn and bread from Masyê and Masyâôî, and *it was* given by them; he also blessed them thus: 'May this corn come up from you, as from the archangels! as it came unto you *from* Aûharmazd *and* the archangels, may it extend from you unto your descendants, without disturbance from the demons;' and two Ahunavairs *were* recited by him, for the staying away of the demon *and* fiend.

14. And, owing to the explanation of the sacred beings, Masyê and Masyâôî attained also to the manufacture of clothing, the tending of sheep, house-building, and primitive carpentry, the agriculture *and* husbandry of the ancients, and the memory of their original state; and *these* proceeded from them through *their* lineage, presenting an example and

[1] Mentioned in Visp. i, 9: ii, 11: ix, 5, and recognized as a spirit in Pahl. Visp. i, 31 (Sp.). The spirit who assists the husbandman, see Études irân. ii, 201.

[2] The MS. has 'his,' as in § 13, by mistake.

[3] Two of the sacred Yathâ-ahû-vairyô formulas.

spreading *in* the world, to artificers among the plenitude of artificers.

15. And after that, the destiny to be carried on came to Sâmak [1], who *was* their son, and the descent of *their* collateral descendants *was* on to each region and each quarter of the world, *to* that extent which the creator chose for that region and quarter; *and* thereby *there* was a completion of the progress and spreading of mankind into the various regions *and* quarters.

16. At another time it came to Vâêgere*d* and Hôshâng [2] of the early law (pê*s*-dâ*d*), for providing in the world the law of husbandry, *or* cultivation of the world, and *of* sovereignty *or* protection of the world. 17. And through their companionship and united force, given by religion, the sovereignty and cultivation *of* the world *were* prepared through progress and a succession of provisions *of* Aûhar-maz*d*'s creatures, *as well as* the religion appointed by Aûharmaz*d*. 18. And through that glory *of destiny* (gadâ) two-thirds of the demons of Mâzanô [3] *and* the seven evil-instructed *ones* [4] of Aêshm *were* destroyed by Hôshâng.

19. After that it came to Tâkhmôrup [5] the well-armed, and through that glory the demon and evil mankind, the wizard and witch, *were* smitten by him; idolatry *was* also cast out by him, and he propagated in *his* time the reverence *and* service of the creator; the evil spirit, converted into the shape of a horse, *was* also carrying him *for* thirty winters.

---

[1] See Bd. XV, 24–26.

[2] Grandsons of Sâmak, see Bd. XV, 28, and Sachau's Albîrûnî's Chronology of Ancient Nations, pp. 206, 212.

[3] The idolators of Mâzandarân. See Yt. XIX, 26.

[4] Called 'seven powers' in Bd. XXVIII, 15.

[5] See Bd. XXXI, 2, and Yt. XIX, 28, 29.

20. And it came, at another time, for the conference with Aûharmazd, to Yim[1] the splendid, the son of Vîvang,ha; and owing to his accepting the four classes of the religion, *which* are priesthood, warriorship, husbandry, and artisanship, *there* are the four classes which are priesthood, warriorship, husbandry, and artisanship, and thereby the world *was* improved, extended, and developed; he also rendered even the creatures, in a measure, immortal, undecaying, hungerless, thirstless, plentiful, and fully-settled. 21. And in the good religion[2] *it* is declared, by the word of the creator Aûharmazd to Yim, thus: 'Then do thou widen my world! (that is, make up *its* measure more), then do thou extend my world! (that is, make *it* up larger), and then thou shouldst accept from me the protection, nourishment, and chieftainship of the world; and do thou effect such watchfulness over *it*, *that* no one shall be able to occasion the wounding or injury of another.' 22. And *this was* accepted and done by Yim, as Aûharmazd commanded him; and through the same glory he widened the earth three-thirds larger than that *which* it was theretofore. 23. And, in that realm of his, the cattle and men of the realm *were* made immortal by him, and the other creations, water, vegetation, and the various foods, imperishable. 24. And this, too, is declared by the good religion, that the world *was* made by him like the supreme heaven in pleasantness; also the enclosure made by Yim, constructed by him according to all the commands of the creator[3], about guarding the creatures from perishing through the winter of

---

[1] See Bd. XXXI, 3–5, and Yt. XIX, 31–33. [2] In Vd. II, 4.
[3] As detailed in Vd. II, 22–31, 40, 41.

Mahrkûs, and likewise many other wonders are reported by the good religion.

25. And it came, at another time, by command of the creator, to Frê*d*ûn the Âspîgân[1] when he was in the pregnant womb, owing to the share of husbandry *in* the avocations of the religion, through allotment from the glory of Yim, and through its triumphant splendour. 26. And Frê*d*ûn, through that triumphant splendour, became a responder *to* Dahâk[2] from the pregnant womb, and that degraded fiend *was* averted and paralysed by him; *having* come to nine years *of age*, he proceeded about his destruction, and through that victory Dahâk *was* smitten by him[3], the creatures *were* saved and relieved thereby, those of Mâzandar and Mâ*d*a *were* smitten, their ravage and mischief *were* removed from the region of Khvanîras, *and* the region of Khvanîras *was* preserved *for his* three sons. 27. And owing to his husbandry, which is the third avocation of the religion, pestilence and disease *were* disturbed *by* the medical treatment even of pestilence itself, and he exhibited to mankind also many other wonders produced and useful occupation for the world.

28. And, in the life-*time* of Frê*d*ûn, the same destiny came to Aîrî*k*[4], son of Frê*d*ûn, owing to introduction *by* the creator, and *was* diffused in him, and he practised humility; the life[5] which is perfect is brought through a prayer from *his* father Frê*d*ûn,

---

[1] See Bd. XXXI, 7, 8, and Yt. XIII, 131; XIX, 36.

[2] The Arab usurper, or usurping dynasty, that conquered Yim in his old age; see Bd. XXXI, 5, 6.

[3] See Yt. XIX, 37.

[4] See Bd. XXXI, 9, 10.

[5] Probably 'destiny;' the initial letter of vakhsh, 'destiny,' has been omitted, and this blunder converts the word into khayâ, 'life.'

and that life[1] came to him from the creator through the blessing of Frê*d*ûn.

29. And it came, through *his* mother, to a descendant of Frê*d*ûn *and* descendant of Aîrî*k*; it proceeded with the angel Nêryôsang to Mânûs*k*îhar[2], and its entire progress was in the lineage of Aîrî*k*. 30. And it came to Mânûs*k*îhar, the monarch of Irân, and through it many wonder-wrought actions *were* performed by him; he smote Salm and Tû*g* in revenge for Aîrî*k*[3], he was a responder *to* the superfluities of foreign countries, he arranged the realm of Irân, improved and fertilised the land of Irân, and made the country of Irân victorious over foreigners.

31. At another time it came to Aûzôbô, son of Tûmâsp[4], a descendant of Mânûs*k*îhar the monarch of Irân; *and*, through that destiny and glory combined, the new-born came to mature activity and the proportions of a man during childhood, through agriculture; he disclosed *his* lamenting mother to the countries of Irân, he marched on to the destruction of foreigners, to drive out *and* make *them* outcast from the land of Irân; he also defeated the village-terrifier of the country of Irân, the wizard who frightened his father *and* fellow-immortals, Frangrâsîyâk of Tûr[5]; and he developed *and* ferti-

[1] See note 5 on preceding page.

[2] Here spelt Nêresang and Mânûs*î*r. The former is the usual spiritual messenger of Aûha*r*ma*zd*; and for the lineage of the latter see Bd. XXXI, 9–14. It appears that the glorious destiny was preserved by the angel Nêryôsang for some generations, and he conveyed it to the grandfather of Mânûs*k*îhar (see Chap. II, 70).

[3] The three sons of Frê*d*ûn, among whom he divided his dominions, with the usual result of triumvirates.

[4] See Bd. XXXI, 23; XXXIV, 6.

[5] See Yt. XIX, 56–64, 77, 82, 93, and Bd. XXXI, 14, 15, 18, 21, 22, 35; XXXIV, 6; where the Av. form Frangrasyan is further

lised the country of Irân, and increased the many streams *and* cultivated lands in the country of Irân.

32. At another time it came to Kerêsâspô the Sâmân [1], owing to the share of warriorship which is the second avocation of the religion, through allotment from the glory of Yim [2]; and, through it, the serpent Srôbŏvar which *was* swallowing horses *and* swallowing men, the golden-heeled demon Gandarepô, and much other production *of* adversity *by* the demon and the fiend—the murderess of the creatures—*were* destroyed by him.

33. At another time it came to Kaî-Kobâ*d* [3], the progenitor of the Kayâns; through it he arranged the realm of Irân, he united the sovereignty with himself in the Kayân race, *and* he thereby occasioned much splendour *and* actions of advantage *to* the creatures.

34. And it came to Pâtakhsrôbô [4], *son* of Aîryêfshvâ [5], *son* of T*â*z, who *was* king of the Arabs, through the mindfulness of the archangel Ashavahis*t*ô, and his enquiry about it from its own tribe [6]—*for* the demon of greediness (*â*zŏ), with *one* similarly

corrupted into Frâsîyâ*v*, as it is also hereafter in Chap. II, 68; Zs. XII, 3.

[1] A famous hero whose exploits, like those of Hercules, have given birth to many legends; see S. B. E., vol. xviii, pp. 369–382.

[2] Compare § 25.

[3] See Yt. XIX, 71; Bd. XXXI, 24, 25, 28; XXXIV, 7.

[4] Or Pâtâsrôbô, spelt Pâtsrôbô in Pahl. Vd. XX, 4 (Sp.).

[5] Or Aîryêfshnîg; evidently the same as Virafsang in Bd. XXXI, 6, which is spelt Avirafshanêg and Âirafshanig in two MSS. of the Irânian Bundahi*s*. Hence we may conclude that Pâtakhsrôbô was a brother of Zâînîgâv, and a great-uncle of Dahâk; but how his daughters could have been married to the three sons of Frê*d*ûn, as stated in the *K*itradâ*d* Nask (see Dk. VIII, xiii, 9), is a chronological difficulty that throws doubt upon this identification.

[6] The people of the primitive faith, who are supposed to have

destined, had rushed for the destruction of him who *was* very gentle to that tribe[1]—*as he had* a full inclination for the ascendancy of the portion whose guidance to the lofty priestly master *was* owing to the archangel Ashavahis*t*ô, just as the fish image[2] of that *other* portion *was* for falling into the river; and *it is* declared *that* he came to the ceremonial of Zaratûs*t*.

35. At another time it came to Kaî-Arsh *and his* brothers[3], the descendants of Kobâ*d*; through it they have been all-experienced and powerful, heedful and performing wonders; and the eldest brother of them, Kaî-Ûs, seized upon the sovereignty of the seven regions, *and* became very illustrious *and* full of glory. 36. *At* the same time it came to Aôshnar[4] who became fully sagacious (pûr-zîr), owing to the glory of Yim, when he was in *his* mother's womb, and many wonders *were* taught by him to *his* mother, through speaking from the mother's womb; also at his birth he vanquished the maleficent spirit by uttering answers *to* the questions *of* the deadly Frâ*k*ih the demon-worshipper. 37. He also attained to the chancellorship (farmâ*d*ârîh) of Kaî-Ûs, and became administrator (râyînî*d*âr) in his realm *of* the seven regions; the frontier speech (vîmand-gôbisnîh) *was* also explained *and* taught by him,

---

already practised most of the duties upheld by Zarathus*t*ra before his appearance as a reformer.

[1] Indicating that the Arab subjects of the king had revolted, because he favoured those of the primitive faith who, no doubt, gained further favour by putting down the rebellion.

[2] Or it may be 'fish priest,' as karapŏ, 'a heathen priest,' and kerpŏ, 'shape, image,' are written alike in Pahlavi letters.

[3] See Yt. XIX, 71; Bd. XXXI, 25.

[4] See Yt. XIII, 131; Dd. XLVIII, 33.

and much other learning of advantage *to* mankind *who* are unaffected by the utterance of replies of a foreigner; he *also* advised the Irânian country with the best-instructed counsel.

38. And *its* coming to Kaî-Sîyâvakhsh[1] the illustrious, through the wondrous-formed Kangd*ez* *being* held by him for the retention *of* protection *for* the much splendour *and* suitable glory of the religion, from which the restoration of time, the re-arrangement of the realm of Irân, *and* the reunion of power *and* triumph with the religion of Aûha*r*ma*zd* are manifest.

39. It came to Kaî-Khûsrôî[2], son of Sîyâvakhsh, *and* through it he smote and vanquished Frangrâsîyâk[3] *of* Tûr, the wizard, and his fellow-miscreation Kêrsêvazd[4] of those of Vakgir[5], and many other very evil devastators of the world; he also joined in the destruction of that idol-temple which *was* on the shore of Lake *K*ê*k*ast[6], *and* demolished that fiendishness which *was* awful. 40. On account of the desirableness of means for the renovation *of the universe, he is also* on a throne (namî*k*ŏ), which is assuredly selected by that destiny, at a secret place where *there* is an immortal preserver for his body until the renovation, through the will of the creator.

41. And it came from him, after Zaratû*s*t of the Spîtâmas came to the conference of the creator

---

[1] See Yt. XIX, 71, 77; Bd. XXXI, 25; Byt. III, 25, 26.

[2] See Yt. XIX, 74, 77, 93; Bd. XXXI, 25.

[3] See § 31.

[4] Brother of Frangrâsîyâk, see Yt. XIX, 77; Bd. XXXI, 15.

[5] Reading Vakgiragânŏ, probably the inhabitants of the Bakyîr mountain, mentioned in Bd. XII, 2, 20 as a stronghold of Frâsiyâ*v* (= Frangrâsîyâk).

[6] See Bd. XVII, 7; Mkh. II, 95.

Aûharmazd, and accepted from the omniscient creator Aûharmazd unmixed freedom from pollution, the comprehensive and also recited acquaintance with the knowledge *and* work of priesthood, warriorship, husbandry, and artisanship, *and* the separate portions of the Mazda-worshipping revelation (dênô) brought to king Kaî-Vistâsp by command of the creator, illuminated by the great splendour in that supreme sovereign of the sacred beings, *and* propagated *by* the learned of the region, in the regions which *are* seven, through the good eloquence which is owing to the succession of creatures until the renovation *of the universe.* 42. And through its production by those who *will be his* sons, Aûshêdar, Aûshêdar-mâh, and Sôshâns[1], the renovation in the existence of the creatures of Aûharmazd is immortal; and a more remindful statement of its splendour, glory, *and* marvellousness is a statement *that* is written and found below[2].

43. And *there* have also been others before Zaratûst, the prophet (vakhshvar) of desired fame in the Mazda-worshipping religion; for it is declared that, at times, some came from the spiritual *beings* to him who *was* more of a leader, *and* mankind have become as captivated by the solicitation *and* interrogation of that affair, as now by the solicitation *and* interrogation of the religion; the necessity for that period is not now necessary, because all mankind

[1] The Pahlavi transcripts of the Avesta names, Ukhshyad-ereta, Ukhshyad-nemangh, and Saoshyãs, of the three apostles expected to revive and renovate the Parsi religion in successive millenniums. According to the imperfect chronology of the Bundahis, the millennium of Aushêdar-mâh has now nearly one-fourth elapsed.

[2] See Chap. XI, 7-11.

are made acquainted with the religion, and Zaratûst of the Spîtâmas, *whose* guardian spirit is righteous, is to be reverenced.

44. Now, that which is declared in the world is written, about the splendour, glory, and marvellousness of the prophet of the Mazda-worshipping religion, the best of creations, *whose* guardian spirit is reverenced, Zaratûst of the Spîtâmas; and ten chapters are published here, as to the information from the Avesta, and *in* benediction *of* the religion of Aûharmazd[1].

45. That of it which is before the birth of that glorious *one* from *his* mother *in* the present *world*.

46. That of it which is from the birth of that illustrious *one* onwards, *till* his coming to a conference *with* Aûharmazd.

47. That of it which is from the conference onwards, till his pre-eminence over prophecy in the world, *and* the acceptance *of* the religion *by* the exalted Kaî-Vistâsp.

48. That of it which is onwards from that, till the departure (vîkhêzô) of that pure soul to the existence which is best.

49. That of it which is also successively after that, in the reign of the obedient king Kaî-Vistâsp.

50. That of it which is after that, until the collapse (angâvisnô) of the sovereignty of Irân.

51. That of it which is also after that, until the end of the millennium of Zaratûst *and* the arrival of Aûshêdar.

52. That of it which is also after that, until *the end of* the millennium of Aûshêdar *and* the arrival of Aûshêdar-mâh.

[1] Then follow the headings of these ten Chapters (II to XI).

53. That of it which is also after that, until the end of the millennium of Aûshê*d*ar-mâh and the arrival of Sôshâns.

54. *And* that of it from the arrival of the Triumphant Benefiter, *until* the wonder *of* the renovation *and* future existence; a statement of them each separately.

CHAPTER II.

1. About the marvellousness of the manifestations before[1] the birth of that most auspicious of offsprings from *his* mother[2].

2. One *marvel* is this which is declared, that the creator passed on that glory of Zaratû*s*t through the material existences of the creatures[3] to Zaratû*s*t; when the command arose from Aûha*r*ma*zd*, the coming of that glory from the spiritual *existence* to the worldly, and *to* the material substance (mâ*d*îyâtŏ) of Zaratû*s*t, is manifested *as* a great wonder to the multitude (va*l* kabedânŏ).
3. *Just* as revelation mentions *it* thus: 'Thereupon, when Aûha*r*ma*zd* had produced the material (dahi*s*nŏ) of Zaratû*s*t, the glory then, in the

---

[1] The MS. has pata*s* for pê*s*.

[2] The contents of this chapter are thus mentioned in the summary of the Spend Nask (Dk. VIII, xiv, 1 in S.B.E., vol. xxxvii, p. 31):—'The Spend *contains* particulars about the origin *and* combination *of* the material *existence*, guardian spirit, *and* soul (or glory) of Zaratû*s*t; how the creation of each one *occurred* in the spiritual *existence*, and *in* what mode *it was* produced for the worldly *existence*; how their connection with the parents *arose*, the coming of the parents together, the combination in the mother, and the birth from the mother; *and* whatever is on the same subject.'

[3] The writer uses two Arabic words: mâ*d*îyâtŏ-i '*h*alqŏ.'

presence of Aûharmazd, fled on *towards* the material of Zaratûst, on to that germ; from that germ it fled on, on *to the light which is endless*[1]; from the light which is endless[2] it fled on, on to that of the sun; from that of the sun it fled on, on *to* the moon; from that moon it fled on, on to those stars; from those stars it fled on, on to the fire which *was* in the house of Zôis[3]; *and* from that fire it fled on, on to the wife of Frâhîmrvanã-zôis[4], when she brought forth that girl who became the mother of Zaratûst.'

4. Of that splendour, escaped at the same time into the earth *and* into the sky, the father-in-law's ignorance is declared, so that it is said by those in the village of the more instructed and invoking Zôîs[5], as to the self-combustion *which* burns the fire, that fuel is not necessary for its use. 5. Then they went on to the governor (kêdŏ), and he explained *to* them concerning that same (that is, he spoke to them) thus: 'The full glory of embodied existence

[1] Perplexed by the repetitions, some copyist has evidently omitted this phrase by mistake.

[2] Pahl. anagar, a transcript of Av. anaghra which is always translated by Pahl. asar, 'endless.' The 'endless light' is the abode of Aûharmazd, see Bd. I, 2.

[3] Written in Pâzand.

[4] Also written in Pâzand. In Bd. XXXII, 10, it is stated that 'the name of the father of the mother of Zaratûst was Frahimravâ' (or Fereâhimruvânâ in the Irânian version); but very little reliance can be placed on such Pâzand readings of names originally written in Pahlavi.

[5] Here written in Pahlavi letters which can also be read Zandîh. In the text, the two preceding adjectives, farhakhtar va-khvân, might be read Farâkht-ruvânân as the beginning of the name. But, as it stands, the text implies that Zôîs, the father-in-law of his son Frâhîm-rvanã's wife, was the master of the house, which is the usual oriental arrangement.

is the glory of life *apart* from the body, so that all diligence devoid of this is only movement.'

6. And *it is* declared that the demons, on account of their defeat by that glory in maintaining[1] adversity for the girl, *were* bringing on to that district three armaments (hênô), winter, the demon of pestilence, and oppressive enemies; and *a suspicion was* cast by them into the minds of those of the district, that this harm happened to the district owing to the witchcraft of this girl; so that those of the district quarreled dreadfully with the parents, as to the witchcraft of antagonism *in* the girl, and about putting *her* out from that district.

7. And the father of that girl spoke even these *words* to those of the district, with much reason, about the unjust assertion of witchcraft relative to the girl, that is: 'When this girl *was* brought forth among those of mine, her whole destiny (vakhsh) *was* afterwards set forth *by* that manifest radiance of fire, where it brought out radiance from all over her in the dark night. 8. When this girl sits in the interior of the house, wherein there is no fire, *and* in the chamber (sarâî) of fire they increase *its* intensity (bûrzŏ), it is lighter there, where *and* when this girl sits, than there where they increase the intensity of the fire; *one* is dazzled by the radiance from her body, *and* that of a wizard *would* not *have* been so glorious.'

9. Even then, owing to the influence (sârînisnŏ) of the demons, and the Kavîg and Karap[2] of the

[1] Reading dârîh, but it may be gârîh for kârîh, 'producing.'

[2] The Karaps were apparently idolatrous priests, especially those before the conversion of Vistâsp by Zaratûst; one being called 'a wizard' in Chap. III, 5, 42-44, another 'unsanctified' in IV, 24.

district, they did not become satisfied; *so* the father ordered the girl to go to Pa*d*îragtarâspô[1], the father of a family in the country (matâ) of the Spîtâmas, in the district (rû*d*astâk) of Alâk; and the girl obeyed the command of *her* father. 10. That disturbance which the demons caused, with evil intention, for the expatriation of that girl, the sacred beings assiduously made the reason for the coming of the girl for marriage to Pôrûshâspô, the father of Zaratû*s*t, through *her* father sending the girl to the dwelling of Pa*d*îragtarâspô, the father of Pôrûshâspô.

11. One *marvel*[2] is this which is declared, that when that girl, in going to that family, stood on the loftiest place in the country of the Spîtâmas, and *it* is surveyed by her, a great wonder is manifested to the girl, *just* as revelation mentions: 'It is their[3]

---

a third is 'deadly' in IV, 67, and a demon himself is a Karap in IV, 61, and has Karaps under his control in II, 45. The following Karaps are named in the time of Zaratû*s*t:—Dûrâsrôbô mentioned in Chap. III, 4–41; Brâ*d*rôk-rêsh in III, 20–34, who is called a Tûrânian in III, 28; Vaêdvôi*s*t in IV, 21–24; and Zâk in IV, 67. Some others are named by other writers. The Kavîgs, Kaîs, or Kîgs are mentioned with the Karaps in Chaps. II, 9; III, 50; IV, 2, 6, 14, 64, 67; VIII, 26, 40, as equally objectionable, but their avocation as officials is not defined. Both classes seem to have held official rank, but whether their titles were tribal or official is uncertain. The Avesta calls them Karapan and Kavi; the latter word being also the royal title of the Kayân dynasty, of which Vi*s*tâsp was a member. Compare Zs. XV, 1–4; XXIII, 8.

[1] So also in §§ 13, 70. In Bd. XXXII, 1, 2, the two old MSS. of the Irânian Bundahi*s* have Padtarâsp thrice and Pîrtarâsp once; K20 has Spîtarsp and Paitiresp; K20b has Padirtarâspô and Paitirispô; and M6 has Padirtarâsp and Paitiresp. Zs. XIII, 6, has Purtarâspô.

[2] One of the marvellous manifestations mentioned in § 1.

[3] Probably we should read: 'It is the voice of those sacred beings' who are mentioned in § 10. As the word yaz*d*ân, 'sacred beings,' is exactly similar, in Pahlavi, to shân (in val*d*shân, 'their'

voice is carried away to her from them; "do thou proceed to that village which is theirs; it is very depressed in height and very wide in breadth, in which he who is living and the cattle mostly walk together; besides, for thy assistance that village is divinely fashioned *and* compassionate."' 12. Thereupon that damsel stopped, and also fully observed that *their* recital seems *to be* for the conveyance of this statement, that my action *should be* such *as was* ordered me *by* my father also. 13. Then that damsel thoroughly washed *her* hands, and proceeded from them to that village which was Pa*d*îragtarâspô's, and the glory came to Pôrûshâspô, the son of Pa*d*îragtarâspô.

14. One *marvel* is this which is declared, that the creator Aûha*r*ma*zd* passed on the guardian spirit (fravâhar) of Zaratû*s*t, to the parents of Zaratû*s*t, through (le-*k*adôn) Hôm[1], by a marvel produced by cultivation. 15. Again, too, revelation says that, when the separation (burînŏ) of the third millennium occurred, at the end of the 3,000 years of spiritual existence without a destroyer, (after the creatures *were* in spiritual existence, *and* before the arrival of the fiend); then the archangels framed Zaratû*s*t together, *and* they seated the guardian spirit within, having a mouth, having a tongue, and the proclaimer *of* the celestial mansions.

---

or 'those'), a copyist would be liable to the blunder of leaving out the final word in writing val*d*shân ya*zd*ân. Or the original writer himself may not have quoted enough of the text he was reading, to make his meaning clear.

[1] A sacred and mythical tree, described in Bd. XVIII, 1–3, and often personified as a sacred being. It is now represented, in Parsi ceremonies, by twigs of a particular plant brought from Persia.

16. Then the three millenniums of Zaratûst[1] *were* the number manifest to them through observation by the eye, *and* it seemed that he became just like an archangel through bodily contact with (ham-kerpîh)[2] the archangels. 17. And when the separation of the third millennium occurred, after the framing of Zaratûst together, and before the conveying of Zaratûst down to the worldly *state*, at the end of the 3,000 years *of* worldly existence with a destroyer, then Aûharmazd argued with Vohûmanô *and* Ashavahistô[3] thus: 'Is his mother beheld by you, so that we may produce Zaratûst?'

18. And Ashavahistô spoke *in* reply thus: 'Thou art aware even of that, *O* propitious *one!* about the Zaratûst we *shall* produce, *and* thou and we have produced, thou knowest, *O* Aûharmazd! *and to us* who are the other archangels do thou announce the place, because its appearance thou knowest, *thou* propitious spirit Aûharmazd!'

19. Then Aûharmazd argued with Vohûmanô and the reminding by Ardavahistô[4], Shatraver, Spendarmad, Khûrdad, *and* Amûrdad[5], *saying*:

---

[1] Meaning the period of Zaratûst's existence merely as a guardian spirit, the first period of the destroyer (§ 17) who then remained powerless in confusion (see Bd. I, 22).

[2] Or 'sheltering with' (ham-karîkîh).

[3] The personifications of the Avesta phrases for 'good thought' and 'perfect rectitude,' who are two of the seven that hold a superior position among sacred beings, somewhat similar to that of archangels. When a Parsi speaks of Aûharmazd as the first of the Ameshaspends, or archangels, he does not put him on an equality with the rest, any more than we put a commander-in-chief on an equality with his troops when we call him a good soldier.

[4] Another pronunciation of Ashavahistô.

[5] These last four archangels are personifications of the Avesta

'The conveying of Zaratûst down does not seem *to be for* me, because, having a mouth *and* having a tongue, *he will be* a proclaimer to the world of embodied beings. 20. If we convey Zaratûst down on to the world of embodied beings, having a mouth *and* having a tongue, *as* a proclaimer *of* the celestial mansion, this is evident: they *will* say, concerning the origin *of* him who is my righteous man, *that* we frame him together with the water, with the land, with the plants, *and* with the animals[1]. 21. Therefore we *will* carry off there, to the village of Pôrûshâspô, him whom they *will* call Zaratûst of good lineage of both natures, both *of* Nêryôsang[2] who is of the archangels, and *of* Yim who is of mankind.'

22. Then the archangels framed together a stem of Hôm the height of a man, excellent in colour, *and* juicy where fresh; also to carry off the guardian spirit of Zaratûst to that stem of theirs, the archangels made it go forth thither from that endless light, and gave it up there also to the instinctive intellect (âsnô vîr). 23. Likewise their carrying off *was* manifest around, and a wall *was* openly displayed round them, but a restless one; the Hôm *was* constantly provided with a mouth, where it was suitable, *and* sap constantly oozed from the Hôm where it was moist.

24. And when thirty[3] years of the 3,000 years of

---

phrases for 'desirable dominion, bountiful devotion, completeness or health, and immortality.'

[1] That is, as an inferior and irresponsible being.

[2] Here spelt Nêrôsang; see Chaps. I, 29; II, 70; and Zs. XIII, 6, for this angel's influence on the royal race.

[3] The MS. has 330 years, but the time intended is evidently that shortly before the birth of Zaratûst, and this third 3,000 years

well-disturbed[1] worldly existence remained, Vohûmanô and Ashavahistô then associated their pre-eminence together, *and* turned off into the embodied existence; there they came up to where two birds had settled in quest of progeny, *and* seven years before the serpents devoured the inexperienced progeny. 25. For their *own* designs, Vohûmanô *and* Ashavahistô went on, and those birds consulted *them* thus: 'We have to offer homage, and our want is that Hôm.'

26. The circumstances of those associated together in pre-eminence and the request of these *for* that Hôm *were* a double marvel; Vohûmanô seized one of those *birds* by both legs, and the other *by* one; he also brought them that Hôm, and gave it up to them there, on that tree within *their* nest. 27. And they uncovered above the serpents, that have gone up to the progeny of the birds; then that guardian spirit of Zaratûst started up, and the serpents on the tree rushed also from them away towards the demons; *but* that guardian spirit of Zaratûst smote them on the jaws, *and* the serpents fell down *and* expired, which *events* have also occurred among them till now, *having* been requisite as regards a depriver of life (gân-gîr) and *any* one of that species. 28. And that Hôm *was* connected with that tree; and on the summit of that tree, there

ended either when Vistâspô accepted the religion, in Zaratûst's forty-second year, or when Zaratûst received the religion in his thirtieth year, but this earlier date is the more likely.

[1] This word, hû-aîbigadîg, is written in Pahlavi precisely like an-aîbigadîg, 'without a destroyer,' though its meaning is the reverse, which is an unexpected cause of perplexity to a cursory reader.

where the nest of the birds was, it grew constantly fresh and golden-coloured[1].

29. After the coming of her who bore Zaratûst, to Pôrûshâspô for marriage, Vohûmanô *and* Ardavahistô, thus associated together in their preeminence, came up there to Pôrûshâspô in the cattle-pasture of the Spîtâmas, and their thoughts *were* confined to that Hôm brought by them. 30. Then Pôrûshâspô walked forth, with spiritual desire, up to the water of the Dâît[2], because the requirement of the spirits is the spiritual knowledge[3] that spirits are ever-beneficial; and that Hôm *was* also seen by him, when it had grown on that tree, on the inside of the nest. 31. Then Pôrûshâspô thought thus: 'It is for me, really (madam-îk-am) to proceed and, even as *there* is no reaching by me up to that Hôm, that tree must be cut down, for apart from that, *O* Hôm of Aûharmazd! thou seemest fresh, so that the benefit of something from thee *will be* advantageous.'

32. Then Pôrûshâspô walked on and washed their clothes acquiescently (patâsîg), and here a great wonder was manifest to Pôrûshâspô. 33. About this it says that, all the while that Pôrûshâspô washed their clothes, Vohûmanô then proceeded from the uppermost third of the tree unto the middle of it, whereon *it was* the desire of Pôrû-

---

[1] Or it may be 'verdant.'

[2] Av. Dâitya, a mythic river in Aîrân-vêg (Bd. XX, 13); a favourite place for religious rites, see Yt. V, 17, 104, 112; IX, 25, 29; XVII, 45, 49, 61. Or it may be merely mayâ-î shêd, 'brilliant water.'

[3] Reading maînôg-dânisnîh, but the MS. has maînôg dênô-dânîh which might be translated 'spiritual knowledge of religion,' though the latter Pahlavi word is unusual.

shâspô to be conveyed. 34. Then Pôrûshâspô, *having* washed the clothes, walked up to it and, thereupon gathering up the whole of that *Hôm*, all of it *was* then also appropriated by him through assistance like that of that *archangel*, *just* as what thou offerest for the food-sustenance of a friend's son of two years *or* three years *of age;* and it seemed to him that *archangel's* joyful payment.

35. Carrying off their Hôm, Pôrûshâspô spoke of it to *his* noble (mas) wife thus: 'So thou, *O* Dûk*d*âûb! shouldst keep their Hôm in custody, all the while that their Hôm fulfils duty and routine.'

36. One *marvel* is this *which is* declared, that the coming of the nature (gôhar) of the body of Zaratû*s*t, through water *and* vegetation, to the bodies of *his* parents, is manifested *as* a great wonder of the creator to the multitude. 37. As revelation mentions *it thus:* 'Thereupon, when Aûha*r*ma*zd* had produced the material (dahi*s*nŏ) of Zaratû*s*t[1], the nature of *his* body then, in the presence of Aûha*r*ma*zd*, fled on *towards* the material of Zaratû*s*t.'

38. About Khûr*d*ad and Mûr*d*ad[2] bringing the cloud-water down in a compassionate manner ever anew, drop by drop, *and* completely warm, for the delight of sheep and men, *and—with* as much seed as the roving of two rampant bulls *would* thereby *cast* upon the plants *which* have grown, all of every species—*they are* casting *it* upon those other plants at that time, even upon the dry *ones;* and the

---

[1] Compare § 3.

[2] These two archangels have special charge of water and vegetation (see Sls. XV, 25–29), and here they are represented as acting in a manner usually ascribed to Ti*s*tar, the Dog-star.

nature of Zaratûst came from that water to those plants.

39. One *marvel* is this *which is* declared, that, in order that the nature of Zaratûst shall come unto *his* parents, after[1] the mounting of the archangels Pôrûshâspô drives six white cows, with yellow ears, up to those plants. 40. And here is manifested a great wonder, *such* as revelation mentions thus: Two[2] of those cows, unimpregnated, *had* become full of milk, and the nature of Zaratûst came from the plants to those cows, and is mingled with the cows' milk; it is owing thereto *that* Pôrûshâspô drove those cows back. 41. And Pôrûshâspô spoke to Dûk*d*âûb thus: '*O* Dûk*d*âûb! in two of those cows, *which are* unimpregnated *and have* not calved, milk *has* appeared; do thou milk those cows, which are the splendour *and* glory of the cows *and of* any embodied existence whatever.' 42. And Dûk*d*âûb arose and, taking that pail of hers which had a four-fold capacity, she also milked from them the milk which *was* in them, and a great *part* of what they gave up to her she had to throw away; and the nature of Zaratûst was in that milk.

43. One *marvel* is this which is manifested in the struggle of the adversary for concealing and spoiling that milk, *just* as revelation mentions thus: Thereupon, at that time, the demons formed *themselves* into an assembly, and the demon of demons growled thus: 'You demons become quite unobservant: that food is really supplied fresh, so that the formation is settled which *will* extend as far as to that

[1] Reading akha*r* instead of adên, 'then.'

[2] In some places the singular number is used, in others the plural.

man who *will be* the righteous Zaratûst; which of you *will* undertake his destruction, all the while that he exists for mankind, so as to make *him* more contemptibly impotent?' 44. *K*êshmak[1], astute in evil, growled thus: 'I *will* undertake his destruction.' 45. Astute in evil, he rushed away with thrice fifty *of* the demons who are Karaps of *K*êshmak; and that village *was* partly uprooted and partly destroyed[2] by him, fellow-workers *were* ruined, and the number of fellow-eaters of broken victuals, attending the great, *was* not broken up, among whom was he that had repelled his authority.

46. *It is* declared that, afterwards, Pôrûshâspô asked again *for* that Hôm from Dûk*d*âûb, and he pounded it, and with that cows' milk[3], into which the nature of the body of Zaratûst had come, he here mingled the guardian spirit of Zaratûst, and the nature of the body came at once into union with it.

47. One *marvel* is this *which is* declared, that Pôrûshâspô *and* Dûk*d*âûb drank up that Hôm and milk, when they were mingled together and announced to Aûhar*m*a*zd*; and here occurred a combination of the glory, guardian spirit, and bodily nature of Zaratûst into a man*child*. 48. And a great wonder is manifested to both of them, through that which revelation mentions thus: Thereupon, both have embraced the first *time*[4] with desire

---

[1] The whirlwind demon; see Bd. XXVIII, 24. Compare Chap. IV, 61.

[2] The usual effects of a hurricane.

[3] The mingling of milk with pounded Hôm still constitutes part of the Parsi ceremonial; see Haug's Essays, 3rd ed., p. 405.

[4] Pahl. 'ko*l*â 2 lâlâ fratûm vapdî*d*ô hav*â*nd.'

for a son, *and* the demons shouted out unto them, in the villainous speech *of* sinfulness, thus: 'Why shouldst thou act like this, vile[1] Pôrûshâspô?' whereupon they started up like people who *are* ashamed. 49. A second *time* they have embraced, and the demons shouted out unto them, in villainous speech; whereupon they started up like people who *are* ashamed. 50. A third *time* they have embraced thus, with desire for a son; and the demons shouted out unto them, in villainous speech; whereupon they started up like people who *are* ashamed. 51. And they spoke with one another about *it*, *and* continued at this duty, and accomplished it[2], *saying*: 'We will not so stop without accomplishing something, not *even* though both Râk and Nô*d*ar *should* arrive here together[3].' 52. Then that man*child* who *was* the righteous Zaratû*s*t became complete, and here *below there* came together the nature of the body, the guardian spirit, and the glory of Zaratû*s*t in the womb *of his* mother.

53. One *marvel* is this which is declared, that, after the combination of Zaratû*s*t in the womb *of his* mother, the demons strove anew wonderfully

[1] Reading anâg, but it may be intended for hanâ=aê, 'O.'

[2] Pahl. '*a*fshân madam hâr s*u*ftŏ, aêghshânŏ pavan akôsh *frâz* va*b*idûntô.'

[3] Evidently an old proverb, implying a fixed determination whatever catastrophe may happen, even if one's ancestors of the eleventh or twelfth generation shall appear. Nô*d*ar (Av. Naotara) was a son of King Mânû*sk*îhar (Bd. XXXI, 13, 23), and Râk was a nephew of Nô*d*ar (Bd. XXXI, 31), doubtless the same as Ragan (Bd. XXXII, 1; XXXIII, 3) which seems to be a Pâzand misreading of Aîri*k*ŏ, or Êri*k*ŏ, see Zs. XVI, 11–13, and compare the genealogies in Chap. II, 70 and Zs. XIII, 6. The proverb is used again in Chap. III, 19, and the names are mentioned in III, 39.

to cause the death of Zaratûst in *his* mother's womb, and she who bore him *was* rendered sickly by them through the sharpest of sharp and afflictive pain, until she wished to ask the wizard physicians for a desirable remedy. 54. And here is manifested a great wonder, just as revelation says: 'It is then a voice of theirs is carried away there to her from the higher region, from Aûharmazd and from the archangels, thus: "Thou damsel who goest! do not proceed thither, because anything *of* theirs is destruction through wizard medical treatment; *for* healthfulness wash *thy* hands thoroughly, *and* those hands shall take firewood, and upon it thou shalt offer meat for the sake of the infant, thou shalt offer up cows' butter *to* the fire for his sake; thou shalt likewise heat *it* at the fire for his sake, and shalt quaff (pâîmês) *it* off at the *proper* time for his sake, and thou *wilt* become well."' 55. Then at once that damsel washed *her* hands thoroughly, and she did just as *she had* heard, and became well[1].

56. One *marvel* is this which is manifested to the multitude when three days remained to his coming[2] *forth;* in the manner of the sun, at the approach of *its* uprising, when its first advancing twilight is diffused, *his* body is then announced as revelation says: 'It is then when in those last three nights during which Zaratûst was in the womb, where he still subsisted three days till afterwards born, *that* the village of Pôrûshâspô became all luminous. 57. Then spoke the horse-owners and cattle-owners of the Spîtâmas, in running away, thus: "It is requisite *to be* forgiven[3]; the village of Pôrûshâspô, on which

[1] Compare Zs. XIV, 2–5.
[2] Literally 'going.'
[3] Apparently an appeal for mercy.

that fire[1] is in every crevice, is disturbed by confusion[2]." 58. Then, on running together again, they said: "It is not fully forgiven for the village of Pôrûshâspô; fire is on it in every crevice *and* it is disturbed by confusion; unto him is born, at his house, a brilliant man*child*."'

59. This, too, is one of the wonders, when the report of the marvellousness of the birth *of* that man*child and of his* great glory, is due to statements of Yim and also others, brilliant in carrying on the destiny which had entered them from the sacred beings. 60. Wherein Yim spoke to the demons thus: 'Here *below* the pure *and* righteous Zaratûst *will* be born, who *will* produce for you who are demons that absence of intercession which is prepared for you (that is, he *will* produce for you a thoroughly-harassed actual inactivity, an absence of intercession so that you are not able to pray on your own account, *and* no one prays for you).'

61. *It is* declared that the report about the birth of Zaratûst, and concerning his prophesying, is explained (avazandî-hastŏ) only by the illustrious, *such* as Yim and Frê*d*ûn *and* many learned people; but the sacred beings are also heard through the tongues of the animals scattered in the world, in order that even that witness shall arise as regards his prophesying. 62. *Just* like that which is declared, that in the reign of Kaî-Ûs *there* was an ox, and a splendour had come to his body from the sacred beings; and whenever a dispute as to the frontier arose between Irân and Tûrân, that ox *was* brought, and the boundary between Irân and Tûrân

---

[1] Assuming that nîram stands for nîr*ă*, a variant of nûrâ.

[2] Or 'terrified with fear.'

was truly shown by him. 63. And because, when an Irânian *had* to seek a decision as to a Tûrânian in a dispute *and* lies occurred, the Tûrânians were constantly convicted through the showing of the boundary *by* the ox, and happened to be defeated by the Irânians—*and*, besides that, their envy also *arose* as to Kaî-Ûs, even of *his* ownership—therefore, on account of *his* possession of that wonder, the Tûrânians proceeded about the smiting and destruction of that ox, and through their sorcery and witchcraft the mind of Kaî-Ûs *was* disturbed about that ox, and he went to a warrior, *whose* name *was* Srîtô[1], *and* ordered him to kill that ox; *so* that man came to smite the ox. 64. And here is manifested a wonder of importance by that ox, *such* as revelation mentions thus: 'To him spoke the ox, in grave words, thus: "Thou shouldst not murder me, *O* Srîtô! thou seventh[2] of those of this race; you *will* atone *for this* malice when Zaratûst, the most desirous of righteousness among the existences, arrives and proclaims thy bad action in revelation; and the distress in thy soul becomes such as is declared by that passage where *it says*: 'As death occurs to him, that of Vadak[3] and the like occurs.'"' 65. *It* is declared that that man, when this wonder *was* thus seen by him *proceeding* from the ox, did not kill *it*, but went back to Kaî-Ûs *and* told *him* what he *had* seen. 66. Kaî-Ûs then still, on account of the amazing deceitfulness of the demons *and* wizards, ordered the same man to smite that ox;

[1] This legend is also told, with further details, in Zs. XII, 7-25.
[2] Compare Zs. XII, 10.
[3] The mother of Dahâk, who first committed adultery in an aggravated form (see Dd. LXXII, 5; LXXVIII, 2).

and that man proceeded also again to the ox, *and* though *it was* carrying *on* still much *of* that talk, he did not lend an ear to *it*, *but* killed *it*.

67. Regarding the sole-created ox[1], too, *it* is declared that, *on* meeting its destruction by the evil spirit, it bellowed thus: 'Though thou thinkest it as to us, *O* evil spirit, astute in evil! that thou art *in* every way a winner by destruction, *it is* not to our destruction thou art even then an attainer *in* every way (that is, *it* is not possible for thee so to annihilate that we *shall* not arise again); even now I proclaim that that man, Zaratûst of the Spîtâmas, *will* arrive in that last revolution, who *will* produce distress for the demons, the assistants of the demon, and also the wicked who are bipeds.'

68. Likewise the marvellousness of Zaratûst's defeat of the demons, owing to his glory and by means of his sagacity, even before he had come into the world by birth; when Frâsîyâv[2] the wizard is amazingly distressed through seeking that glory of his by desire of the demons, just as revelation[3] mentions thus: 'Thereupon Frâsîyâv, the very powerful Tûrânian, rushed away, *O* Zaratûst of the Spîtâmas! to the wide-formed ocean a first, a second, and a third time; and he wished to obtain that glory which is specially for those *of* the countries of Irân, *for* the born and the unborn, and which is *for* the righteous *one*; *but* he did not attain to that glory.'

---

[1] Pahl. tôrâ-î aêvak-dâdŏ, the primeval ox, from whom the animals and plants have all descended (see Bd. III, 14, 17, 18; IV, 1–5; X, 1; XIV, 1–3; XXVII, 2).

[2] The same person as Frangrâsîyâk of Chaps. I, 31, 39; II, 69; XI, 3.

[3] In Yt. XIX, 56–62; V, 42.

69. And this, too, *is mentioned*, that to all the seven regions the villain Frangrâsîyâk rushed away, and the glory of Zaratû*s*t *was* sought by him [1].

70. Here is an enumeration *of* the worthy lineage of Zaratû*s*t [2]:—Zaratû*s*t *was son* of Pôrûshâspô, *son* of Pa*d*îragtarâspô, of Urugadhasp*, of Haê*k*a*d*aspô*, of *K*ikhshnu*s**, of Paêtrasp*, of Areǵadhar*s*n*, of Hardhar*, of Spîtâm, of Vaêdi*s*t*, of Nayâzem* [3], of Aîrî*k* [3], of Dûrâsrôbô, of Mânû*sk*îhar monarch of Irân, of Mânû*s*-khûrnar, of Mânû*s*-khûrnâk whom Nêrôksang implanted in [4] Vîzak*, *daughter* of Airyak*, *son* of Thritak*, of Bitak*, of Frazû*s*ak*, of Zû*s*ak*, of Fragûzak* [5], of Gûzak* [6], *daughter* of Aîrî*k*, *son* of Frê*d*ûn monarch of Khvanîras, *son* of Pûr-tô*r*â the Âspîgân, of Nêvak-tô*r*â the Âspîgân, of Sôg-tô*r*â the Âspîgân, of Bôr-tô*r*â the Âspîgân, of Ka*r*dâr-tô*r*â [7] the Âspîgân, of Sîyah-tô*r*â the Âspîgân, of Spêtô-tô*r*â the Âspîgân, of Gêfar-tô*r*â the Âspîgân, of Ramak-tô*r*â [8] the Âspîgân, of Vanô-fravi*s*n the Âspîgân, of Yim monarch of the seven

[1] See Yt. XIX, 82.

[2] Compare the genealogy in Zs. XIII, 6; Bd. XXXII, 1, and that quoted there from the Vigîrka*r*d-i Dênîg. The names marked here with an asterisk are written in Pâzand, or partly so.

[3] Ayazem, of Ragan, in Bd. The latter name is Rag*is*n in Vig., but Êri*k*ô in Zs. XVI, 13.

[4] This wants confirmation, but varzî*d* *b*ên can hardly be a name as assumed in Vig., where it is altered to Varzî*d*-dên.

[5] The g is of the old form like s.

[6] The G is omitted, but see Bd. XXXI, 14.

[7] Or Kûtâl-tô*r*â; this generation is omitted both in the Vigîrka*r*d and Bundahi*s*.

[8] This generation is interlined in the MS. of the Dînka*r*d. The Bundahi*s*, XXXI, 7, also omits Nêvak-tô*r*â; and the Vigîrka*r*d omits Bôr-tô*r*â, Sîyah-tô*r*â, Spêtô-tô*r*â, and Ramak-tô*r*â. The termination tô*r*â is merely the Zvâri*s* equivalent of gau. In Irânian MSS. the Pahlavi î and û are practically written alike in most cases.

regions, *son* of Vîvangha, of Ayang,ha*d**, of Anan-g,ha*d**, *son* of Hôshâng the Pê*s*dâ*d*ian monarch of the seven regions, *son* of Fravâk, of Sîyâmak, of Masyâ, of Gâyômar*d* the first man.

CHAPTER III.

1. About the marvellousness which is manifested after the birth of that most auspicious of offsprings from *his* mother, till his coming to a conference *with* Aûha*r*ma*zd*[1].

2. One *marvel* is this *which is* declared, that on being born he laughed outright; the seven midwives (dayah)[2], who sat around him, were quite frightened thereby; and those terrified ones spoke thus: 'What was this, on account of grandeur or contempt? when, like the worthy man whose pleasure is due to activity, the man's child so laughs at the birth owing to him.' 3. Pôrûshâspô also spoke thus: 'Bring out this man*child* to the sheep*skin* clothing which is soft; the affair *was* owing to thee, owing to the virtue of thee who art Dûk*d*âûb, that the advent of glory and coming of radiance to this man*child was* openly seen when he laughed outright at his birth.'

4. One *marvel* is this which is declared, that Pôrûshâspô afterwards went to a Karap, Dûrâsrôbô *by* name, who was the most renowned for witchcraft in that district, and informed him of the birth of Zaratû*s*t *and* the wonders which were manifested

---

[1] The contents of this chapter refer chiefly to 'the rearing of Zaratûst.' For the other matters mentioned in Dk. VIII, xiv, 2, see Zs. XIV, 6–12.

[2] Sls. X, 15 prescribes 'ten women.' Zs. XIV, 13 mentions 'seven wizards (yâtûkŏ).'

therein; he *also* brought *him* to the house for the purpose of seeing Zaratûst. 5. That wizard, owing to the coming *on* of vexation at that glory in Zaratûst, desired with evil intention a really mischievous deceit (shê*d*ŏ), to compress with *his* paws (gôv) the tender head of that full-glorious child, to cause *his* death. 6. And here is manifested a great wonder to the multitude, just as revelation mentions *it* thus: 'Thereupon the paws of that deadly *one* (mar) *are* driven back to behind him (that is, reversed (aûskûn) backwards); nor ever after *did* that deadly *one* become again a devourer of meat with *his* jaws by means of those paws.' 7. That Karap also, besides that, examined the marks *and* evil specks on Zaratûst[1]; and Pôrûshâspô, *in* awful alarm as to the dispersion *of* the emanation of splendour (âp-dihîh) from Zaratûst, hastened (sârînî*d*) to make Zaratûst invisible.

8. One *marvel* is this *which is* declared, that the Karap Dûrâsrôbô, through witchcraft, cast such fear of Zaratûst into the mind *of* Pôrûshâspô, *and* so injured the mind of Pôrûshâspô, that, owing only to that very fear as regards himself, he asked the Karap for the death of Zaratûst. 9. Also about[2] the mode of putting to death for which Pôrûshâspô, owing to the distraction (vishôpisnŏ) by which he becomes helpless, asks Dûrâsrôbô; and that Karap is bringing much firewood together, and to shelter (nipâyî*d*anŏ) Zaratûst amid that firewood, to stir up a fire, and to make *it* blaze with the wood were the remedy he arranged (vîrâstŏ); and Pôrûshâspô acted accord-

[1] Compare Zs. XVI, 1–3.

[2] Pahl. madam-m*á*, where m*á*=*k*i, 'what? whatever,' is used for -i*k*, 'also,' as often happens.

ingly. 10. And here is manifested a great wonder to the multitude, just as revelation mentions it thus: 'Neither *was* fire among the vegetation on a tree (that is, it does not come on), nor *has* fire seized upon plants; *but* on rushed, at dawn[1], that son-loving mother, and she came forth to him intelligently (hûshûmônd), and seizing him, thereby removed him with *her* right hand aloft as he sat[2].'

11. One *marvel* is this which is declared, that after Pôrûshâspô spoke to the Karap Dûrâsrôbô about the fire not burning *the child*, he asked anew about putting Zaratûst to death; *then* to ensconce (nipâyî*d*anŏ) Zaratûst in a narrow path, and despatch many oxen on that path, so that he *may* be trampled on *by* the feet of the oxen *at* night, were the remedy that Karap proposed (girâyî*d*ŏ) to Pôrûshâspô; and Pôrûshâspô acted accordingly. 12. Here also is manifested a wonder of grandeur to the multitude, just as revelation mentions: 'It *was* that ox walked on which *had* become sorrowful (that is, its sorrow was great owing to another ox) and *it was* aged and walked before that *one* (before the leading ox), it *also* hastened before that *other* (that is, it stood up before Zaratûst), *and* he *was* greatly pitied by it for the whole day, so that it kept away the oxen from him, *being* the first *that* walked thither *and* the last *that* walked away; on rushed at dawn that son-loving mother, forth to *him* she came intelli-

[1] Reading pavan aûsh, but it might be pavan hûsh, 'with sense,' here and in § 14, where there is nothing to indicate that the child was out all night, but in §§ 12, 18 he is evidently rescued the next morning.

[2] Pahl. 'madam pavan aûstakŏ.' Compare Zs. XVI, 7.

gently, and seizing him, thereby removed him with *her* right hand aloft as he sat[1].'

13. One *marvel* is this which is declared, that Pôrûshâspô came a second time (îdanŏ) to that Karap also about the oxen not trampling on Zaratûst, *and* asked anew about the mode *of* putting Zaratûst to death; *then* to ensconce Zaratûst *near* a drinking-pool (*â*vkhûr) in the domain (gêhân), and to drive many horses to that drinking-pool, so that he may be trampled on by the hoofs of the horses, were the substituted[2] remedy that Karap proposed; *and* Pôrûshâspô acted accordingly. 14. And here is manifested a great wonder to the multitude, just as revelation mentions thus: 'That horse walked on which *had* become fully-hoofed (that is, its hoofs were very thick); *it is* yellow-eared and it walks before that *one* (before the leading horse), and it hastens before that *other* (that is, it stood up before Zaratûst), and *was* the first *that* walked on thither, *and* the last *that* walked away; on rushed at dawn that son-loving mother, forth to him she came intelligently, and seizing him, thereby removed him with *her* right hand aloft as he sat[3].'

15. One *marvel* is this *which is* declared, that Pôrûshâspô *came* again to that Karap, spoke also about the horses, too, not trampling on Zaratûst, and asked anew as to what *may be* the mode *of* putting

---

[1] Compare Zs. XVI, 5.

[2] Possibly 'supplementary' or 'gratuitous.' The word is nîrmatŏ which, as a noun, means the gratuity or honorarium paid to a priest for acting as a substitute for another. Its etymology is obscure, unless it be an abbreviation of nîrûmandî, 'strength,' used in the legal sense of 'refresher.'

[3] Compare Zs. XVI, 6.

Zaratûst to death; *then* to have Zaratûst carried off into the den (sûrâk) where a wolf's cubs (hûnûskân) *are* slaughtered, so that when the wolf arrives *and* sees the slaughtered cubs, she *will* wrathfully growl *and* mangle Zaratûst in revenge for those cubs, was the remedy that Karap proposed; and Pôrûshâspô acted accordingly. 16. *And* here is manifested a great wonder to the multitude, just as revelation mentions: 'It is when that wolf came on, several Yûgyâsts [1], towards Zaratûst, the wolf *was* struck dumb by the assistance of the sacred beings, so that its mouth *was* down *at* the cubs, one with the other.'

17. One *marvel* is this which is declared, that Srôsh [2] the righteous *and* Vohûmanô proceeded to him, and a woolly (kûrûsak) *sheep* was brought by them unto him; the nurses (dâyagân) [3] also *were* terrified, apart from him, the whole night. 18. *Then* on rushed at dawn that son-loving mother, forwards from the position *of* that woolly *sheep* she walked, and she, the mistress of the domain (zan-î gehân), spoke thus: 'Thou runnest on violently (ûtayûtŏ) in excess;' for she considered in this *way*, that 'the wolf is so much better to that son than thou art [4] good to me, when I shall show *his* [5] bone or blood in thy sight [6].' 19. Forwards to him has she come

[1] The Yûgyâst is a distance of sixteen Roman miles of a thousand paces each (see Dk. VIII, xx, 19, note). But the writer of the scripture here quoted could have had no idea of the distance he was mentioning.

[2] A sacred being who personifies 'obedience,' and is a special protector of man, particularly at night.

[3] It may also be read dehîgân, 'the country-folk.'

[4] Or '*she* would be.'

[5] Or 'they show *my*.'

[6] This seems to be a bitter reproach addressed to her husband; but the ambiguity of the Pahlavi makes its exact meaning rather uncertain.

intelligently and, seizing him, she thereby removed him, through the grace (dahisnŏ) of the sacred beings, aloft as he sat; and she, the mistress of the domain, spoke thus: 'I *shall* not give thee up again, *my* son, not *even* though both Râk and Nô*d*ar *should* arrive here together[1].'

20. And *it* is declared that, afterwards, the Karap Dûrâsrôbô, with a malicious disciple, came to the same district and noticed about the advancement of Zaratûst; and they saw no means for injuring *or* putting *him* to death, but his condition (mindavam) *was* a marvel as full of vigour as this which is declared, that Brâ*d*rôk-rêsh, the Karap, growled thus: —21. 'Then I, *who* am the most far-seeing of the people in that district of ours as to witchcraft, see upon their district that well-directing (that is, he understands good commands) produce *of* development (that is, the increase which continually becomes more, which *has* come and which *will* arrive), with good flocks (that is, he understands to keep good sheep), with good herds (that is, he understands to keep a herd which is better *than* another's), the well-exerting (that is, he understands to do work which is better *than* another's), well-fighting (that is, he understands to do battle well), and perfectly liberal (that is, he understands to exercise beneficial liberality) bantling (hûnûskŏ) of Pôrûshâspô[2], in the three nights while he was begotten out of

[1] See Chap. II, 51. Compare Dk. V, ii, 4; Zs. XVI, 8–13.

[2] The Pahlavi version of an Avesta text, here translated, is a fair specimen of the complication produced by appending a gloss to every epithet. It is useful as a combination of translation and lexicon, but it is apt to be perplexing, unless all the glosses are carefully omitted by the reader who can dispense with a lexicon.

his parents. 22. Unto him *will* Vohûmanô come in the embodied world (that is, Vohûmanô *will* come unto Zaratû*s*t), and conducting him unto a conference, his good religion *will* extend into the seven regions *of* the earth; and so I *shall* not even let him produce in *his* mind (that is, he *will* not know) where *and* how I *shall* murder him; and a token of this matter, that *one* speaks truly, is this, that I state *it* beforehand, promptly after the full hearing of the statement of the matter, when you heard this statement.'

23. Pôrûshâspô advanced, conveyed in a four-in-hand chariot [1]; then, on hearing that statement, *and* when they had heard that statement, Pôrûshâspô started forth, conveyed in that four-in-hand chariot. 24. And Pôrûshâspô spoke to Brâ*d*rôk-rêsh, the Karap, thus: 'Brâ*d*rôk-rêsh, *thou* Karap! whatever men they shall behold, cry out when at birth; even the offspring of that secluded person they behold in death, cry out when at birth [2]; *but* what *was* that which *they* beheld *at* the birth of my son? 25. When at birth he laughed outright; *was* that also beheld *in* thy son, when at birth did he laugh outright? 26. When Vohûmanô comes unto him, into *this* embodied existence, *it* is also said by him on *his* return: "*O* Pôrûshâspô! where is thy servant [3]?" So, *O* Karap! concerning him who is my son, *it is* beheld that *he was* seen sagaciously by thee.'

For restoring the original Avesta, the Pahlavi translation, without the glosses, is usually the best guide.

[1] Pahl. 4-ayûgi*s*nŏ râê (Av. *k*athruyukhta and ratha).

[2] This seems to be the meaning of Pahl. 'zag-*ík* tanŏ armê*s*tô-dahi*s*nîh pavan *fráz* khadîtund margîh, amat pavan zerkhûni*s*nŏ, ba*r*â bekhûnd.'

[3] Pahl. 'Pôrûshâspô! aêghat bandakŏ?'

27. And[1] when Pôrûshâspô enquired of him thus: 'What was the *matter* with thee when, through bringing thee unto that son of mine, *he was* thereby offered; and thou lookedst long up away from him in height, and thou lookedst long down away from him in depth, and thou lookedst long out away from him in different directions?' 28. The Tûrânian, Brâ*d*rôk-rêsh the Karap, spoke *in* reply thus: 'When through bringing me unto that son *was thy* offering of him, and I[2] looked long up away from him in height, then the radiance *and* glory out of him kept together up to the sun, *and* through him[3] I have accompanied *them* on the boundary *of its* radiance *and* glory; so that I saw this, that mankind through speaking to the soul may attain to the firmament of the sun; *but* this, namely, how the routine (dâ*d*istânŏ) is in the supreme heaven, *was* not seen by me. 29. When through bringing me unto that son of thine *was thy* offering of him, and I looked long down in depth away from *thy* offering of him, then the radiance and glory out of him kept together unto the sky which is below this earth, and through him[4] to the boundary of *its* radiance and glory; *but* this, namely, how the routine is in that sky, *was* not seen by me. 30. And when through bringing me unto that son of thine *was thy* offering of him, and I looked long out away from him in different directions, then the radiance *and* glory from him kept together for adorning this earth, *and*

[1] The first five words of § 28 are here inserted in the MS., so as to combine the two sentences in a perplexing manner.

[2] The MS. has *a*fat for *a*fam by mistake. [3] Or 'that.'

[4] The differences of form in §§ 28–30 are probably due to errors of copyists.

through him I have accompanied *them* on the boundary of *its* radiance *and* glory; so that I saw this, that only from the action of this *one* the future existence *will* arise; but the routine of the future existence *was* not seen by me. 31. This son of thine thinks thus: "I *will* make a grander material existence than that of *any* other;" so he *will* also make thy spiritual *one*, where thou goest; *and* this son of thine *will* remain in the great protection *of* Vistâsp, not in thine.'

32. One *marvel* is this which is declared, that when Zaratûst was seven years old, that Dûrâsrôbô being joined by Brâ*d*rôk-rêsh the Karap at the village of Pôrûshâspô, on account of the little previous seeing of Zaratûst *by the latter*, they saw Zaratûst in that neighbourhood when a hut (kâ*d*akŏ) was constructed by him with the children; and they sat with evil intention to injure the mind of Zaratûst through witchcraft, and for that reason fear and terror *were* cast by them upon the children. 33. Here a great wonder became manifest to them, owing to the powerful intellect, cautiousness, and practice of Zaratûst, just as revelation mentions thus: 'When the other children were excessively terrified at their own silliness of speech, Zaratûst did not quite close the eye in his mind as regards them.'

34. One *marvel* is this *which is* declared, that when these two Karaps came to the dwelling of Pôrûshâspô, he ordered the preparation of food for their eating; and his prepared food is chewed up (f*râz* khayâî-aît), *with* a gobletful (pûr dôlakŏ) of mare's milk. 35. He also spoke to Dûrâsrôbô thus: 'Thou art the most spirit-worshipping[1] of mankind

[1] Literally 'demon-worshipping;' it is not clear that idolatry is

in our district; do thou worship this of mine.' 36. A great marvel, owing to the sagacity of Zaratûst at a childish age, is just as revelation mentions that Zaratûst spoke thus: 'I worship this, *O* father! *it is* not that which it is necessary for me to worship *that* he should worship.' 37. And Pôrûshâspô spoke thus: '*It is* not that of mine thou worshippest, *and* it is that of mine he should worship.' 38. As many as three times those persons (gabrâân) carried on those assertions; *when* up stood Zaratûst and spoke concerning them, and he broke forth with that eternal statement[1], namely: 'The righteous I reverence, men *or* women; the poor I reverence, men *or* women; *not* the wicked, men or women; when any one whatever shall join Pôrûshâspô, where he shall be celebrating worship, the worship shall then be suitable to the worshippers, that is, he shall worship that which it is necessary to worship.'

39. One *marvel* is this which is declared, that afterwards Dûrâsrôbô the Karap shouted to Zaratûst thus: 'Evil was thy reckoning[2] which, owing to the conduct of fate (bâhar), I, the foremost of the existences embodied in Râk and Nôdâr[3], bring to thee; I am made further worthy where thy fate is carried away from me; now is the joy (parkân) which I convey to him[4] through bringing *it* on, and this

intended, but rather some form of worship antecedent to Zoroastrian Mazda-worship which latter had not yet been established. The author of this legend must have supposed that it differed very little from the religion of Pôrûshâspô.

[1] Reading sakhûn-i leyalmin which is written in Pahlavi exactly like dashinô rigeld, 'the right foot.'

[2] Pahl. marakŏ, possibly for marg, 'death.'

[3] See Chap. II, 51, note.

[4] Probably referring to his companion Brâdrôk-rêsh who, accord-

will occur, so that I *may* observe he *will* kill thee with the evil eye in the house.' 40. And here is a great wonder which became manifest about Zaratûst, in the sagacity of *his* reply to that deadly *one* at that childish age, which *was* just like this which revelation mentions, that Zaratûst spoke thus: 'Without the joy of a murderer I observe, with propitiousness and complete mindfulness, that it is thee I notice in that house which is thine [1].'

41. One *marvel* is that which, after this reply of Zaratûst to Dûrâsrôbô, became manifest in that Karap, just as revelation mentions thus: 'The deadly *one* became disabled and stupefied as long as the milking of ten mares *in* milk whose milker is *only* one.'

42. One *marvel* is this *which is* declared, that when that wizard emerged from *that* stupefaction, he then shouted again to Zaratûst *in* the same manner, Zaratûst uttered that same reply, *and* the deadly *one* became anew disabled and stupefied as long as the milking of twenty mares full of milk whose milker *is only one.*

43. One *marvel* is this which is declared, that again when that wizard emerged from *that* stupefaction, he then shouted to Zaratûst *in* the same manner, Zaratûst uttered that same reply, *and* the deadly *one* becomes anew disabled and stupefied as long as the milking of thirty mares full of milk whose milker is *only* one.

44. One *marvel* is this *which is* declared, that when that wizard emerged from that stupefaction, he

ing to most accounts, was the murderer of Zaratûst in his old age. This tradition is mentioned in Dk. VII only here and in § 22.

[1] Alluding to Dûrâsrôbô's own fate, see § 45.

then grumbled thus: 'Do ye have the horse driven for us, and turn round the chariot wherein you harness *it*; for really this smiting *one* (ganâk) *will* destroy me through the arrival of the *sacred* text *and* through *his* possession of authority.' *So* they had the horse driven, and *it was* harnessed to the chariot by them. 45. And here is manifested a great wonder to the multitude, just as revelation mentions thus: 'When he *had* proceeded several Yûgyâsts[1] in driving, he stopped in his distress through being terrified, *and* this occurred which I mention for a warning[2], his semen *was* expelled, so that it arose in his skin and burst it[3], and *his* loin thereby broke from *his* thigh; he then died outright, then his progeny, and then the offspring of his progeny.'

46. One *marvel* is this which is declared that, even before the coming *of Zaratûst* to a conference[4], *there* is manifested in him a mind which is more capacious than the whole world, *and* more exalted than every worldly possession, with an understanding whose strength is perfectly selected, an intellect of all-acquiring power, and a sagacity of all-deciding ability; also with the much heedfulness *of* the kingly glory, and the full desire for righteousness, the efficacious diligence and authority, and even the superiority in mightiness and grandeur of the priestly glory. 47. Also the handsomeness of body *and* completeness of strength which are in the character *of* these four classes of his, which are priesthood,

---

[1] See § 16 n.

[2] Pahl. 'avŏ pês yema*le*lûnam.'

[3] Or 'in his back and broke it,' if we suppose that pôst, 'skin,' stands for pôst, 'back.' Compare the same legend in Zs. XIX, 1–8.

[4] With the sacred beings.

warriorship, husbandry, and artisanship; *besides* a perfect friendship for the sacred beings *and* the good, *and* an awful enmity for the demons *and* the vile. 48. That is the nature by which the habits (dâ*d*ŏîh) of mankind *and* bipeds, the perfection and completeness of the sacred beings through the creativeness of Aûha*r*ma*zd*, and its *own* commemoration *of them* are provided. 49. So that the sacred beings shall bring a report, as to his superiority, from every one of those who are *and* were *and* will be, *and* of his coming for reminding *us of* Aûha*r*ma*zd* and *of* the lord-and-mastership (ahû-va-ra*d*îh) of the world, *also of* the preservation of the creations therein (ay*î*pŏ-dahi*s*nân), from the destroyer, by the tongue of the many-mannered (kabed-sarâ*d*akŏ) sage, the fully-virtuous *one* of the age producing no harm (avazand-dahîg) in the world. 50. And the demons on this *account*, that this is *he* whom many Kîgs[1] *and* Karaps *have* to influence the good to confound *and* destroy, then also kept *their* promise and practised friendship.

51. And on the completion of thirty years beyond his birth[2], the archangel Vohûmanô came on in commemoration of Aûha*r*ma*zd*, when *he was* bringing his Hôm-water (mayâ-î Hômîgân)[3] from the

[1] See Chap. II, 9 n.

[2] The remaining contents of this and the following chapter are thus summarized in Dk. VIII, xiv, 3, 4:—'His attainment on maturity, at thirty years *of age*, to a conference *with* Aûha*r*ma*zd*; and the occurrence of seven conferences in ten years. Many marvels, owing to him are published therein, just as there are *some* which, collected *and* selected, are noticed by the Dînka*r*d manuscript,' that is, in this seventh book, in which, however, the details of the seven conferences do not occur; but some are mentioned in Zs. XXI, 8–XXII, 13.

[3] See Visp. XI, 2.

river Aêvatâk[1], just as this which revelation mentions thus: 'When Zaratûst came forth to the third effluent (ba*r*â-ta*g*is*n*îh), that of the good Dâitî, he further proceeded through that; and when he marched onwards from that, a man *was* seen by him, who marched from the southern quarter. 52. That was Vohûmanô, and it seemed *to* him *that* Vohûmanô *was* of early form (so that he is more discerning as to a person) and foreseeing (that is, he was beforehand in everything); it seemed *to* him *that* Vohûmanô *was* as much *in* height as three men's spears; and it seemed *to* him, *as to* Vohûmanô that a glossy twig (arûs tâk) *was* brought by him in *his* hand, through carrying off which branch the plant *was* not injured by him; that became the spiritual twig of the religion, and this *was* indicated by it, that it is necessary to proceed as uninjuriously by the religion. 53. There is *some one* who says that it became a reminder of the spiritual *existence*, and this *was* indicated by it, that it is necessary to proceed as uninjuriously in the world, so that peace may exist with every one.

54. When he came onward to the fourth effluent, as far as the Aûshân-rû*d* of the good Dâitî (which was the name of it) and *he was* in it, Zaratûst *was* bringing the Hôm-water from the middle of it; and on the ascent Zaratûst, bringing his right foot out of the Aûshân-rû*d*, covered *himself* with his clothes, and upon that Vohûmanô, advancing, joined him in front.

[1] Literally 'single-flowing.' In Bd. XXIX, 4, 5, it is Nâîvtâk which has been translated as 'navigable' in Bd. XX, 34, and as 'flowing in a channel' in Dk. VIII, xxxvii, 38, 42; IX, xvi, 16.—From § 54 it appears to have been a channel of the good Dâitî river which flows from Aîrân-vê*g* (see Bd. XX, 13).

55. And that man enquired of him thus: 'Who art thou; from whom of them art thou[1]?' *He replied:* 'I am Zaratûst[2] of the Spîtâmas.'

56. The words of Vohûmanô *were:* '*O* Zaratûst of the Spîtâmas! about what is thy foremost distress (that is, for what is thy need when thou becomest quite distressed); about what is thy foremost endeavour; and for what is the tendency of thy desire (lak kâmakŏ-dahisnîh)?' 57. The reply of Zaratûst *was* thus: 'About righteousness, I consider *my* foremost distress; about righteousness *my* foremost endeavour; and for righteousness the tendency of my desire (that is, my need is for that thing, and I am a distressed seeker of righteousness).'

58. The words of Vohûmanô *were:* '*O* Zaratûst of the Spîtâmas! that which is righteousness is existing (that is, a real thing is, as *it were*, that which is righteousness), so that whatever is that which is righteousness is thus what is one's own.' 59. And Zaratûst spoke thus: 'That which is righteousness exists, and concerning that I am completely clear and aware; *but* where *and* how is that radiance which is that whose arrival is through Vohûmanô.'

60. And Vohûmanô spoke to him thus: '*O* Zaratûst of the Spîtâmas! deposit this one garment which thou carriest, so that we *may* confer with him *by*

---

[1] See Pahl. Yas. XLII, 7 c (Sp.).

[2] According to the numbering of the folios in the old Bombay MS., written in 1659, nine folios were here separated from it last century. They contained the text as far as the end of Chap. IV, and the first eight of them were found at Naosâri about twenty years ago and copied. But all Indian copies, written before that time, omit this mislaid text. See S. B. E., vol. xxxvii, pp. xxxvi, xxxvii.

whom thou art produced *and by* whom I am produced, who is the most propitious of spirits, who is the most beneficent of existences, and who is he *that* I, who am Vohûmanô, am testifying (that is, I am a reminder of him).'

61. Thereupon, Zaratûst thought thus: 'Good is he who is the creator, who is better than this reminder.' 62. Then they proceeded in company, Vohûmanô and Zaratûst; Vohûmanô *first and* Zaratûst after.

CHAPTER IV.

1. About the marvellousness which is manifested from the first conference onwards till the end of the seventh conference which occurred within the duration of ten years, also his pre-eminence in prophecy in the world, *and* the acceptance of the religion *by* the exalted Kaî-Vistâsp, as *happened* after the ten years of conference.

2. In *the first* two years, one *marvel* is this which is declared, that when he was back from the first conference, he then, by the first command of the lord *and* creator Aûharmazd, recited the unique formula (âyînŏ) in an assemblage (ram) of Kîgs and Karaps, the prophecy of his Mazda-worshipping religion and commemoration of Aûharmazd, as he chanted with a loud voice, *and* invited mankind to the religion of Aûharmazd. 3. Just as this *passage* of revelation mentions thus: 'Thereupon, the thorough inspection for this material existence of those with a *sacred* girdle, provided with dwellings *and* provided with cattle, *was* altogether arranged by Zaratûst.'

4. And when their announcement (nivêdisnŏ) for

speaking to be heard *was* issued [1], then Zaratûst, on becoming exalted, called out unto the embodied world of righteousness to extol righteousness and to scorn the demons [2]. 5. 'The homage of the Mazda-worship of Zaratûst, *and* the ceremonial and obeisance for the archangels *are* the best for you I assert; and of deprecation (ayazisnîh) for the demons next-of-kin marriage is really the best intimation, so that, from the information which is given *as to* the trustworthiness of a good work, the greatest are the most intimate of them, *those of* father *and* daughter, son *and* she who bore *him*, and brother *and* sister.'

6. *It is* declared that, upon those words, innumerable demon-worshipping Kîgs and Karaps have rushed upon Zaratûst and strove for his death, just like this which revelation states:—'It is then a number (mar) have run away who have sat in the vicinity of Tûr's progeny (hûnûskŏ) [3], the arbitrator; and the shame of the brother of Tûr arose, like *that of* a person whose shame *was* that they spoke of his next-of-kin marriage so that he might contract it.'

7. This Tûr *was* Aûrvâîtâ-dang [4] the Tûr, the scanty giver, *who* was like a great sovereign of that

[1] From this point §§ 4–8 and 11 have been already translated in S. B. E., vol. xviii, pp. 412, 413, in illustration of the meaning of Khvêtûk-das in Sasanian times and later.

[2] Av. staomî ashem; nâismî daêvô (Yas. XI, 19; XII, 1).

[3] An opprobrious term for the progeny of evil beings and animals, also used by a Karap when speaking of Zaratûst in Chap. III, 21.

[4] As this name has not been found in the extant Avesta, its correct reading is uncertain. In Zs. XX, 8, it can be read Aûrvaîtŏ-dih, in which dih is the Pahl. translation of Av. dang,hu, of which dang is a Pahl. transliteration; and the whole name may mean 'friendly to the province,' which seems suitable to this particular ruler. The MS. appears to have dêng.

quarter; many troops and *much* power *were* also maintained by him, and the multitude (mar) told him they would seize the great *one* from *him* who is little.

8. *But* the progeny of Aûrvâîtâ-dang the Tûr, the scanty giver, *spoke* thus: '*Should* we for that *speech* destroy him, this great *one* who mingles together those propitious words *for* us—where we are thus without doubt *as to* one thing therein, *such* as next-of-kin marriage, that it is not necessary to contract *it*—it would make us ever doubtful whether it *might* be necessary to contract it.'

9. And Aûrvâîtâ-dang the Tûr, the scanty giver, spoke thus: 'Thou shalt not destroy that man whom mine eyes *have* seen *as* the most loving-eyed of the whole embodied existence; he *will* attain strength, for it *has* not seemed to me, when thou destroyest him on this account, *that* wisdom *has* arisen *for* a long time; so that no rule (âhankŏ) *of* wisdom *will* arise, in this earth, which is so counselling (hangamanig) as this *one* is (that is, when they destroy a man who is counselling, wisdom *will* not arise *for* a long while).'

10. Aûrvâîtâ-dang the Tûr, the scanty giver to his own *people*, also spoke thus: 'For me thou art a pure *man* who is counselling.'

11. And Zaratûst spoke thus: 'I *shall* not always be that quiet speaker, by[1] whom that I *have* mentioned is the most propitious *thing* to be obtained; and of interfering[2] speaking and managing the temper *there* is a next-of-kin marriage, and the high-

[1] Or 'from.'

[2] It may be 'parenthetical or ambiguous.'

priest *who has* contracted[1] *it* is to perform the ceremonial.'

12. And here the good spiritual lordship and mightiness of glory of Zaratûst, those which are provided for commemoration *of* the supreme lord and creator Aûharmazd, are manifested *as* a great wonder to the multitude, *and there* is rendered visible the great pre-eminence which is in him *as* a prophet *of* the creatures, which for the baseness (nankîh) of the deceitful Agash[2], the secret-moving and deceiving-natured, is the concealed control of a good disposition. 13. Then idleness, like even the habit of fear and nature of apostasy, is an attractor of every one of the multitude, when it extends to much length; little by little, too, that guide and combatant becomes a petitioner for greatness, *and it is* manifest through that compassion (tang-libbemâîh) and superior mindfulness of his, *and* through the glory of that stout champion, *there are* much fame *and* treasure.

14. The nobles of Aûrvâîtâ-dang the Tûr, the ruler of the land, *were* angry and clamourers for Zaratûst's death; but he invited the Kîgs and Karaps to the religion of Aûharmazd, just as this *passage* of revelation states that Zaratûst also spoke thus: 'Worldly righteousness, *O* Aûrvâîtâ-dang, *thou* Tûr *and* scanty giver! is the whole *of the worship of* the demons and the termination of the Mazda-worship of Zaratûst.' 15. And Aûrvâîtâ-dang the Tûr, the scanty giver, spoke thus: '*O* Zaratûst of the Spîtâmas! thou shalt not attract me to this evil in which thou really art.'

---

[1] Or, perhaps, 'celebrated.'

[2] The demon of the evil eye (see Bd. XXVIII, 33); Av. Aghashi, Vd. XX, 3, 7, 9.

16. Zaratûst also spoke thus: 'Aûharmazd enquired of me thus: "O Zaratûst! when thou hast come away to us, among the spiritual lords, who of the people in thy material existence *was* the protector of the powerful men who *are* warriors, *that was* most seeking benefit, most seeking cattle, most extensively associating, most fully-supplying (that is, he gives out most things), and most hospitable[1] (*that is, one* saw the door of a prince's (khidîvŏ) treasury)?" I replied to him thus: "Aûrvâitâ-dang the Tûr, the scanty giver."'

17. 'And he spoke *in* reply to me thus: "Him, O Zaratûst! thou shalt attract, first of the men *who are* warriors, to thinking about, speaking about, and acting about this religion which is Aûharmazd's and Zaratûst's. 18. If you attract him, O Zaratûst! and he believes in it and also gives currency to this *religion* of thine, and sits before *thee* in discipleship, this that *one* calls discipleship of thine he shall undertake, and the religion he hears fully he shall propagate (rûbâk vabîdûnyên); he is also ever after, O Zaratûst! the first of the men *who are* warriors, the *one* most seeking benefit, most seeking cattle, most extensively associating, and most hospitable of those who have yet been born *and* who *will* henceforth be born. 19. And if you do not attract him, O Zaratûst! and he does not believe in it, nor gives currency *to* this *religion* of thine, nor hears *it*, nor even sits before thee, nor would sit before thee, so that *it is* obvious to me that *he* is not attracted, thou shalt speak unto him thus, O Zaratûst: 'Thou art a stricken supplicant for righteousness, and a producer of lamentation for the souls of Tanâpûhar sinners

[1] Literally 'most many-doored.'

worthy of death;' for even so it is, and for this reason he becomes worthy of death, because the existence of the religion is known to him." 20. What I tell thee, *O* Aûrvâîtâ-dang, *thou* Tûr *and* scanty giver! is that thou art a stricken supplicant *for* righteousness, a producer of lamentation for the souls of Tan*â*pûhar sinners worthy of death.'

21. One prodigy of the demons is specified, who *was* the enemy of whatever sacred beings *there are*, a Karap, Vaêdvôi*s*t[1] *by* name, *of* those unsanctified (aya*s*tân) *by* Aûha*r*maz*d*[2]. 22. And Aûha*r*maz*d* spoke thus: 'I so befriend that man, *O* Zaratû*s*t! who is put forward by me over the creatures, whom thou shalt invite (khvânê*s*), I *who* am Aûha*r*maz*d*, because I am through righteousness opposed to harm (that is, through virtue I keep harm away from the creatures), *and* the archangels are opposed to harm. 23. Therefore do thou proceed, *O* Zaratû*s*t! *and* thou shalt demand from him for me (that is, keep as my property) a hundred youths of vigour (tôsh tal)[3], girls, and teams of four horses; so do thou speak to him thus: "*O* Vêdvoî*s*t! Aûha*r*maz*d* demands from thee a hundred youths of vigour, girls, *and* teams of four horses; if thou givest *them*

[1] Here written in Pâzand, but the Pahlavi form, Vêdvoî*s*t, occurs in §§ 23, 24.

[2] Or '*of* the non-worshippers *of* Aûha*r*maz*d*.'

[3] For an instance of gifts of slaves see the Pahlavi inscription on an engraved stone from Baghdâd, in *Indian Antiquary*, vol. xi, p. 224, ll. 2, 3 of inscription: 'kevan bîdûn va-kanîgakô . . . lakhvâr . . . shed*r*ûnam . . . va-zak shibâ rî*d*ô va-shibâ kanîgakôân shed*r*ûnt:'—'Now . . . I send back a slave-boy and slave-girl . . . and those seven slave-boys and seven slave-girls are sent.' This inscription was probably engraved in the seventh century, judging from the forms of the letters.

to him, splendour and glory are thine through that giving; and if thou dost not give to him, evil destiny is thine through that not-giving."'

24. Then Zaratûst walked on to that Vêdvoîst of those unsanctified, and spoke to him thus: '*O* Vêdvoîst of the unsanctified! that *which* Aûharmazd demands from thee is a hundred youths of vigour, girls, and teams of four horses; if thou givest them to him, splendour *and* glory are thine through that giving; and if thou dost not give to him, evil destiny is thine through that not-giving.' 25. And that Karap shouted in reply *to* Zaratûst thus: 'For me *there* is no more from thee (that is, there is no opulence for me from thy action), nor from Aûharmazd; I am more of a divinity (bagtar) *and* am more forward in opulence than even Aûharmazd; many droves of a thousand swine are also acquired by me.'

26. On went Zaratûst, up to Aûharmazd *and* up to the archangels, and Zaratûst spoke thus: '*O* Aûharmazd, propitious spirit, creator of the world of embodied *beings, thou* righteous *one!* thus spoke he *in* reply to me: "For me *there* is no more from thee, nor from Aûharmazd; I am more of a divinity than thee *or* even Aûharmazd, and many droves of a thousand swine are acquired by me."'

27. And Aûharmazd spoke thus: 'Owing to the splendour and glory of those which are ours, *O* Zaratûst! that man has acquired arrogance (that is, the cattle we produced are the many cattle of his arrogance). 28. This *will be* his retribution for it then, however, when he does not reach further alive at the end of the third night[1]; in that third night

[1] Apparently the third night after death, on the passing away of

they *will* have stood aloof from alongside his life (that is, they *will* have stood away from assisting it); those seven of them who are radiant and bright-eyed (s*p*ê*d*ŏ dôîsar) make him rush up on high, and up there on high *he* shall be fed upon mouldy bread (parnân).'

29. One *marvel* is the great healthfulness owing to the Hôm-water *and* the bringing of this *by* Zaratûst from the river Dâîtî, which is manifested when Vohûmanô *was* conveying *him* to the conference. 30. Just as is declared in the words of Aûha*r*ma*zd* to Zaratû*s*t thus: 'For them is the Hôm-water which thou bringest, *O* Zaratû*s*t! not for those demon-worshipping people *who* worship the demons, or for a satisfier of courtezans (*g*êh-vi*g*âr); they shall sprinkle it on to that bull thou shalt bring forward, who is a four-year-old of exhausted vigour, black-haired and useful; *on* drinking up the water, that bull *will* become quite sound from that infirmity.'

31. Thereupon, Zaratû*s*t went on first into the embodied existence, on which dwelt, at the end of Sagâstân [1], that same Parsha*d* *whose* title was Tô*r*â (*the Bull*). 32. Parsha*d*-tô*r*â [2] also spoke to him

which the soul is supposed to have its destination determined, until the resurrection (see Hâ*d*ôkht Nask, II, 18; III, 17). If the seven sacred beings who stand aloof from him be the archangels, they treat Vêdvoî*s*t very leniently; but this legend treats of a period which it assumes to be earlier than the laws of Zaratû*s*t.

[1] The modern Sîstân, bordering upon Afghânistân and Bulû*k*istân.

[2] Av. Parsha*d*-gau, mentioned twice in Yt. XIII, 96, 127, but it is not certain that both allusions refer to the same individual. The name also occurs in Bd. XXIX, 5, but only in one old MS.; in all others another name is given, though the locality appears to be

thus: '*O* Zaratû*s*t of the Spîtâmas! give me this Hôm-water which thou bringest.' 33. And Zaratû*s*t spoke thus: 'Do thou praise righteousness, *O* Parsha*d*-tô*r*â! and scorn the demons; *also* utter the profession [1] of the Maz*d*a-worship of Zaratû*s*t among the iniquitous.' 34. *It was* praised by Parsha*d*-tô*r*â, and the demons were scorned by him; yet he did not speak among the iniquitous as to his accepting the Maz*d*a-worship of Zaratû*s*t. 35. Forward to him *came* Zaratû*s*t at that praise of righteousness, for him *was* that Hôm-water which Zaratû*s*t brought; not for those demon-worshipping people *who* have worshipped the demons, *but* for that bull of his *which* Zaratû*s*t brought forward, a four-year-old of exhausted vigour, black-haired and useful; owing to that bringing forward of the water, the bull became quite sound from that infirmity.

36. One *marvel* is that which is declared regarding the rushing of the evil spirit for the slaughter of Zaratû*s*t, just as revelation [2] mentions thus: 'From the northern quarter forth rushed the deadly evil spirit, and thus shouted he, astute in evil, the deadly evil spirit: "Rush on, *O* fiend! and destroy the righteous Zaratû*s*t." 37. On to him they rushed, the fiend, the demon Bû*d*, and secret-moving Pestilence, the deceiver. 38. Zaratû*s*t chanted aloud the Ahunavair; the fiend *was* confounded at that, *and* away they rushed, the demon Bû*d* and secret-moving Pestilence, the deceiver. 39. And the fiends shouted thus: "Thou art scornfully observing, *O* evil spirit! (that is, anything to the purpose thou

nearly the same. In § 31 the first part of the name is here written Parshê*d*.

[1] The Fravarânê, Yas. XI, 16. [2] Pahl. Vd. XIX, 1-4.

dost not thoroughly observe, and what thou orderest *us* to do is not possible); the death of him who is Zaratûst of the Spîtâmas is not contemplated by us." 40. Owing to the full glory of the righteous Zaratûst, he perceived in *his* mind thus: "The wicked demons, astute in evil, consult together about my death;" and up stood Zaratûst, forth went Zaratûst.' 41. Here is manifested a great wonder to the multitude, in that which is mentioned thus: 'And a stone *was* put forth by the righteous Zaratûst, *that* was held in *his* hand, and the size of a hut, *and* which was obtained by him from the creator Aûharmazd, the spiritual Yathâ-ahû-vairyô [1].'

42. And one *marvel* is this which is manifested not only in the country of Irân to Irânians, but in every land and to every race: the shattering of the demons' bodies *through* the chanting of the Ahunavair aloud *by* Zaratûst. 43. Just as that which *a passage* [2] mentions thus: 'I worship the resources of the Kayân glory, with which the righteous Zaratûst was associated in thinking about, speaking about, *and* acting about the religion which was, of all embodied existences, the most righteous in righteousness, the most lordly in sovereignty, the most radiant in radiance, and the most glorious in glory. 44. At *his* appearance [3] the demons have fallen before him, at *his* appearance their semen (mâyagân) also drops, at *his* appearance the courtezan is also withdrawn by them from mankind;

---

[1] The first three words of the Ahunavair formula.

[2] See Yt. XIX, 78–81.

[3] Reading vên*âv*dahakih, but the first letter is omitted in all three occurrences of the word.

on hearing[1] him *they* lamented, very violently is it lamented by the demons. 45. By the Ahunavair, which the righteous Zaratûst chanted aloud to them, all the demons are seized *and* buried in the earth, where the complete shattering of their bodies is manifest.' 46. So that, after the shattering of their bodies, it became evident to those in the world *that* they were not able to do mischief in the bodily form of a demon, and they have been declared of the nature of sacred beings to mankind, *but* mankind fully understood that they are not sacred beings, but demons.

47. Zaratûst revealed (gushûftŏ) to mankind by the word of Aûharmazd, how in this religion *the latter* tells in words to Zaratûst where *and* how, in the embodied existence, mankind consider a demon as exalted *or* as a high-priest, because they are where they say that they must consider *some one* as high-priest. 48. *So* Aûharmazd spoke *to* Zaratûst thus: 'How do they who are good people, *O* Zaratûst! consider a demon as exalted? and how are they that even tell a demon thus: "We should accept you," because the demons speak thus: "It *will* happen to you"?'

49. And Zaratûst spoke thus: 'Only for the *reason*, *O* Aûharmazd! *that* people hasten on to that which is a jungly plain without dwellings, where no one resides from the departure of light until sun-

[1] If the word be Pahlavi, it is probably intended for snâyân, 'hearing'; but it may be merely an approximate transcript of Av. snaodhentis, which word, if this be the case, must have puzzled Sasanian scholars as much as it does those of the present time. As a transcript, the word might be read snôdîyân, and we might guess the meaning of the phrase to be 'thereupon weeping *they* lamented.'

rise arrives, when *it is* two Hâsars[1] of night, and again silently (agôp) from sunset until their returning together when the two Hâsars of night are gone, they hear that no work, no men, and no voices of dogs are there. 50. Then they say as to that, on arriving back, thus: "We have consulted with the demons there; when we request (zâêm) monarchy (sâstârîh) *and* leadership from them, they give them to us; when we request the possession of flocks and opulence from them, they give them to us."'

51. *Then Aûharmazd spoke thus:* 'How can they do such a thing for them, *O* Zaratûst! (that is, how does it happen *that it is* continually given by them *for* those that speak thus: "It happened to us")?'

52. And Zaratûst spoke thus: 'They speak variously, *O* Aûharmazd! as to that generosity; there is *one* who speaks thus: "I have ever after been possessing more flocks, so long as I am *in* consultation with the demons;" and there is *another* who speaks thus: "I have ever after been worse and more ill-fated, so long as we are *in* consultation with those demons;" according as they possess a full subsistence for them*selves* from the demons (that is, when they diversely subsist fully *on* whatever they bespeak from the demons).' 53. Zaratûst also spoke thus: 'So they speak about it, *O* Aûharmazd! thus: "Observe further, where any one of us returns *he* is either shrunk together (that is, he holds *his* head down to *his* chest), or shrunk away (that is, he looks quite aside), or is only pleasantly

[1] Av. hâthra, which, as a measure of time, varies from one to two hours (see Farh. Oîm, p. 43, ll. 1–3).

cast down and, owing to acquiescence in him, the demons tempt (nes,hûnd) *him* away out of mankind."'

54. And Aûharmazd spoke thus: 'According to thy wish, do thou, *O* Zaratûst! fully observe thy existence, upwards from the head, downwards from the sole[1] of the foot, and afar *on* various sides; and thou shouldst beseech before and behind and *in* every direction, for we *are* not as to thee as the demons *are* as to mankind, we give away everything only in invisibility; but the demons, through close connection, when they rush out, tempt only with pleasantness. 55. Even unto thee, *O* Zaratûst! a fiend *will* rush, a female, golden-bodied *and* full-bosomed (so that she wears a bodice), and she rushes to request companionship from thee; a female, golden-bodied *and* full-bosomed, to request conversation from thee, to request co-operation from thee. 56. *But* thou shouldst not grant her companionship, nor conversation, nor shalt thou prescribe *any* conduct for her; afterwards, to revert her downwards, thou shalt utter aloud that triumphant saying the Yathâ-ahû-vairyô.'

57. Zaratûst proceeded to the habitable *and* friendly world, for the purpose of fully observing that beaten track (khâpisnŏ) of the embodied existence; then that fiend came forward when he sat in the vicinity of a garment—that garment[2] which, when Vohûmanô *was* conveying *him* to the conference, *was* deposited by him—a female, golden-bodied *and* full-bosomed, and companionship, con-

[1] Assuming that lêlyâ stands for zêrih; the only difference, in Pahlavi writing, being in the first letter.

[2] See Chap. III, 60.

versation, and co-operation *were* requested by her from him; she also whined (dandî*d*ŏ): 'I am Spenda*r*ma*d*[1].'

58. And Zaratû*s*t spoke thus: 'She who is Spenda*r*ma*d* *was* fully observed by me in the light of a cloudless day, and that Spenda*r*ma*d* appeared *to* me fine behind and fine before and fine all round (that is, *in* all positions she was handsome); do thou turn *thy* back, *and* I *shall* know if thou art Spenda*r*ma*d*.'

59. And the fiend spoke to him thus: '*O* Zaratû*s*t of the Spîtâmas! where we are, those who are females are handsome in front, *but* frightfully hideous behind; *so* do not make a demand for my back.' 60. After she *had* protested a third *time*, the fiend turned *her* back, and she *was* seen by Zaratû*s*t behind in the groin; and when matter was exuded, *it was* full of serpents, toads, lizards, centipedes, and frogs.

61. And that triumphant saying, the Yathâ-ahû-vairyô, was uttered aloud by Zaratû*s*t; then that fiend *was* annihilated, and *K*êshmak[2] the Karap rushed forth. 62. And he grumbled in leaving, thus: 'The misery which is here *below* is such as I have obtained, because, owing to thee, I thought that thy sacred beings *were* more joyful than any heroes who through defeat go to hell; I proceed more joyfully *than* the sacred beings, as regards the life in the body, so that I fully deceive the life in thy body, and thou art fully deceived by me as regards thine.'

[1] The female archangel Bountiful Devotion, in whose special charge are the earth and virtuous women; see Sls. XV, 5, 20-24.

[2] See Chap. II, 44, 45.

63. Zaratûst also revealed (gushûftŏ) this secret to mankind, and their knowledge *how* to test a demon is manifested therein, even by a great wonder of the same nature to mankind: the visible rushing of the demons into the world before Zaratûst, *and* their bodies *being* afterwards shattered by the loud chanting of revelation *by* Zaratûst from the Avesta announced, which *was* the acceptance of *its* truth by the ruler Vistâsp and the people of that time; and if this *had* not been so, *and* Vistâsp *and* those of *his* time *were* not accepting the Avesta which *was* announced by *Zaratûst in* this fashion, through *their* considering *it* false, it would not have reached unto us.

64. One *marvel* is this, with which, too, he who *was* Zaratûst became aware from revelation, about the vileness *and* perverted religion of Zâk of the deadly Karaps of Vistâsp and many other Kaîs and Karaps who *were* at the residence of Vistâsp, their combination for the death of Zaratûst, the preparation for severe abuse of him to Vistâsp, and influencing Vistâsp for his death by command of Vistâsp, *which* extends to awful imprisonment and punishment. 65. Afterwards, too, his knowledge about *his* preservation therefrom, the manifestation of his wondrousness, and the evidence concerning *his* attainment unto prophesying; *also* after the continuance of the last questioning *of* the ten years of conference, *his* departure alone, by the advice *and* command of Aûharmazd, to the residence of Vistâsp and the precinct (var) of that terrible conflict. 66. *His* uttering, on the horse-course (aspânvar) of Vistâsp, a reminder of the power and triumph of Aûharmazd over himself, *as* he invited Vistâsp to

the religion of Aûharmazd; and with great wisdom Vistâsp heard the words of Zaratûst, on account of his own complete mindfulness and spiritual knowledge of ritual, *and* would have asked for an outpouring of prophecy.

67. *But* thereupon, too—before the words of Zaratûst *were fully* heard by him, *and* he could have understood the character of Zaratûst—owing to the demonizing of the deadly Zâk and the rest *of* those Kîgs *and* Karaps, *spoken* out with slanderous knowledge *and* perverse actions to Vistâsp about Zaratûst, *there* then *occurred* his consignment of Zaratûst to that confinement *and* punishment as stated in the words of Zaratûst thus: 'I have spoken about their three enquiries, and I am bound by thirty of them, I with thirty-three fetters of murderers, wicked ones, and demon-worshippers [1]. 68. But the hunger of manhood's inclination [2] violently affected the strength of my legs, but the hunger of manhood's inclination violently affected the force of my arms, but the hunger of manhood's inclination violently affected the hearing of my ears, but the hunger of manhood's inclination violently affected the sight of my eyes, and it would force away my bosom up to *my* back (so that it [3] would stay behind at my back) through the continuance of that deadly hunger of manhood's inclination.'

69. And here, through the mightiness of Zaratûst —*who* proceeded alone to the terrible combat *with*

[1] Compare Zs. XXIII, 5.

[2] Reading gûsn-girâîh; but it might be dûs-vîrâîh, 'bad provision.' He was left to starve to death in prison.

[3] The bosom. The idea of the writer appears to have been that in case of utter starvation the chest would totally collapse, so that the breast bone would touch the spine.

evil, where *there* became manifest, in the mode which is written, the descent of his life into so much punishment, due to hunger and thirst, heavy fetters, *and* other misery unto which the strength of human nature is attaining, *but* unto which *it* is not destined —is manifested a great wonder to king Vi*s*tâsp and his officials, when *his* full-glorious person *was* found by them alive in awfulness, imprisonment, and those other transformations (pa*d*ga*s*takîh) of long-continued starvation.

70. One *marvel* is this, that the sacred beings contrived, for the sake of (va*l* vahân-î) his preservation from that awfulness, a body possessing life, *and* on his account it became lifeless and imperceptible; afterwards, in the great session of Vi*s*tâsp and the assembly of the world, Zaratû*s*t, through the strength and blessedness of the true word, restored the same body anew, like that which is issuing in the statement of the wonder about the splendid horse of Vi*s*tâsp[1].

71. One *marvel* is *his* telling and disclosing the thoughts of king Vi*s*tâsp and *of* those of the realm, and many other concealed matters, through spiritual perception.

72. One *marvel* is several matters of evil deceit (va*d* *g*amâs) which Dahâk had done in B*á*pêl[2]

[1] This very slight allusion to the cure of Vi*s*tâsp's horse by Zaratû*s*t is sufficient to show that this legend existed in the ninth century; but the writer of the Dînka*r*d seems inclined to trace it back to a tale that he vaguely relates in the earlier part of this section, and which he evidently found in older writings; this tale, however, does not mention a horse, but only an animated body. The Persian Zaratû*s*t-nâma developes the legend of the sick horse, whose legs are drawn up to its belly, into 160 couplets.

[2] Babylon; see Yt. V, 29–31; XV, 19–21.

through witchcraft, *and* mankind had come to idol-worship through that seduction, *and its* increase was the destruction of the world; *but* through the triumphant words of the religion, which Zaratû*s*t proclaimed opposing it, that witchcraft is all dissipated and disabled.

73. One *marvel* is this which is manifested, with wonders owing to Zaratû*s*t, in controversy about the religion with the famous learned of the realm, among whom, known for learning *in* the world, *are* the investigators (girâyagânŏ) of the words of speech; *and* among those *things* which *are* more surprisingly controversial *are* those later (sibastar) words which *are* to save their creatures by a later religion. 74. Also to proclaim its truth intelligibly, and to make king Vi*s*tâsp *and* those previously learned *men* without doubt as to the truth of the religion, the creator Aûha*r*ma*zd* sends some *spirits*, Vohûmanô, Ashavahi*s*tô, and the propitious fire[1], as a reminder to Vi*s*tâsp about the true prophesying of Zaratû*s*t, *and* the desire of Aûha*r*ma*zd* for the acceptance of the religion *of* Ma*zd*a-worship *by* Vi*s*tâsp *and for its* propagation in the world.

75. The wondrousness which is manifested to Vi*s*tâsp *and* those of the realm—both through the travelling (vâzî*d*anŏ) of those archangels down from the sky to the earth, and in *their* travelling to the abode of Vi*s*tâsp—*was* like this which revelation mentions thus: 'Then he who is the creator Aûha*r*ma*zd* spoke *to* them, to Vohûmanô, Ashavahi*s*tô, and also the fire of Aûha*r*ma*zd*, the propitious, thus: "Proceed! you *who* are archangels, unto the

[1] Compare Zs. XXIII, 7.

abode of Vi*s*tâsp, whose resources (*a*fzâr) are cattle *and* who is far *and* widely famed, with a view to *his* reliance upon this religion (that is, till he shall stand up for this religion); and, as regards the answering words of the righteous Zaratû*s*t of the Spîtâmas, to approve the nature (zag *s*ân) of those words." 76. The archangels proceeded unto the abode of Vi*s*tâsp, whose resources are cattle *and who* is far *and* widely famed; their radiance, in that lofty residence, seemed to him, that Vi*s*tâsp, a heaven *of* complete light, owing to their great power and triumph; this *was* so that, when he thus looked upon it, the exalted Kaî-Vi*s*tâsp trembled, all his courtiers (pê*s*akŏ) trembled, all his chieftains (pa*d*ŏ) were confused, *and* he of the superior class *was* like the driver of a chariot-horse.

77. 'And the fire of Aûha*r*ma*zd* spoke, in the words of heroes, thus: "Fear not, for *there* is no fearing for thee, *thou* exalted Kaî-Vi*s*tâsp! they have not come for alarming thy abode, *as* a reminder of the deputed envoys of Ar*g*âsp[1]; *there* have not come, for alarming thy abode, the two Khyôns of

[1] Av. Areg*a*d-aspa, king of the *Hv*yaonas (Pahl. Khyôns), mentioned in Yt. V, 109, 113, 116; XVII, 50; XIX, 87. His war with Vi*s*tâsp, for the purpose of compelling the latter to abjure his new religion, is described in the Yâ*d*kâr-î Zarîrân (see Geiger in *Sitzungsberichten der p.-p. und h. Classe der k. bayer. Akad. der Wiss.* 1890, Bd. II, pp. 43–84). Ar*g*âsp sends two envoys, Vîdraf*s* the wizard and Nâmkhvâst of the Hazârs, to demand Vi*s*tâsp's submission; this is refused defiantly by advice of Zarîr, the king's brother; and both nations prepare for war. When the Irânians meet the Khyôns, Vi*s*tâsp consults his vazîr *G*âmâsp, who prognosticates prodigious slaughter. And, after losing most of their chieftains (including twenty-three brothers and sons of Vi*s*tâsp), the Irânians utterly annihilate the Khyôn army. This war is called the 'war of the religion' in Bd. XII, 33; Byt. III, 9.

Argâsp who demand tribute and revenue (sâk va-bâzŏ); and *there has* not come, for alarming thy abode, the all-overpowering thief who is an injurer, *or* the dog who is a highwayman. 78. We are three who have come over (taristŏ) to thy abode, Vohûmanô, Ashavahistô, and also the fire of the propitious lord; of these thy knowledge is most wisely most just. 79. If thou helpest vision, so that it becomes wisdom for thee, the worldly *existence* requires the good religion of the Mazda-worshippers, which proceeds purely through the recitation which Zaratûst of the Spîtâmas *teaches.* 80. Do thou chant the Ahunavair, do thou praise perfect righteousness [1], and utter no worship [2] for the demons! because the desire of Aûharmazd, as regards thee, is *for thy* reliance upon this religion; *it* is also the desire *of* the archangels, and the desire, as regards thee, *of* the other sacred beings who are beneficent (sapîr-dahakŏ) *and* righteous.

81. '"And as the recompense in this life, if you praise the good *and* pure religion of the righteous Zaratûst of the Spîtâmas, we *will* give unto thee a long reign and sovereignty, and the long lifetime of a life of 150 years; we *will* give unto thee Good Integrity and Rectitude [3] which is long-continued in desire for constantly assisting, good for assistance

---

[1] That is, recite the Yathâ-ahû-vairyô and the Ashem-vohû formulas.

[2] Pahl. a-afzisnîh, literally, a 'non-worship,' which may mean something worse than 'no worship;' but 'execration or malediction' is usually expressed by gazisn, 'cursing,' which is written exactly like yazisn, 'worship.'

[3] Pahl. Aharîsvang and Râê-astisnîh, the equivalents of Av. Ashis-vanguhi and Rasãstât who are spiritual personifications of the qualities mentioned in the text.

through constantly assisting, and not passing away; and we *will* give unto thee a son, Pêshyôtan[1] is *his* name, he is immortal, *and* so is undecaying, hungerless, and thirstless, living and predominant in both existences, *those* of the embodied *beings* and of the spirits. 82. *But*, as the recompense in this life, if you do not praise the good *and* pure religion of the righteous Zaratûst of the Spîtâmas, we *will* not convey thee up on high, and we *will* order thine end; the vultures which *are* mindful of decay *will* see *and* eat up those *and* these of thine, thy blood *will* reach the ground, and the waters *will* not reach thy body."'

83. One *marvel* is that *connected* with the confidence (vâvarî-hastanŏ) of Vistâsp in the religion, even through that occurrence of the speech of the archangels; and, afterwards, the obedience (patyasâî?) *of* his thoughts in the case of the delays through the bloodshed owing to Argâsp[2] the Khyôn and his attendant heroes (pas-gurdânŏ) throughout the same Khyôns, because of the acceptance of the religion. 84. Also, for the sake of daily *and* visibly showing to Vistâsp the certified victory over Argâsp and the Khyôns, and his own superior position, unceasing rule, splendour, and glory, the creator Aûharmazd sends, at the same time, the angel Nêryôsang[3] to the abode of Vistâsp, as a reminder for the archangel Ashavahistô to give to Vistâsp to drink of that fountain of life, for looking

[1] Written Pêshyâôtanŏ, both here and in Chap. V, 12. He is the immortal priestly ruler of Kangdez, who was expected to come to restore the religion in Irân in the time of Aûshêdar, see Bd. XXIX, 5; Byt. III, 25–32, 36–42, 51, 52.

[2] Here written Argadâspô; see § 77.

[3] Written Nêrôksang here and in § 85.

into the existence of the spirits, the enlightening food by means of which great glory *and* beauty *are* seen by Vistâsp.

85. Just as this *passage* of revelation mentions thus: 'And he who is the creator Aûharmazd spoke to the angel Nêryôsang thus: "Proceed *and* travel, *O* Nêryôsang the assembler[1]! unto the abode of Vistâsp, whose resources are cattle *and who* is far *and* widely famed, and thou shalt say this to Ashavahistô, thus: '*O* Ashavahistô! do thou authoritatively take this fine saucer (tastô), which is fully finer than the other saucers that *are* made (that is, the cup (gâm) is as fine *as* is possible to make for royalty), *and* carry up to Vistâsp the Hôm and Vars[2] (mûi) which are for us; and do thou give it[3] unto the ruler Vistâsp to drink up, by whose word it is accepted.'" 86. Ashavahistô authoritatively taking the fine saucer from him, also, thereupon, gave it unto the exalted ruler Kaî-Vistâsp to drink *from*[4]; and the ruler of the country (dîh), the exalted Kaî-Vistâsp, lay down when divested of *his* robes, and he spoke to Hûtôs[5] thus: "You, *O* Hûtôs! are *she*

[1] Compare Vd. XXII, 7.

[2] A lock of three, five, or seven hairs from the tail of a white bull, that is tied to a metal thumb-ring which is put into the Hôm-strainer when the Hôm-juice is about to be poured through it. See Haug's Essays, 3rd ed., pp. 397–403. This ring and lock of hair may be the relic of a hair-sieve that may have been used for straining the Hôm-juice in former times.

[3] The saucer, or cup, of strained Hôm-juice.

[4] The foregoing twenty-six words, excepting two, have been here repeated by the writer of the old Bombay MS., after turning over a folio.

[5] Av. Hutaosa, wife of Vistâsp and descendant of Nôdar (Av. Naotara); see Yt. XV, 35, 36. According to the later authority of the Yâdkar-î Zarîrân, § 48, she was also a sister of Vistâsp.

whom the prompt ability (têzŏ hûnar) of Zaratûst of the Spîtâmas should reach; *and* through the diligence of the prompt ability of Zaratûst of the Spîtâmas, you[1] would expound the religion of Aûharmazd and Zaratûst."'

87. One *marvel* is this which is declared, that when Vistâsp, accepting the religion, praises righteousness, the demons in hell are disabled, and the demon Aeshm[2] rushes to the country of the Khyôns *and to* Argâsp, the deadly *one* of the Khyôns, because he was the mightiest of the tyrants at that time; and the *most* hideous of all, of so many of them in the country of the Khyôns, are poured out by him for war.

88. And here, too, is manifested a great wonder also to the host (ram) of Irân who have been coming there, unto the residence of Argâsp the Khyôn, like this which revelation mentions thus: 'Then, just at the time his legion is separately displayed, Aeshm the unredeemable (tanâpûharak) adheres (gêrevêdŏ) to him, as *being himself* without escort (agurôh), and quite opposes (barâ sperezêdŏ) him, because: "You, who are a Khyôn, *have* become unlucky through want of success after you engage *in conflict*."' 89. Henceforth, it is not that the victory *of* Irân *has* come over foreigners *and* Khyôns—through companionship at the abode *of* that man who is mightier by the birth *of* Zaratûst

The similarity of her name to that of Atossa, the wife and sister of Cambyses, whom Darius afterwards married, is striking.

[1] As the verbal forms of the present third person singular and second person plural are alike in Pahlavi, it is doubtful which personal pronoun to use.

[2] The demon of Wrath; see Bd. XXVIII, 15–17.

of the Spîtâmas—when that hideous sovereignty *of* Argâsp, the deadly Khyôn, is swallowed up by him (*Vistâsp*), for the confusion of the deadly species (that is, *they are* further smitten by him, one through the other; and are swallowed together by him, mutually struggling and through mutually devouring). 90. And apart from him, that bitter *and* well-hardened Khyôn that is quite disabled by him the good *Vistâsp*, that deadly *fiend* is disturbed about him of eloquent abilities (*Zaratûst*); and so he grumbled at the hideous sovereignty thus: 'Prompt ability comes into existence *and* the Khyôn came; thereupon prompt ability comes into existence *and* the Irânian has come[1].'

. . . .

CHAPTER V.

1. About the marvellousness which is manifested from the acceptance of the religion *by* Vistâsp onwards till the departure (vîkhêzô) of Zaratûst, *whose* guardian spirit is reverenced, to the best existence, when seventy-seven years[2] had elapsed onwards from *his* birth, forty-seven onwards from

---

[1] According to the numbering of the folios of the old MS. of 1659 (brought from Persia to India in 1783) one folio, numbered 313 in Persian words, is here missing. It has not yet been found in India, and, owing to folio 312 apparently completing a sentence, and folio 314 evidently beginning a new chapter, the loss of text is hardly perceptible. It would have filled the next two pages.

[2] The MS. has '57 years,' through پنجاه '50' being written instead of هفتاد '70'; but see Chap. III, 51 which states the interval of thirty years between his birth and conference.

his conference, *and* thirty-five years onwards from the acceptance of the religion *by* Vistâsp[1].

2. One *marvel* is this *which is* declared that, when Zaratûst chanted revelation in the abode of Vistâsp, *it was* manifest *to* the eye that it is danced to *with* joyfulness, both by the cattle *and* beasts *of burden*, and *by* the spirit of the fires which *are* in the abode. 3. By *which*, too, a great wonder is proclaimed, like this *which* revelation mentions thus: '*There* seemed a righteous joyfulness of all the cattle, beasts *of burden*, and fires of the place, *and there* seemed a powerfulness of every kind of well-prepared spirits and of those quitting the abode (mân-hishânŏ), "that will make us[2] henceforth powerful through religion," when they fully heard those words which *were* spoken by the righteous Zaratûst of the Spîtâmas.'

4. And one *marvel* is the provision, *by* Zaratûst, *of* the achievement of ordeal, that indicator of the acquitted *and* incriminated for sentence *by* the judge, in obscure legal proceedings; *of* which *it* is said in revelation *there are* about (*k*îgûn) thirty-three kinds. 5. These, too, the disciples of Zaratûst kept in use, after that *time*, until the collapse of the monarchy of Irân; and the custom *of* one of them is that of pouring melted metal on the breast, as in the achievement of the saintly (hû-fravar*d*ŏ) Âtûrpâ*d* son of Mâ*r*aspend, through whose preservation a know-

[1] The contents of this chapter and the next, as far as VI, 11, may be connected with the following summary in Dk. VIII, xiv, 9:—'Information also *as to* many other things which are marvellous, and *as to* a summary of the statements of these seven enquiries, which is *derived* from knowledge of every kind.' For the seven enquiries, see Zs. XXII.

[2] Or, perhaps, 'make the abode.'

ledge about the religion *was* diffused in the world; and of the manifestation, too, through that great wonder, this is also said, on the same subject, in the good religion, that of those many, when they behold that rite of ordeal, it convinces the wicked ones[1].

6. One *marvel* is that which is afterwards manifested, after the former captivity of Zaratûst[2] and his speaking about the religion to Vistâsp and those of the realm[3], *such* as the acceptance of the religion *by* Vistâsp *and* that which Zaratûst said to him at *his* original arrival, as regards the declaration of a ruler's religion, thus: 'Thine is this disposition, *and* this religion which is calling (khrôsakŏ) is a property *of* that description *which* thou puttest together, *O* Kaî-Vistâsp! so that *if* thou wilt accept this disposition of thine, thou wilt possess this religion which exists (that is, the learning of learnings), *and be* the ruler that shall cause *its* progress; thou *wilt* possess in this disposition of thine, as *it were*, a new support (stûnakŏ), *and* any one *will* uphold *thee* by upholding *it*, as thou art the possessor of the support of this religion.' 7. Also the victory of Vistâsp over Argâsp the Khyôn and other foreigners in that awful battle[4], just as Zaratûst explained unto Vistâsp in revelation; *and* much which is declared by revelation.

8. One *marvel* is the disclosure by Zaratûst, in complete beneficence, medical knowledge, acquaintance with character, and other professional retentiveness (pîshakŏ-gîrûkîh), secretly *and* completely, of *what* is necessary for legal knowledge and spiritual

[1] §§ 4, 5 are already translated in AV. p. 145.
[2] See Chap. IV, 67–69.
[3] See Chap. IV, 73.
[4] See Chap. IV, 88–90.

perception; also the indication, by revelation, of the rites for driving out pestilence (sêgŏ), overpowering the demon and witch, and disabling sorcery and witchcraft. 9. The curing *of* disease, the counteraction of wolves *and* noxious creatures, the liberating of rain, *and* the confining of hail, spiders, locusts, and other terrors of corn *and* plants *and* adversaries of animals, *by* the marvellous rites which are also relating to the worship of Khûrdad *and* Amûrdad[1], and many other rites which *were* kept in use until the collapse of the monarchy of Irân; and there are *some* which have remained even *till* now[2], *and* are manifested with a trifle of marvellousness by the sacred fires. 10. And the disclosure to mankind *of* many running waters from marvellous streams (ardâyâ), and remedies for sickness which *are* mixed (fargardakŏ) by well-considering physicians; many *are* spiritual and celestial, gaseous (vâyîg) and earthy; and the worldly advantage of others, too, is the praise (lâfŏ) which ought to come to one for angelic[3] wisdom.

11. One is the marvel of the Avesta itself, which, according to all the best reports *of* the world, is a compendium of all the supremest statements of wisdom.

12. One *marvel* is the coming of this also to

---

[1] These two archangels personify health and immortality, respectively (see Chap. II, 19), and are supposed to have special charge of water and plants.

[2] The ninth century, unless this phrase be copied from one of the sources of the Dînkard.

[3] The MS. has yazdânŏ-khiradŏîh which has the meaning given in the text; but this word can also be read gehânŏ-khiradŏîh, 'worldly wisdom,' though gêhânŏ is the more usual orthography.

Vi*s*tâsp, which the archangels announced as a recompense for accepting the religion [1], as he saw Pêshyôtan the happy ruler, that immortal and undecaying son, not wanting food, large-bodied, completely strong, fully glorious, mighty, victorious, and resembling the sacred beings; the unique splendour of Pêshyôtan for the sovereignty of Kangd*ez in* yonder *world*, as allotted to him *by* the creator Aûha*r*ma*zd*, is manifested even through that great wonder to the multitude [2].

CHAPTER VI.

1. About the marvellousness which is manifested after the departure (vîkhê*z*ŏ) of Zaratû*s*t, whose guardian spirit is reverenced, to the best existence, *and* in the life*time* of Vi*s*tâsp.

2. One *marvel* is this which is declared by revelation, about the provision of a chariot [3] by Srîtô [4] of the Vîsraps [5]; this is through a famous wonder and

---

[1] See Chap. IV, 81.

[2] It is singular that nothing is stated here about the death or departure of Zaratû*s*t, which event, according to § 1, ought to have concluded this chapter. But in Chap. III, 39, Dûrâsrôb evidently foretells that Zaratû*s*t will be killed by the evil eye of Brâ*d*rôk-rêsh. In Dk. V, iii, 2, the killing of Zaratû*s*t by Brâ*d*rô-rêsh the Tûr is merely mentioned. In Zs. XXIII, 9, it is stated that Zaratû*s*t passes away (vi*d*îrê*d*ŏ) forty-seven years after his conference and preaching to Vi*s*tâsp. While the modern Persian Zaratû*s*t-nâma does not mention his death, though it speaks of Bartarûsh as his chief enemy in his younger days. But compare Chap. III, 22.

[3] Pahl. r*dê* which is written exactly like the Pahlavi ciphers for twenty-two and, no doubt, stands for Av. ratha.

[4] So spelt ten times in §§ 2–11, but here Srâtô. It is also Srîtô in Dk. V, iii, 2.

[5] Pahl. Vîsrapân in §§ 9, 11 and Dk. V, iii, 2; but here it is

the coming of a report about the marvellousness of that chariot to Vi*s*tâsp, Vi*s*tâsp's begging that chariot from Srîtô, and Srîtô *saying* in reply to Vi*s*tâsp: 'That chariot is for a righteous man, *in* which the soul of Srîtô in the life*time* of Srîtô's body[1], *and* that of that man in the life*time* of his body, come visibly together once in the worldly existence.' 3. And the soul of Srîtô, through the generosity of that Srîtô, presents that chariot to the eyesight of that man of righteousness; thereby it becomes evident he had seen *it*, and is told not to act in another manner. 4. The exalted Kaî-Vi*s*tâsp, as becoming from revelation more particularly aware of this marvel about the future at that time, and for the sake of this marvel being published to the worldly existence (gêhânîgîh), and of *his* becoming

---

Visrapân, and in § 7 the first letter is omitted, leaving only îsrapân. In Pahl. Vd. XX, 11 (Sp.) we have Srît-î سدوسر (in L4), which latter name may also be îsrapânŏ, though more likely to be read Sêr*z*ânŏ when considered by itself. It is almost certain that the person mentioned in Pahl. Vd. XX, 11 is intended to be the same as that named here in the text. But it is doubtful if this person be the Av. Thrita son of Sâyu*z*dri (or Sâi*z*dri) of Yt. V, 72; XIII, 113. As the legend in the text appears to refer to the soul of Srîtô, or Thrita, revisiting the world to meet Vi*s*tâsp, this Srîtô may have been the warrior Srîtô, the seventh brother, employed by Kaî-Ûs, about 350 years earlier, to kill the frontier-settling ox of that time, but there seem to be no means of so identifying him with absolute certainty.

[1] This is the literal meaning of the Pahl. 'mûn rûbân-î Srîtô pavan zîndagîh-î Srîtô tanŏ,' but it is not quite consistent with Srîtô's return to the earth as a spirit. The Indian copyists seem to have observed this, as they have omitted several words, so as to alter the meaning to the following:—'That chariot is for a man of the righteous, *with* whom Srîtô in the life*time* of that *man's* body comes visibly together, &c.' But the sentence is not quite grammatical.

more invoking *for* the supremacy of the Maz*d*a-worshipping religion, became discernible by those of the realm, is sought for, *and* is most attended.

5. A great wonder became manifest to Vi*s*tâsp and those of the world, just as revelation mentions thus: 'Thereupon the archangels are letting forth the soul of that *Srîtô* from the light of the supreme heaven, from the light on to the earth created by Aûhar*m*az*d*; *and* the soul of Vi*s*tâsp proceeded from him into the light to meet *it*. 6. Vi*s*tâsp proceeded on to the propitious south (rapîtvînŏ); he *was* producing more gain than the gainers, and he *was* more inquisitive than the inquisitive; to all whom he saw he spoke, and unto such as spoke he listened; when he gazed at them looking simultaneously they stood up, *and* obeisance *was* offered by them unto the soul *and* person of Vi*s*tâsp.'

7. Immediately upon that no delay occurred until *there* came on at a run—*besides* the soul of Srîtô of the Vîsraps—the most horrid (agrandtûm) of demons, from the horrid northern quarter of the horrid destroyer (za*d*âr), that was himself black, and his deeds, too, were very black. 8. And as he comes himself, so also he grumbles *to* the soul of Srîtô thus: 'Give a maintenance (khvârag) *to* Vi*s*tâsp who is thy driver[1], for the sake of good fellowship and service, and for that, righteousness is suitable unto a pure *one*; do not *give it* as a thing which is protective (that is, do not *give it* for the sake of worldly gratuity), *but* for love of the righteousness which is owing to the perfect existences.'

9. When those words were fully heard by Srîtô of

[1] This speech seems intended as veiled irony.

the Vîsraps, the early bestower (levînŏ-vakhsh), he stood still and so he spoke in words thus: 'For righteousness I give thee, *O* mighty Kaî-Vistâsp! this chariot which is without a driver, only for love of the righteousness which is owing to the perfect existences.' 10. As much for righteousness as is best for righteousness, and as much for the soul as is best for the soul, the gift of the whole *was* secured (that is, its acceptance *was* announced as often as three times).

11. Then that chariot became two chariots, one spiritual and the other worldly; in the worldly *one* the exalted Kaî-Vistâsp travelled forth unto the village of the Nôdars[1] in the joyfulness *of* good thoughts, and in the spiritual *one* the soul of Srîtô of the Vîsraps travelled forth unto the best existence.

12. One *marvel* is this which is declared that in fifty-seven years onwards from the acceptance of the religion *by* Zaratûst[2], the arrival of the religion is published in the seven regions[3]; *and* within the life*time* of Vistâsp, the circumstance (aêdûnŏîh) is manifested by the coming of *some* from *other* regions to Frashôstar of the Hvôbas[4] for enquiry *about* the

[1] Nôdar (Av. Naotara) was a son of king Mânûskîhar (Bd. XXXI, 13) and an ancestor of king Vistâsp. Vistâsp being a descendant of Kaî-Kavâd (Bd. XXXI, 28, 29) who was the adopted son of Aûzôbô (Bd. XXXI, 24) a son of Zâgh, son of Masvâk, son of Nôdar (Bd. XXXI, 23 corrected from XXXIII, 5). Hûtôs, the wife of Vistâsp, was also of the village of the Nôdars (Yt. XV, 35).

[2] That is fifty-seven years after the conference of Zaratûst (see Chap. V, 1).

[3] See the summary in Dk. VIII, xiv, 10:—'Likewise, about the communication of Zaratûst's knowledge of the Mazda-worshipping religion to the world, his attracting mankind to the religion, *and* the ages, after Zaratûst, until the renovation *of the universe*.'

[4] Av. Ferashaostrô Hvôgvô (Yas. LI, 17); he was a brother

religion, *even* as revelation mentions thus: 'Two whose names are thus, Spîtôîs[1] and Arezrâspô[2], who have hastened unto Frashôstar of the Hvôbas in search of wisdom.'

13. Thus much splendour and wonder *of* Vistâsp *and* those of the realm regarding Zaratûst[3], and thus much due to the coming of the archangels from the sky to the earth before Vistâsp, as evidence about the true prophesying *of* Zaratûst[4]; and that, too, about Pêshyôtan[5], the chariot of Srîtô[6], and other subjects seen written above, *are* declared by the Avesta, which is the same that they accepted from Zaratûst, as the culmination[7] (*av*arîgânîh) of Aûharmazd's words. 14. And if this splendour, glory, *and* wonder that *are* written above as regards *what* those learned *men* of the realm saw—which *are* in the statement revealed by the Avesta—*had* not occurred, king Vistâsp *and* those learned *men* of the realm would not have seen what this Avesta had revealed to them—which *was* thus much splendour *and* wonder reported by it to them—*and* not one word about leaving *its* preservation to us would be annexed.

of Gâmâsp (Dk. V, ii, 12; iii, 4; Zs. XXIII, 10), and the father of Zaratûst's wife Hvôvi. The Hvôvas (Pahl. Hvôbas) were a numerous family.

[1] Av. gen. Spitôis (Yt. XIII, 121). He was high-priest of Fradadafsh, the south-east region.

[2] Av. Erezrâspa (ibid.) He was high-priest of Vîdadafsh, the south-west region (see Bd. XXIX, 1). These foreign envoys were brothers, each being a son of Uspãsnu.

[3] See Chap. IV, 73.

[4] See Chap. IV, 74–82.

[5] See Chap. V, 12.

[6] See §§ 2–11.

[7] See Chap. V, 11.

CHAPTER VII.

1. About the marvellousness which is manifested after *the time of* Vistâsp until the collapse (hangaftanŏ) *of* the sovereignty *of* Irân.

2. There is marvellousness *which* is manifested after Vistâsp until the collapse of the sovereignty of Irân, apart from the blessedness of ordeal, the accomplishment of other Avestic rites, the great power over the sacred fires, *and* many other religious observances *which* were connected with the disciples of Zaratûst.

3. Even after the devastation which happened owing to Alexander, those who *were* rulers after him brought back much to the collection from a scattered state[1]; *and* there are *some* who *have* ordered the keeping *of it* in the treasury of Shapân[2].

4. Likewise there is to be brought *forward* what *there is* concerning the names of rulers *and* high-priests, *such* as arrive for it at times *and* periods, which *are* each consecutive, as organizers *of* the religion and the world; also of the tyrant *or* apostate, who is manifest at various periods, for the disturbance of the religion *and* monarchy and the penance of the world, *with* the coming of the penitential *one*.

---

[1] Referring to king Valkhas the Askânian (probably Vologeses I, see S. B. E., vol. xxxvii, p. 413); possibly also to Ardashîr Pâpakân.

[2] So here, but usually written Shapîgân, and sometimes Shaspîgân. It was no doubt a royal treasury, and Dk. V, iii, 4, calls it so, but uses the words gangŏ-î khûdâyân, in which Gâmâsp is said to have deposited the Avesta and Zand written in gold upon ox-hides. If Shapîgân be a corruption of shâyagân, 'royal,' it is singular that some copyist has not corrected the spelling.

5. *Such* as Vohûmanô, son *of* Spend-dâ*d*[1], of the rulers, about whom it says even this in the Avesta, that *he is* Vohûmanô, the just, who is the most efficient of the assembly of Ma*zd*a-worshippers. 6. And *S*ênôv[2] of the high-priests, as about him it says even this: 'The religion becomes a hundred years *old* when *S*ênôv is born, and two hundred years when he passes away; he was also the first Ma*zd*a-worshipper *with* a life of a hundred *years*, *and* who walks forth upon this earth with a hundred disciples.'

7. Also Alexander of the devastators, as it says even this of him in revelation[3], that *in* those three winters, which *are* of like purpose (ham-ay*âz*akô), that Aeshm[4] would set up a deadly king in the impenitent world, who is the evil-destined Alexander.

8. And of the high-priests *are* Ar*e*zvâk[5], the interpretation of whose name is 'the pure word;' Srûtvôk-spâ*d*âk[5], the interpretation of whose name is 'the propitious recitation;' Zrayang,h*a*u[6], the interpretation of whose name is 'the ocean existence;' and Spe*n*tô-khratv*a*u[6], the interpretation of

[1] Av. Spe*n*tô-dâta of Yt. XIII, 103, a son of Vi*s*tâsp, with whom Avesta dynastic history ends. He was the Persian Isfendiyâr, and his son Vohûmanô is unknown to the Avesta. The *K*itradâ*d* Nask (Dk. VIII, xiii, 18) mentions a 'Namûn, son of Spend-shê*d*,' which probably stands for 'Vohûmanô, son of Spend-dâ*d*,' but this appears to have been in a Pahlavi supplement compiled in Sasanian times. He is also mentioned in Bd. XXXIV, 8, a chapter 'about the computation of years by the Arabs,' according to the Irânian Bundahi*s*.

[2] Av. Saêna of Yt. XIII, 97, where the last clause of the passage here translated from the Avesta occurs. Compare Zs. XXIII, 11.

[3] Not in the extant Avesta.

[4] The demon of Wrath.

[5] Av. gen. Erezv*a*u and Srûtô-spâd*a*u in Yt. XIII, 115.

[6] These two names are written in their Av. gen. forms, as they occur in Yt. XIII, 115.

whose name is 'the propitious wisdom.' 9. Because it says even this about them, namely: 'I mention thy manifestation, *and* also the tokens of its publicity when this religion of thy Maz*d*a-worshippers becomes four hundred years *old*[1]; in this law benightedness (lêlyâîh) arises, *and* the embodied existences see the manifestation through calculation *of* the planets and also the stars; and whoever, too, *are* mine are *so* for a century, through the average opinion *of* thirty medium winters for a man[2]; *and* the righteous Arezvâk and those three others are they of the most righteous existences, over whom they *are* the most masterly *and* most authoritative in that time.' 10. And this, too, that they who glorify the religion of the Maz*d*a-worshippers in the fifth and sixth centuries *are* they; *and* no persons save *their* souls, except *those* who remain for the arrival of the four[3] interpretations that *arise* through the authority of these four individuals, Arezvâk, Srûtô-spâdh*a*u[4], Zrayang,h*a*u, *and* Spe*n*tô-khratv*a*u who, all four of them, seek *their* thoughts, words, *and* deeds in the *sacred* text (mânsar).

11. Also Rashn-rêsh[5] is the apostate of that

[1] If the chronology in Bd. XXXIV, 7, 8 were correct, the interval between the first revelation of the religion and the death of Alexander would be 272 years, and this would make the 400th year of the religion coincide with B.C. 195.

[2] That is, for a generation. The meaning appears to be, that these four successive high-priests insure the continuance of orthodox religion for more than a century, or well into the sixth century of the religion, as mentioned in § 10.

[3] The MS. has the cipher for 'three,' by mistake.

[4] Here written in Avesta characters.

[5] In Dk. III, cxcviii, 2, this apostate is said to have been an

time, as *some one*[1] says unto Rashn, *one* of the sacred beings, and about many besides this *one*, thus: 'All who are creatures of the beneficent spirit are distressed by their persecution, *but* put trust in those men, Arezvâk *and* those three others.'

12. And of the organizers of the period is Artakhshatar[2], son of Pâpak, as it says even this about him, namely: 'Which is that ruler who is powerful, more striving than the Kayâns, *and* mighty, an embodiment of the *sacred* commandments and awfully armed[3]; in whose abode Aharîsvang[4], the virtuous *and* radiant, walks forth in maiden form, beneficent and very strong, well-formed, high-girded, *and* truthful, of illustrious race *and* noble? 13. Whoever it is that, on the occurrence of strife, seeks prosperity for *him*self with his own arm; whoever it is that, on the occurrence of strife, encounters the enemies with his own arm.'

14. Tanvasar[5] is also for his assistance, as it says

---

associate (ham-pâîgar) of the Christian ecclesiastic Akvân, and yells out ten admonitions contradicting those of the righteous Sênôv who is mentioned in § 6 (see Peshotan's edition, vol. v, pp. 239, 311). It does not follow that he was a contemporary of Sênôv, and here he seems to be placed fully two centuries later.

[1] Probably Aûharmazd.

[2] The founder of the Sâsânian dynasty, who reigned as king of the kings of Persia, A.D. 226–241.

[3] Most of these qualities are applied to the angel Srôsh, the personification of obedience (see Yas. LVII, 1); also to Kavi Vistâspa and Karsna, son of Zbaurvant, in Yt. XIII, 99, 106.

[4] Av. Ashis vanguhi, 'good rectitude,' personified as a female angel; her description is given in Yt. XIII, 107, and is similar to that of Anâhita in Yt. V, 64.

[5] So spelt here and in §§ 17, 18, thrice in all; it is also thrice spelt Tansar, in Dk. III, last chapter, 7; IV, 25, 25, and this mis-spelling has led to the mis-pronunciation Tôsar. It appears, however, that Tanvasar is a transposition of Tanvars, 'hairy-

this, too, about them: 'Zaratûst asked again thus: "Who is he who is the most salutary *for* a country, which the demons *have* exhausted of everything virtuous, over which his authority is brought and *which* is wicked and teaching falsehood?" 15. Aûharmazd spoke thus: "An autocrat (sâstâr), to cure a country, who *has* not gone *mad* (that is, he does not annoy the good) and is well-directing (that is, he gives virtuous commands), who is *also* of noble race, and likewise a priest who is acquainted with war, of a famous province, *and* righteous, are most salutary *for* that country. 16. And I tell thee this, that the apostasy of destruction is *just* like the four-legged wolf which the world gives up to running astray (vardak-takhshisnîh) (that is, owing to its action *they are* leading *it* off as astray; which is so that even he who is not opulent is rendered sickly, that they (*the apostates*) may take away his things by the hand of the assassin (khûnyân); and they shall lead the world, the dwelling for *his* residence, into wandering. 17. But that wicked (*av*ârûnŏ) strife descended upon that country, besides that wicked demon-worship, besides that wicked slander; and not even that wicked strife, nor that wicked demon-worship, nor that wicked slander, is dissipated from

bodied,' because we are told that Tansar, or Tanvasar, was so called on account of all his limbs being covered with hair (vars). This statement occurs in the introduction to Tanvasar's letter to Gushnaspshâh (Ar. *G*asnasf-shâh), king of Padashkhvârgar (Ar. Farshvâdgar) and Tabaristân; and is made on the authority of an old Pahlavi copyist, Bahrâm Khûrzâd, whose Pahlavi was translated into Arabic by Ibn al-Muqaffa in the middle of the eighth century, and that into Persian early in the thirteenth century (see Darmesteter's edition in Journal Asiatique for 1894, pp. 185–250, 502–555).

that country until *the time* when they attach the grant of approval to him, the spiritual leader, the eloquent (pûr-gûftâr), truthful-speaking, *and* righteous Tanvasar. 18. And it is when they grant approval to the spiritual leader, the truthful speaker of eloquence, the righteous Tanvasar, that those *of* the country obtain redress (bêsh*â*z*a*gânîh) when they seek *it*, and no deviation (anâyûînakŏîh) from the religion of Zaratû*s*t."'

19. As to the nature of the questions *and* statements of the organizer of the religion, Âtû*r*pâ*d*[1] son of Mâ*r*aspend, about the connection of the glory with the race, it also says this, that 'though righteousness *may* arise from the statements and prosperity of the Tûrânians when extracted by questions, *it is* said that its acceptance occurs there through complete mindfulness[2]; they benefit the embodied world of righteousness, and produce distress for the fiend; in like manner, they rely upon Vohûmanô, *and* Zaratû*s*t is their delight through the report *of* the birth *of* Zaratû*s*t from us who are archangels. 20. This liberality for thee is *from* us who are archangels, *and* Âtû*r*pâ*d*, the very best well-destined *man* arose; and this, too, do thou say about him, that it is the steel age in which that man, the organizer of development *and* organizer of righteousness, Âtû*r*pâ*d* son of Mâ*r*aspend, of the convocation, begets Avarethrab*a*u[3].'

[1] A high-priest who was prime minister of king Shahpûhar II (A.D. 309–379). He is often mentioned in Pahlavi writings, but in the Avesta he is only alluded to, apparently, by the title Râ*s*tarevaghe*n*t in Yt. XIII, 106.

[2] A translation of Av. spe*n*ta-ârmaiti, the archangel Spendâ*r*ma*d*.

[3] So written, all three times in Pâzand. He is the Avarethra-

21. This Avarethrabau, too, is an organizer whose righteous guardian spirit we reverence, and *in* memory of Mânûskîhar, the well-destined, and a progenitor of Âtûrpâd[1], it says that 'only from him *comes* Avarethrabau;' and *then also arises* this *one* of the adversaries of the religion, the apostate of apostates, whom they have even called the Mazdag-like (Mazdagîg-ik)[2]. 22. As it says this, too, about them, namely: 'This religion of mine thou dost survey with thoughts of spiritual life, thou dost very thoroughly inspect *it*, O Zaratûst! when many, aware of apostates, call the performance of righteousness and even the priesthood innocence, and few are frank and practising *it*.' 23. In the revelation of the Mazda-worshippers is this, namely: 'Thoroughly look into revelation, and seek a remedy for them and any whatever of them who have become disturbing in the embodied existence, and uncaptivated *by* the orthodox (âyîn-aûmônd) righteousness which is owing to the perfect existences; and so they divide the religion of the Mazda-worshippers through division of race, they speak regarding the action *of* their own *followers*, and give the endowment to their own. 24. They grant supplies of food, so that they *may* say the food is proportional to the hunger; they speak of procreation, *and* say that they say lineage is through the mothers; and they approve of wolfishness, so that they would act something like

bangh, son of Râstare-vaghent of Yt. XIII, 106, better known as Zaratûst, son of Âtûrpâd in his old age, for whom the Andar'z-î Âtûrpâd-î Mâraspendân was written.

[1] Whose pedigree is traced back to Mânûskîhar in Bd. XXXIII, 3.

[2] Probably some disciple of Mânih, the heretic who had been put to death A.D. 276–7. Mazdag was put to death A.D. 528. See S.B.E., vol. xxxvii, pp. 257 n, 278 n.

wolves *in* the performance of gratifying their desires, like that of the wolf's progeny behind the mother. 25. Moreover, they form their lineage through the mothers; buying their women *as* sheep, they shall carry off for profit even that son *or* brother who is the progeny, those that we have produced for your companionship; you are not predominant, but *have* remained in companionship; you do not even believe them, *but* you do not establish an ordeal, although *it is* evident that you will be acquitted; they lie even to *their* children, so that the advance of the promise-breaker is through them, and even in their own persons[1].'

26. Here it speaks about the organization of the religion *by* the glorified[2] Khûsrôî, son of Kavâ*d*, thus: 'Upon their lingering behind, a man is produced who is righteous, the Glorified *one*[2], an approver (khênî*d*âr) of speech who is wise, whom the convocation, on hearing the words that he utters, speaks *of* as a high-priest; that is when he gives out penance (srôshîgîh), so that he may effect the punishment of sinners. 27. The constant outpouring of perplexity (pê*k* shârî*d*an) *by* the perverters is the fear of that hero, as regards that

[1] This quotation, from a Pahlavi version of an Avesta text, would probably be very applicable to the state of the Persian people at many periods in the fourth and fifth centuries, when heresy was prevalent and orthodox Zoroastrianism was by no means universal. Some of the evils mentioned are inseparable from slavery at all times.

[2] Literally 'immortal-soulled,' Anôshak-rûbân, the usual title of king Khûsrô I, who reigned A. D. 531–578. Before he became king, A. D. 528 or 529, he had summoned an assembly of priests to condemn the heretic Mazdag, when the last important revision of the Pahlavi versions of the Avesta probably took place (see Byt. I, 6–8, and Nöldeke's Gesch. der Sas. pp. 463–466).

convocation, when he casts *them forth* by expulsion from the vicinity, so that he may make *them* extinguished very quickly; owing to that, they, *whose* producer is even he who is a person destroying the righteous man, become gloomy on account of the Glorified *one*, through *his* smiting the spiritual life of apostasy; *just* as now, when he who is gloomy, *and* of scattered intellect, is gloomy owing to you *of* the Spîtâmas.' 28. This, too, it states, namely: 'In every way, I tell thee, *O* Zaratûst of the Spîtâmas! that their time is mistrustful (avâvar) as to him who is an open friend, *and* most deceitful both *to* the wicked and the righteous; the Glorified *one* is a controller (ayûkhtâr) exalting the creatures, *and* whoever is possessing the creatures of the righteous *ones*[1], so that he remains again at work in the doings of the Glorified *one*, is *he* who is a combiner *of* the actions *and* an utterer of the true replies *of* that Glorified *one*.'

29. And about the occurrence of a symptom of the devastators of the sovereignty *and* religion of the country of Irân one wonder, which is associated with the religion, is even this *which* it mentions thus: 'Thereupon, when the first symptom of a ravager *of* the country occurs, *O* righteous Zaratûst! then the more aggressive and more unmerciful *in* malice becomes the tyrant of the country, and through him, too, they ravage (rêshênd) the house, through him the village, through him the community, through him the province, *and* through him even the whole *of* that manifestation *in* the country *of* any teaching whatever that occurs *through* the ravager *of* the country; and so the country should

[1] Of the good spirits.

keep a man who is observant *and* learned on the watch, because information is in his mind. 30. *Thereupon, when the second symptom of a ravager of the country occurs, &c.*[1] . . . .

31. Thereupon, when the third symptom *of* a ravager *of* the country occurs, the priestly people are disturbing the tradition, so that they speak nothing wisely; it is even on this account they do not accept them, and it is not when *one* speaks truly *that* the ravager *of* the country believes them, and through him, too, they ravage the house, through him the village, *through him the community*, through him the province, and through him even the whole *of* that manifestation *in* the country *of* any teaching whatever *that* occurs *through* the ravager *of* the country; and so, too, the country should keep a man who is observant *and* learned on the watch, because information is in his mind. 32. Thereupon, when the fourth symptom of a ravager *of* the country occurs, it upsets the replenishment of the fires, and upsets those men of the righteous, so that they shall not undertake the care of them; and thus they shall not convey the holy-water to him who is a priestly authority, so that they may not produce the seizing upon the stipend *of* the priestly authorities *by* him who is the ravager *of* the country; through him, too, they ravage the house, through him the village, through him the community, through him *the province, and through him* even the whole *of* that

[1] The whole of this section is omitted in the old MS., evidently by mistake. Perhaps the second symptom of devastation was connected with the evil deeds of the warrior class, but this is very uncertain. Passages of four or five words are also omitted by the MS. in §§ 31, 32.

manifestation *in* the country *of* any teaching whatever *that* occurs *through* the ravager *of* the country; *and* so, too, the country should keep a man who is observant *and* learned on the watch, because information is in his mind.'

33. About the collapse of the sovereignty of Irân, it also states this, namely: 'That very villain (mar), *O* Zaratûst! brings those provinces on to running astray, so that he may make those quite dissevered which constitute the existence of that powerful sovereignty; and then he is a thorough assailant *of* the righteous, then he is an assailant *of* the righteous with eagerness. 34. That same deadly *one* (mar), *O* Zaratûst! does not continue living long afterwards; moreover his offspring disappear (that is, they perish utterly); but his soul falls to the bottom of the gloomy existence which is horrible hell, and upon their bodies every kind *of* unseemly unhappiness comes from themselves, owing to their own actions when they give approval to the imprisonment of a guardian of spiritual *affairs* who is eloquent, true-speaking, *and* righteous. 35. Against that deadly *one* he contends, *O* Zaratûst! for the spiritual lordship *and* priestly authority that I approve *as* good *for* the whole embodied existence; also against the preparation of a decree to produce evil decisions, *and* against the dismissal of litigants, whether heterodox or orthodox, who are of a family of serfs of a far-situated village and are making petitions.'

36. 'And *as to* the land, too, over which he wanders, the evil spirit utterly devastates their country through pestilence and other misery; and, moreover, strife which is tormenting falls upon that

country, besides demon-worship which is iniquitous, *and* besides slander which is iniquitous. 37. And the strife which is iniquitous is not to be dissipated (*a*pâsî-aîtanŏ) from that country, nor the demon-worshippers who *are* iniquitous, nor the slander which is iniquitous, before the *time* when they give approval to him, to the priest who is a guardian of spiritual *affairs*, who is eloquent, true-speaking, and righteous; and it is when they give him approval, that they obtain healthfulness *for* their country when they pray *for it*, and not irregularly from him, *O* Zaratûst!'

38. And this which is recounted is a statement that is execrated (nafrîg-aitŏ) by many, details from the Avesta as to occurrences *that will* arise after Vistâsp until the dispersion (an*gâv*isnŏ) of the sovereignty of Irân from the country of Irân; *it is also* declared that this which is written happened *to* the knowledge of those of the world. 39. This, too, is about the evidence of the above:—'And if this which is declared from the Avesta, as to *what* happens after Kaî-Vistâsp until the end of the sovereignty of Irân, should not have happened, and *it being* the pre-eminence of the Avesta which really became this present treasure, it thereby ensues, owing to its position in that *former* [1], and the manifest absence of the destruction of those rulers *and* high-priests from Vistâsp onwards in this *latter* [2], that it could not be connected with us [3].'

---

[1] The above declaration from the Avesta.

[2] The present Avesta itself.

[3] Meaning perhaps that, for some good reason, it could not be communicated to us in the extant Avesta. If § 39 be not a later addition to this chapter, it implies that the prophetical quotations from the Avesta, regarding the history of the religion after the time

CHAPTER VIII.

1. About the marvellousness which is manifested and is openly specified after the collapsing of the sovereignty of Irân *and* the country of Irân; *also* the end of the millennium of Zaratûst and the arrival of Aûshêdar the descendant of Zaratûst[1].

2. There is this marvellousness, really overthrowing the blessedness of the knowledge of former government, revealed by the Avesta about the ninth and tenth centuries, that which is an indicator of circumstances (aêdûnŏîh) now visible, *such* as the dispersion of the sovereignty of Irân from the country of Irân, the disturbance of just law *and* custom, the predominance of *those with* dishevelled hair[2], *and* the haughty profession of ecclesiastics[3]. 3. Also the collection and even connection of all their four systems of belief (vâvarî-hastanŏ)[4] to-

of Vistâsp, were no more extant in the Avesta, when the Dînkard was compiled, than they are now.

[1] The contents of Chaps. VII–XI have some connection with the following summary in Dk. VIII, xiv, 11, 12:—'*And* about the nature of the advancement of the people of the period, the separation *of* centuries and millenniums, *and* the signs, wonders, and perplexity which are manifested in the world at the end of each millennium in the world. Also as to the birth *and* arrival of Aûshêdar, son of Zaratûst, at the end of the first millennium, and a report of him and his time, *and of* the many destroyers of the organizers of the period between Zaratûst's millennium and the coming of Aûshêdar.'

[2] This meaning for vigârdŏ-vars is chiefly based upon the use of vigârd in AV. XXXIV, 5, for a woman's hair being 'combed.' These invaders of Irân from the east, at the end of the first millennium of the religion, are mentioned in Byt. II, 22, 24, 28; III, 1, 6, 13. They are called 'Turkish demons' in § 47.

[3] The Byzantine Christians.

[4] Zoroastrianism, Muhammadanism, Christianity, and either Judaism or Idolatry.

gether for the upper rank; the coming of *one* working with the sacred beings to the inferior, the transient, and the captive of the period; and the dispersion and downfall of dependent and public men in their time.

4. The disappearance of a disposition for wisdom from the foreigners *in* the countries of Irân, which is an indication of shame *at* the truth of the religion, and *at* the praise, peace, liberality, *and* other goodness whose provision *has* lodgement in a disposition for wisdom. 5. Also the abundance *of* the decisions of apostasy, the falsehood, deceit, slander, quarrelsomeness, fraudulence, ingratitude, discord, stinginess, and other vileness whose real connection is a disposition to devour, neglecting heedfulness for the archangels of fire, water, and worldly *existence*[1]. 6. The oppressiveness of infidelity *and* idol-worship, the scarcity *of* freedom, the extreme predominance of avarice in the individuals (tanô) of mankind, the plenitude of different opinions about witchcraft, *and* the much inclination of many for paralyzing the religion of the sacred beings.

7. The annihilation of the sovereignty of mankind one over the other, the desolation of localities and settlements by severe actual distress, and the evil foreign potentates who *are*, one after the other, scattering the valiant; the destruction among cattle *and* the defilement *of* the spirit of enjoyment, owing to the lodgement of lamentation and weeping *in* the countries of Irân, the clamour of the demon-worshipper in the country, *and* the unobtainable stature, non-existent strength, blighted destiny, and short

---

[1] Ashavahistô, Khûrdad, and Spendarmad.

life of mankind. 8. Also the abundance of ordinances (âyinŏ)[1] of various descriptions, the approval of the apostate among tyrants and the non-approval of the Zoti[2] who is well-disposed and wise, the coming of the Zoti to want, *and* all the other adversity, disruption, and running astray which *are* overpowering even in districts *and* localities of the countries of Irân.

9. The maintenance of no ritual (*a*pandîh) of the religion of the sacred beings; the weakness, suffering, and evil habits *of* those of the good religion; the lamentation and recantation (khûstûkîh) of the upholders of the religion; *and* the wickedness and extermination of good works in most of the countries of Irân. 10. Also much other misery in these two centuries is recounted in the Avesta, which passed away with them and is also now so visible therein, and manifestly occurs in them.

11. This, too, is a statement (nisang-1) as to them, *which* revelation mentions thus: 'That is the age mingled with iron (that is, from every side they perceive *it is* of iron) in which they bring forth into life him who is a sturdy praying apostate. 12. This is their sturdiness, that their approval is unobservant of both doctrines (âînakŏ); and this is their praying, that whenever *it is* possible for them they shall cause misery to others; *also* when an old man publicly advances into a crowd (galakŏ) of youths, owing to the evil times in which that man who is learned is born, they are unfriendly *to him* (that is, they are no friends of the high-priests of the priestly assembly). 13. They are freely speaking (that is,

[1] Or it may be hênô, 'squadrons.'

[2] The chief officiating priest in religious ceremonies.

they utter phrases smoothly), they are wicked and are fully maliciously talking, so that they shall make the statements of priests and high-priests useless; they also tear asunder the spiritual lordship *and* priestly authority, and shall bring the ruler *and* priestly authority into evil behaviour as vicious, but they bring together those *who are* singular. 14. Anything they say is always mischief (agîh), and that district which had a judge they cast into the smiting precinct, into hell; it is misery without any intermission they shall inflict therein, till they attain unto damnation (darvandîh) through the recitation they persevere in, *both* he who is the evil progeny disseminated by the apostate *and* he who is the villainous wolf full of disaster *and* full of depravity.'

15. 'Here *below* they fight, the friend with him who is a friend, they also defraud (zîvênd) him of his own work (that is, whenever *it is* possible for them, they shall seize upon his property), and they give it to him from whom they obtain prosperity in return; if not, they seek him who is acting as a confederate (nishîn-gûn), and they make that other *one* defraud the poor *man* (so that they shall seize upon his property); they also cheat him when he shall make complaint. 16. I *shall* not again produce such for thee, no friend here for him who is a friend, no brother for him who is a brother, no son for him who is a father, nor yet a father *for* him who is a son; admonished, *but* not convinced, they become the abode of the will of the place, so that they subsist in every single place where it is necessary for them *to be*, in each that is necessary for them they march on together, and on the way they reflect upon the path of blessedness and the

manifold learning they utter owing to knowledge of me[1].'

17. 'These three, our increase, learning, *and* reward, we fully understand through the ascendancy *of* him who is ignoble, *and* through the downfall *of* him who is noble *and* superior to him of little thorough instruction who, in every thing, *will* be at the foot of the tyrant. 18. Thinking of a priest *one* becomes spiritual, thinking of a tyrant *one* becomes a Kavîg[2]; a demon *in* disposition is an incipient demon, a Kavîg *in* disposition is himself attracted towards a youth.'

19. Then, when character and wisdom recede from the countries of Irân (that is, they depart), so *that* destitution and also winter, produced by demons who are worshipping the demon, rush together from the vicinity of disaster (vôighn) on to the countries of Irân, where even rain becomes scanty and pestilence is secretly advancing and deceiving, so that deaths become numerous; thus even *he* of perverted wisdom, who is wicked, and the apostate also, who is unrighteous, rush together in companionship. 20. As what *one* says they *all* exclaim thus: 'Consume and destroy, *O* ruler! for *it* is to be consumed and destroyed by thee; destroy even the fire, consume even as food those who are the protection of the association enforcing *religious* obedience, and those leading on the poor *man* of the righteous dispensation by their guidance.' 21. So that they shall make him thoroughly detached and smite him;

[1] So far, this statement (§§ 11–16) seems to be ascribed to Aûharmazd; but what follows (§§ 17, 18, 20) appears to represent the sentiments of some Irânians of those later times.

[2] See Chap. II, 9 n.

likewise wisdom is the wealth they bring him, *and* it is when property is being carried off by them, *that* the wisdom conveyed by them arises.

22. 'And in that age, *O* righteous *one of* the Spîtâmas! the coming of my desire is not purely for thee, nor is a thorough belief *of* the departure of life, so that the bringing *and* conducting of a speaker of promises (mitragôv) is not necessary; those of the perfect apostate injure this discourse of thine, the Avesta and Zand, so that they shall make *it* thoroughly weak; *and* those of the perfect apostate harass their own souls, for love of the wealth which he produced.'

23. And about the ninth and tenth centuries this also it says, that, '*as* that age proceeds, this is what occurs, *O* Zaratûst of the Spîtâmas! when many apostates utter the righteousness of priestly instruction and authority, *which* is wickedness towards me, they cause begging for water, they wither vegetation, and they put down all excellence which is due to the manifestation of righteousness.'

24. Again Zaratûst enquired of him thus: 'What do they so produce by that, *O* Aûharmazd! when they cause begging for water, they wither vegetation, and they put down all excellence due to the manifestation of righteousness?' 25. And Aûharmazd spoke thus: 'They so produce those *things* among them, *O* Zaratûst! when they mention a greater reward for bantlings *and* relations than that of their own souls (that is, they talk more concerning their allowance, where it is that for their own). 26. Moreover, they give to the Kîgs *and* Karaps, for some repute *with* the shepherd people of the husbandman, and with the swift-horsed people *of* the warrior, as

though they would provide us[1] here *below* with a large share of meat, that they would make our privilege, just as we[1] here supply him with meat whom we render greatly precious. 27. The property *of* even a wicked *man* here *below*, O Zaratûst! in the average opinion among the disorganized (anârâstânŏ) is a dignified provision (that is, we form a strong opinion, the approval *of which* is more to be asserted as *being* the opinion of a poor righteous *man*, about a worthy righteous *man* whose manifest righteousness is a homage (franâmisnŏ) to duty *and* good works).'

28. Again he enquired of him thus: 'Is there so perfect a manifestation here *below*, in the age of the worldly existence of the religion of the Mazda-worshippers (that is, is there a lodgement of the religion of the Mazda-worshippers in any one)?' 29. And Aûharmazd spoke thus: 'It is so, among those men of mine[2], O Zaratûst! for here *below there* are priests who are eloquent, and they, too, are men voluble and requisite in the embodied existence, all-beneficent and producing the destruction *of* harm and the wizard; the people of the wicked tyrant say also regarding them, *that*, excepting thee, O Zaratûst! they rightly practise righteousness more largely, more powerfully, *and* more volubly. 30. Blind are those *of* the fiend, who are consulting with thee and are unaware of the tyrant; and observant are also those *of* the fiend who consult with them and think of *their* intelligence, and oppose the imbecile (anâkâsîh-aûmônd) apostate who is near them, so that

[1] The archangels.

[2] Reading minam, instead of madam which is unintelligible here.

they say[1] this, namely: "*As to* this which thou tellest us, *it* is evidently not so as thou sayest," of which they speak thus: "This duty of thy man is not mine (that is, it is not necessary for me to perform) nor thine (that is, it is not necessary even *for* thee to perform), because *it* is not this which is righteousness (that is, not a good work)." 31. For this *one* is produced for these words *and* thoughts of thine, *of* whom thou, too, art aware, he who is whatever is here *below* of Aûshê*d*ar[2] of thoughtful controversy, *O* Zaratû*s*t of the Spîtâmas! for he brings into notice, through the intermingling of his own soul, *him* who is righteous, or has not become *so*.'

32. This, too, he says, namely: '*Of* those, *O* Zaratû*s*t of the Spîtâmas! who come in the ninth and tenth centuries, I tell thee that they are *of* the fiend *of* Greed (Âzî); it is in *her* womb that they are to be fashioned, they who assist those who would be vicious, through pre-eminence in leadership, or through excellence in subserviency.'

33. And this, too, it says about them: 'Those men are much to be destroyed;' so it is said by Aûha*r*ma*zd* that 'these who are righteous, who carry away a corpse in this world, distress their fire, according to every high-priest[3], and even long-flowing water; their bodies, which are really cesspools[4] of a terrible character, become very assisting for the tormentors whose corpses are grievously wicked. 34. Concerning them I tell thee, *O* Zara-

[1] To the apostate.

[2] See §§ 55-60 and Chap. I, 42 n. Here spelt Aûkhshê*d*ar.

[3] Reading dastûr, instead of vastûr.

[4] Pahl. mayâ-vakhdûn = Pers. âb-gîr.

tûst of the Spîtâmas! that, in the ninth and tenth centuries, *there* come those who are the brood of the fiend and the wound-producer (reshgâr)[1] of the evil spirit; even one of them is more to be destroyed than ten demon-worshippers[2]; they also produce extermination for these who are mine, for these of my religion, whom they call a provision for destruction (that is, when it is possible to live in our way, and *ours* are wicked, they diminish in superiority). 35. Even the iniquity that they shall commit in leadership and subserviency, the sin which is smiting thee, they call a trifle (khalakŏ), *O* pure *one* of the Spîtâmas! and the smiter, they say, is *he* whom these of thy religion of Ma*zd*a-worshippers smite. 36. Besides thee, *O* Zaratûst! they distress those *duties*, too, which *are* to be acquired *by* thy people (lagânŏ); they think scornfully of this ceremonial of thine, scornfully of *thy* worship, *O* Zaratûst! *and* they think scornfully of both the two blessed utterances[3], the Avesta and Zand, which *were* proclaimed *to* thee *by* me who am the most propitious of spirits. 37. They foster villainous outrage, *and* they say the best work for mankind is immoderate fighting whose joyfulness is due to actions that are villainous; those, too, *that* they exterminate are the existences *due to* the spirits, they exterminate their own souls, they exterminate the embodied existences *of* the world; *and* they produce lamentation for the soul, *and* even the religion, as regards what is the mode of controlling orthodox people *together* with the iniquitous of the same period.'

38. And this, too, it says, that Zaratûst enquired

[1] Or it may be riyâgâr, 'hypocrite.'

[2] Or 'idolators.'

[3] Pahl. vâfrîgânîh = Av. urvâtâ.

of Aûharmazd thus: 'So what *shall* we prescribe for those who are not capable, through *being* poor (that is, they have no means), nor have they troops, nor a protector over *them*, and they have many persecutors?' 39. *And* Aûharmazd spoke thus: 'The strong-minded[1] man, through understanding, is a token of the development of those who, not being in the army, are capable; their persecutors also are many, and the passing over of authority is owing to the iniquitous of the same period.'

40. This, too, it says, that Zaratûst enquired thus: 'Is he, *O* Aûharmazd! who is a Kaî *or* a Karap, or he who is a most evil ruler in authority, mingled again with the good?' 41. *And* Aûharmazd spoke thus: 'Even he[2].'

42. Zaratûst *also* enquired thus: 'Is he, too, *O* Aûharmazd! who is *one of* those of the good sovereignty, mingled again with the good; or these, *such* as the Kaîsar and Khâkân[3]?' 43. And Aûharmazd spoke thus: 'Even that *former*, *O* Zaratûst!'

44. About the same iniquitous[4] this, too, he says, namely: 'When they are aware and understand about the sayings (galimakŏ) due to righteousness, they are pleased, so that a bribe seems better to them than duty and good works; they love the darkness *rather* than light, the existence they love

[1] Assuming that tôshtŏ-mînisnŏ is a miswriting of toshînŏ-mînisnŏ.

[2] That is, after expiating his misdeeds by his allotted punishment. The last thirteen Pahlavi words of §§ 42, 43 are also added here by mistake in the MS.

[3] The Byzantine emperor and the sovereign Khân of the invaders from the east.

[4] Mentioned in §§ 37, 39.

is the worst existence *rather* than the best existence, *and* they promote difficulty. 45. Concerning them, too, I tell thee that they are more to be destroyed than the leaping (shas*p*ŏ) serpent which is like a wolf *or* a lion, and they ever advance in malice *and* persecution from that *time* till when that man arrives who is *K*itrô-mêhônŏ [1] the righteous, with the victorious club. 46. He *has* marched with fifty triplets of men [2] who are disciples, powerful and tall, looking after duties and ordinances, wide-shouldered, stout-armed, *and* very hairy (kabed-milîh), so that their appearance is rough and of a black colour [3], wherefore the demon and the iniquity *proceeding* from him fear them. 47. He also smites the evil spirit, *together* with *his* creatures; *and* those three manifest branches, that worship the fiend with simultaneous worship, are really these who march for eminent service on horses, even the Turkish demons with dishevelled hair, the Arab, and also She*d*âspô [4] the ecclesiastical Arûman.

[1] So spelt here, but in Dk. IX, xli, 6, it is *K*itrag-mêhônŏ, and other slight variations occur in the best MSS. of Bd. XX, 7, 31; XXIX, 5; Byt. III, 25, 26; Dd. XC, 3; but they can all be traced to an original *K*itrô-mêhan = Av. *K*ithrô-maêthanem, 'of the racial home,' a title applied both to the river and the immortal sacerdotal ruler of Kangd*ez*. The latter is supposed to be Pêshyôtanŏ, a son of king Vi*s*tâsp, who is expected to restore religious rites in Irân and throughout the world.

[2] With 150 disciples, as stated in Byt. III, 27, 29, 42. Here it is written levat*â* 50 3-gabrâân.

[3] Byt. III, 27, 29, 42, states that they wear black marten fur.

[4] In Byt. III, 3, 5, 8, 21, this name is written Shê*d*âspîh which can also be read Shê*d*â*s*fa*s*, and is probably a corrupt pronunciation of the name of some Byzantine emperor or general (such as Theodosius) who had signally defeated the Persians some time in the fifth to seventh century, in which period Zaratû*s*t's millennium probably ended.

48. 'And he *has* then to attract men, contented and discontented, mostly through the incentive of duty; he who is not contented (that is, not agreeing with what he says) contentedly pays respect to him, *O* Zaratûst! (so that he brings him into the religion). 49. Likewise, through that club, he makes *one* press in the same manner: so that *one* is distressed by his hand to hold *others in* contempt, through the valiant arm and through the youthful bodily organs. 50. And he attaches power and triumph to his religion of Aûharmazd, and through that power and triumph they become ever respected thenceforth, when those arrive who are the sons of Zaratûst, who shall produce the renovation in an existence undecaying *and* immortal, hungerless and thirstless, the long-continued perpetuity including all.'

51. And about the separation (burînakô) of the ten centuries in the one millennium of Zaratûst, *and* the tidings of Aûshêdar[1], son of Zaratûst, it says also this, namely: 'When that century fully elapses which is the first of the religion of the Mazda-worshippers, from *the time when* Zaratûst came forward to *his* conference, what is the separation of *this* first century?' 52. And Aûharmazd spoke thus: 'The sun conceals *itself*.' 53. 'What is the separation after the second, third, fourth, *fifth*, sixth, seventh, eighth, ninth, *or* tenth century?' 54. And Aûharmazd spoke thus: 'The sun conceals *itself*.'

55. Then, when thirty winters of the tenth century are unelapsed (that is, thirty winters *are* remaining) a maiden, who is Shemig-abû[2], walks up

[1] See Chap. I, 42.

[2] 'Having a renowned father,' the Zvâris of Av. Srûtad-fedhri, Yt. XIII, 141.

to the water; she that is the mother of that famous Aûshêdar, and her former lineage is from Vôhûrôkô-î Frahânyân[1] in the family of Îsadvâstar, the son of Zaratûst *that* is brought forth by Arang. 56. Then she sits in that water *and* drinks *it*, and she kindles in a high degree those germs which were the third *of* the last that the righteous Zaratûst *was* dropping forth originally, and they introduce that son whose name is the Developer *of* Righteousness[2]. 57. Though *she* is fifteen years old, the girl (kanîg) *has* not before that associated with men[3]; nor afterwards, when she becomes pregnant, *has she done so* before the time when she gives birth.

58. When that man becomes thirty years old, the sun stands still in the zenith (bâlistŏ) of the sky *for* the duration of ten days *and* ten nights, and it arrives again at that place where it *was* first appointed by allotment, where it occupies one finger-*breadth* out of the four finger-*breadths*, and it shines over all the regions which are seven. 59. So, too, *O* Zaratûst! of them themselves, their declaration is thus, that they know that the separation of the millennium, which this religion *has* heard about by listening, is thus; *and* of those who do not even then know, that it is something which is different.

60. Then, when that man becomes thirty years old, he confers with the archangels, the good rulers *and* good providers; *on* the morrow, in the daylight of the day, *it is* moreover manifest, when the *embodied* existence is thus undistressed—without

[1] See Yt. XIII, 97.

[2] The Pahlavi interpretation of Aûshêdar which is an imperfect transcript of the Av. Ukhshyad-ereta of Yt. XIII, 128.

[3] Pahl. 'levatâ gabrâânŏ barâ vepayîdŏ.'

a Kaî and without a Karap (that is, not deaf and blind to the affairs of the sacred beings), and is to be appropriated (that is, has not made its own self apart *from* the affairs of the sacred beings), and is produced full of life—that it has become extending (vâlân), and remains again great *in* various places in Aîrân-vê*g* where the good Dâitî[1] *is*.

61. These are the characteristics as regards the two centuries which are the ninth and tenth; the accuracy of what *was* to come has continued *and* this has happened, and both are declared as regards the accuracy which is stated on evidence as to what *will* happen.

Chapter IX.

1. About the marvellousness which is after the end of the millennium of Zaratû*s*t and the arrival of Aûshê*d*ar, until the end of the millennium of Aûshê*d*ar and the arrival of Aûshê*d*ar-mâh; and as to tidings of the same period.

2. The marvellousness of Aûshê*d*ar as to birth[2], glory of person, sayings and actions; the standing of the sun ten days amid the sky[3]; the perishing of the fiend of the four-legged race; the production of a three-spring cloudless influence[4] for vegetation; the weakening of superfluity *and* destitution; the extreme strengthening of alliance; the gratification *due to* the good friendship of foreigners; the great increase of the wisdom of religion; and the praise

---

[1] See Chap. III, 51, 54; Bd. XX, 13. It is the name of a river.

[2] See Chap. VIII, 55–57.

[3] See Chap. VIII, 58.

[4] Pahl. '3-zarem*dê* an-*av*argarîh.'

of Aûshê*d*ar's smiting *with* a serpent-scourge of several kinds *in* the religion of the Maz*d*a-worshippers.

3. The mightiness of the resources in the fifth century of the same millennium; the manifestation of the wizard Mahrkûs[1] for seven years, in the year which is reported in all the regions which are seven; the coming on *and* arrival of the winter of Mahrkûs, the perishing of most *of* mankind *and* animals within three winters and in the fourth, through the awfulness *of* those winters *and* the witchcraft of Mahrkûs; and the dying away of Mahrkûs of scanty progeny (gas*û*kŏ-zahi*s*nŏ), during the fourth winter, through the Dâhmân Âf*r*în[2]. 4. The opening of the enclosure made by Yim, the coming of mankind *and* animals therefrom, *and* the complete progress of mankind and animals again, arising specially from them.

5. After those winters, the abundant and great increase in the milk of cattle, and the abundant nourishment *of* mankind by milk; the less distress of body *in* cattle, the fullness and prosperity *of* the world, the celebrity of assembled mankind, *and* the great increase of liberality. 6. Also the feebleness

[1] Av. Mahrkûsha of Westergaard's Fragment VIII, 2, who is evidently a wizard or fiend; according to Pahl. Vd. II, 49 (Sp.) the evil winter which was foretold to Yim is called the winter of Markûs. In later times this name has been understood as Heb. Malkôs, 'autumnal rain;' so the idea of the fatal freezing winter of Mahrkûs, the intender of death, was abandoned for that of the deluging rain of Malkôs, as in Mkh. XXVII, 28. In Dd. XXXVII, 94, both snow and rain are mentioned as produced by Mahrkûs or Markûs (as it is always written in Pahlavi), and in Sd. IX, 5 only his name is stated. The most complete account of him is given in our text.

[2] The *Â*f*r*în of the Ameshâspends.

of poverty among mankind, *just* like what revelation mentions thus: 'Even so he, *O* Zaratûst! though he be more unfortunate than he who is accepting *from him*, is like the creator whose bounty of permanent liberality does thus, in the embodied existence, remain in his dwelling.'

7. And this, too, it says, namely: 'When that winter passes away, *of* which *it is* said that *it is* boisterous and destructive[1], then a wild beast, black and wide-travelling, walks up to the Maz*d*a-worshippers, and thus it thinks, that they *who* worship Maz*d*a *will* therefore not finally hate us more than him who is their own progeny, the son whom they thus bring up *as* a Maz*d*a-worshipper here *below, in* fondness *and* freedom from malice towards well-yielding cattle.

8. 'Then Ashavahi*s*tô calls out to the Maz*d*a-worshippers from the upper region, *and* thus he speaks: "You are for the worship of Maz*d*a; let no one *of you* become such a slaughterer of cattle as the slaughterers you have been before. 9. Recommend increase in gifts, recommend neighbourliness in person; are you worshipping Maz*d*a? do you slaughter cattle? do you slaughter those of them which give you assistance, which speak to you thus: 'On account of your helpfulness *one* tells you that you are worshipping Maz*d*a *and* you *may* eat?' I *am* in neighbourliness before that, until *the time* when you exclaim: 'Mine *are* the serpent and toad.'

10. '"And you recommend increase, you recommend neighbourliness, *and* the Maz*d*a-worshippers slaughter cattle, even those of them who give them

[1] The Pahlavi version of Av. 'stakhrahê meretô zaya' in Westerg. Frag. VIII, 2.

assistance, so that you are worshipping Mazda *and* you eat; I *am* in neighbourliness before that, until *the time* when you exclaim: 'Mine *are* the serpent *and* toad.'

11. '"Contentedly the Mazda-worshippers slaughter cattle, contentedly the cattle of the Mazda-worshippers let *them* butcher[1], and contented are the cattle when they do not butcher *them*; contentedly the Mazda-worshippers eat cattle, *and* contented *are the cattle* when they eat them. 12. And then, when *there* are spirits, the slaughterers and whatever they slaughter, the butchers *and* whatever they butcher, *and* the eaters and whatever they eat *are* alike watched *by them*."'

13. And this, too, it says, namely: 'When that century fully elapses, which is the fifth in the second millennium as regards the religion of the Mazda-worshippers, then of all those who *are* upon the earth, the existences which are both wicked and righteous, two-thirds *in* the land of Irân are righteous and one-*third* wicked; and so likewise the Tûrânians *and* those who *are* around Irân remain non-Irânian around Irân; the chief increase in dwellings here *below*, of those in the embodied existence, remains *just* as now.'

14. And this, too, it says, namely: 'When that millennium *has* fully elapsed, which is the first of the religion of the Mazda-worshippers, what is the separation after the first century?' 15. And Aûharmazd spoke thus: 'The sun conceals *itself*.' 16. 'And what is the separation after the second, third, fourth, fifth, sixth, seventh, eighth, ninth, *or* tenth

---

[1] Assuming that bûr'zâvand stands for bûrînênd which occurs in § 12.

century?' 17. And Aûharmazd spoke thus: 'The sun conceals *itself*.'

18. Then, when thirty winters of the tenth century *are* unelapsed (arânakŏ), a maiden, who is Shapîr-abû [1], walks up to the water; *she* that is the mother of that good Aûshêdar-mâh [2], and her former lineage is from Vôhû-rôkô-î Frahânyân [3] in the family of Îsadvâstar, the son of Zaratûst *that* is brought forth by Arang. 19. Then she sits in that water *and* drinks *it*, *and* she kindles in a high degree those germs which were the second *of* the last that the righteous Zaratûst *was* dropping forth originally, and they introduce that son whose name is the Developer *of* Worship [4] (that is, he augments liberality). 20. Though fifteen years old, the damsel (zihânakŏ) *has* not before that associated with men; nor yet afterwards, when she becomes pregnant, *has she done so* before the time when she gives birth [5].

21. When that man becomes thirty years old, the sun stands still in the zenith of the sky *for* the duration of twenty days *and* nights [6], *and* it shines over all the regions which are seven. 22. So, too, the declaration of them themselves is that they know

[1] 'Having a good father,' the Zvâris of Av. Vanghu-fedhri, Yt. XIII, 142.

[2] See Chap. I, 42.

[3] See Chap. VIII, 55–57.

[4] The Pahlavi interpretation of Aûshêdar-mâh which is an imperfect transcript of the Av. Ukhshyad-nemangh of Yt. XIII, 128.

[5] Compare the summary in Dk. VIII, xiv, 13, as follows:—'The arrival of Aûshêdar-mâh, son of Zaratûst, at the end of the second millennium; information *about* him and his time, *and* the destroyers *of* the organizers who *were* within the millennium *of* Aûshêdar.'

[6] The MS. omits a clause here, which occurs in Chap. VIII, 58, possibly by mistake, as part of it is given in Chap. X, 19.

that the separation of the millennium, which this religion *has* heard about by listening, is even thus; *and* of those who do not even then know, that it is something which is different.

23. When that man becomes thirty years old, he confers with the archangels, the good rulers *and* good providers; *on* the morrow, in the daylight of the day, *it is* moreover manifest, when the embodied existence is *thus* undistressed—without a Kaî and without a Karap (that is, not blind *and* not deaf to the affairs of the sacred beings), and is to be appropriated (that is, has not made its own self apart *from* the affairs of the sacred beings), and is produced full of life—that it has become extending, and is again great *in* various places in Aîrân-vê*g* where the good Dâitî *is*.

CHAPTER X.

1. About the marvellousness which is after the end of the millennium of Aûshê*d*ar and the arrival of Aûshê*d*ar-mâh, until the end of the millennium of Aûshê*d*ar-mâh and the arrival of Sôshâns; *and* as to tidings *of* the same period.

2. The marvellousness of Aûshê*d*ar-mâh as to birth[1], glory of person, sayings, and actions; the standing of the sun amid the sky twenty days long[2]; and the increase of the milk of cattle arrives at a maximum (*av*artûm), *just* as what it says, that *one* milks only one mature cow (tô*r*â az) for a thousand men, *and* that he brings as much milk as a thousand men *require;* also the feebleness of

[1] See Chap. IX, 18–20.

[2] See Chap. IX, 21.

hunger and thirst is *just* as it says, that by only a single ration *one* becomes satisfied *for* three nights, *and* whoever eats a leg *of* mutton *has* plenty for him*self for* three days *and* nights. 3. The diminution *of* decay and extension (vêshîh) of life, the increase of humility and peace, *and* the perfection *of* liberality and enjoyment in the world.

4. Like this which revelation states, that, when the first ten winters in the last millennium pass away, the Maz*d*a-worshippers then make enquiry together thus: '*Are* we really more hairy-headed (sar-vars-*ik*-tar) than occurred before, owing to the well-yielding cattle, so that food and clothing are less necessary for us? Has affection come to us more completely, owing to those cattle, than it was ours before? *Have* we grown up less deteriorated in the hair, by old age, than *those* grown up before? *Are* the thoughts, words, *and* deeds of our women and children more instructed than they were before? 5. And *has* this thing occurred, that he is classed as disqualified who in training a child has become quite retrogressive (pas-ûruzd), and is *his* penalty arranged? Does the fiend think of the Karap class, and *are they* utterly destroyed by her through those whose thoughts are most evil, devoid of righteousness, *and* devoid of a liking for righteousness? 6. Near here, in the disturbance of the existences, does that happen as heard by us from the ancients, when listening *to* the true proclaimers of the Maz*d*a-worshippers? And now, even when our numbers *are* so greatly maintaining this dispensation, do we sanctify (aharâyînem) righteousness (that is, do we perform duty and good works) more vociferously *and* more strenuously?'

7. This, too, it says, even that no one passes away in the last millennium, other than those whom they smite with a scaffold weapon [1], and *those* who pass away from old age. 8. When fifty-three years of that millennium of his have remained, the sweetness and oiliness in milk *and* vegetables are so completed that, on account of the freedom of mankind from wanting meat, they shall leave off the eating of meat, and their food becomes milk and vegetables. 9. When three years have remained, they shall leave off even the drinking of milk, and their food *and* drink become water and vegetables.

10. And in his millennium *are* the breaking (lânakŏ) of the fetters of Dahâk [2], the rousing of Kerê*s*âspô [3] for the smiting of Dahâk, the arrival of Kaî-Khûsrô [4] and his companions for the assistance of Sôshâns in the production of the renovation *of the universe*, and the provision of most *of* mankind with the Gâthic disposition and law; also the occurrence of many other wonders and marvels is manifest in that millennium of his.

11. And this, too, it says, namely: 'When that millennium *has* fully elapsed, which is the second of the religion *of* the Maz*d*a-worshippers, what is the separation after the first century?' 12. And Aûhar*m*az*d* spoke thus: 'The sun conceals *itself*.' 13. 'And what is the separation after the second,

[1] Reading pavan dâr snesh, as in some modern copies; but the old MS. of 1659 has run the last two words together, so as to produce pavan dârêgûsh, 'as destitute,' which must be wrong.

[2] For details see Byt. III, 55–57; Bd. XXIX, 9; Dd. XXXVII, 97; Dk. IX, xv, 2. It may be noticed that this release of the demoniacal tyrant is expected to follow the triumph of strict vegetarianism.

[3] See further Byt. III, 59–61; Bd. XXIX, 7, 8.

[4] See Mkh. XXVII, 59–63; LVII, 7; Dd. XXXVI, 3.

third, fourth, fifth, sixth, seventh, eighth, ninth, *or* tenth century?' 14. And Aûharmazd spoke thus: 'The sun conceals *itself*.'

15. And when thirty winters of the tenth century *are* unelapsed, that maiden, who is Gôbâk-abû[1], walks up to the water; she that is the mother of that testifying Sôshâns who is the guide to conveying away the opposition of the destroyer, and her former lineage is from Vôhû-rôkô-î Frahânyân[2] in the family of Îsadvâstar, the son of Zaratûst *that* is brought forth by Arang. 16. 'That maiden whose title is All-overpowerer is thus all-overpowering, because through giving birth she brings forth him who overpowers all, both the affliction owing to demons, and also that owing to mankind[3].' 17. Then she sits in that water, when she is fifteen years old, *and* it introduces *into* the girl him 'whose name is the Triumphant Benefiter, and *his* title is the Body-maker; such a benefiter as benefits (savînêdŏ) the whole embodied existence, and such a *body*-maker, alike possessing body and possessing life, as petitions about the disturbance of the embodied existences *and* mankind[4].' 18. Not before that *has she* associated with men; nor yet afterwards, when she becomes pregnant, *has she done so* before the time when she gives birth[5].

---

[1] 'Having a testifying father,' the Pahlavi of Av. Eredad-fedhri, Yt. XIII, 142.

[2] See Chap. VIII, 55–57.

[3] The Pahlavi version of Yt. XIII, 142, latter clause.

[4] From the Pahlavi version of Yt. XIII, 129.

[5] Compare the summary in Dk. VIII, xiv, 14, 15, as follows:—'The coming and arrival of Sôshâns, son of Zaratûst, at the end of the third millennium, the destroyers *of* the organizers who *were* within the millennium of Aûshêdar-mâh, the arrival of Sôshâns,

19. When that man becomes thirty years old, the sun stands still in the zenith of the sky *for* the duration of thirty days *and* nights, and it arrives again at that place where it *was* appointed by allotment.

CHAPTER XI.

1. About the marvellousness which is after the end of the millennium of Aûshê*d*ar-mâh and the arrival of the Triumphant Benefiter, until the end of the fifty-seventh year of Sôshâns and the production of the renovation among the existences.

2. Concerning the marvellousness of Sôshâns as to splendour *and* glory of person, it says that 'when the coming of the last rotation of those rotations of the seasons of Aûshê*d*ar-mâh *occurs*, the man Sôshâns is born[1] whose food is spiritual *and* body sunny (that is, his body is as radiant as the sun);' also this, that 'he looks on all sides with six-eyed power (6-dôîsarîh), *and* sees the remedy for persecution by the fiend.'

3. This, too, that with him is the triumphant Kayân glory 'which the mighty Frê*d*ûn[2] bore when *Az*-î Dahâk[3] *was* smitten by him; also Kaî-Khûsrôî[4] *was* bearing it when the Tûr Frangrâsîyâk[5] *was* smitten by him; also Frangrâsîyâk bore it when the Drvê Zênîgâk[6] *was* smitten by him; *and* Kaî-

and information *about* Sôshâns and his time. Also, as to the renovation *of the universe and* the future existence, *it* is declared *that* they arise in his time.'

[1] The date here indicated seems to be about twenty-eight years later than that intended in Chap. X, 15-19.

[2] See Chap. I, 25.

[3] See Chap. I, 26.

[4] See Chap. I, 39.

[5] See Chap. I, 31, 39.

[6] Av. Drv*a*u Zainigâu*s*, an Arab chieftain who invaded Irân

Vi*s*tâsp[1] shall bear it when you fully attract him to righteousness, *and* through it he shall carry off the fiend *from* the concerns of the world of righteousness[2].'

4. And this, too, that in fifty-seven *of* his years *there* occur the annihilation of the fiendishness of the two-legged race *and* others, and the subjugation of disease and decrepitude, *of* death and persecution, and *of* the original evil *of* tyranny, apostasy, and depravity; *there* arise a perpetual verdant growth of vegetation *and* the primitive gift *of* joyfulness; *and there* are seventeen years *of* vegetable-eating, thirty years *of* water-drinking, *and* ten years *of* spiritual food.

5. And all the splendour, glory, and power, which *have* arisen in all those possessing splendour, glory, *and* power, *are* in him on whom they arrive together and for those who are his, when many inferior human beings are aroused splendid *and* powerful; and through their power and glory all the troops of the fiend are smitten. 6. And all mankind remain of one accord in the religion of Aûha*r*ma*zd*, owing to the will of the creator, the command *of* that *apostle*, and the resources of his companions.

7. At the end of the fifty-seven years the fiend *and* Aharman are annihilated, the renovation *for* the future existence occurs, *and* the whole of the good creation is provided with purity *and* perfect

in early times and killed many with his evil eye, till the Irânians invited Frangrâsîyâk to destroy him (see Darmesteter's French translation of part of Chap. XLI of Irânian Bundahi*s* in Annales du Musée Guimet, vol. xxii, p. 401).

[1] See Chap. I, 41.

[2] From a Pahlavi version of Yt. XIX, 92, 93, with the second and third clauses transposed.

splendour. 8. *Just* as revelation states thus: 'When that millennium *has* fully elapsed, which is the third of the religion of the Maz*d*a-worshippers, that Maz*d*a-worshipper whose name is so Triumphant[1] then marches forward from the water Kanyisâ[2] with a thousand companions and also maidens *of* restrained disposition and blindly-striving behaviour[3]; and he smites the wicked people who *are* tyrannical, and annihilates them.'

9. Then those Maz*d*a-worshippers smite, and none are smiting them. 10. Then those Maz*d*a-worshippers produce a longing for a renovation among the existences, *one* ever-living, ever-beneficial, and ever desiring a Lord. 11. 'Then I, who am Aûhar*m*az*d*, produce the renovation according to the longing among the existences, *one* ever-living, ever-beneficial, *and ever* desiring a Lord.'

---

[1] See Chap. X, 17.

[2] Reading the name as Pâzand; if it were Pahlavi it would have to be read Kânmâsâî, because Irânian Pâz. yi is very like Pahl. mâ. It is Kyânsih in Bd. XIII, 16; XX, 34; XXI, 6, 7, and represents Av. Kãsava, the brackish lake or sea of Sagastân.

[3] Reading 'va-bigar-*îk*-i vand khîm va-kûr-*k*akhŏ râs,' and assuming that bigar is Ar. bikr, as an Arabic word is occasionally used in the Dînka*r*d (see Chap. II, 2 n) though very rarely. Bd. XXX, 17, mentions 'fifteen men and fifteen damsels' as assisting Sôshâns at the time of the renovation of the universe.

DÎNKA*RD*.—BOOK V.

CHAPTER I.

1. The triumph of the creator Aûharmazd, *and* glory of complete wisdom, is the divine (ahûîg) religion of Mazda-worship.

2. The fifth *book* is about the sayings of the saintly Âtûr-farnbag[1], son of Farukhzâd, *who* was the leader of the orthodox, even as to the manuscript which is called Gyêmarâ[2]. 3. The collected replies of Âtûr-

---

[1] He was the leader of the orthodox about A.D. 815–835, and held a religious disputation with the heretic Abâlis in the presence of the Khalîfah Al-Mâmûn (A.D. 813–833), as detailed in the Mâdigân-î Gugastak Abâlis. He was also the first compiler of the Dînkard, probably of its first two Books, which are not yet discovered, as well as of some of the materials for the other Books. (See S. B. E., vol. xxxvii, p. 411, n. 1.)

[2] The name of this MS. can be only guessed. It occurs three times in each of the two MS. authorities, B and K43, and the simplest reading of five of these six occurrences would be Sîmrâ, so that the remaining one (Sarmâ) may be neglected as a corruption. A final â in Pahlavi is a very certain indication of a Semitic word, for if a final of similar form occurs in an Irânian word, it represents either h or kh; so if the name were Irânian, its most probable reading would be Sîmurkh. But, in § 3, it is intimated that the MS. belonged to an ancient tribe, or congregation (ram); it also seems, from Chap. IV, 8, 9, that the religion of this tribe was not so inconsistent with Zoroastrianism as to prevent its members being taught that orthodox faith; and §§ 4, 5 of the present chapter appear to quote from that MS. some

farnbag, son of Farukhzâd, the leader of the orthodox, about several significant questions that *are* the wonder of the moderns, which *are* like the friendly words, spoken by him *as to* those of the ancient tribe[1] (kâdmon-ramân) who call *it* really their Gyêmarâ, which *are* obtaining[2] a like wonder for them openly accessible to him[3].

4. About the unswerving *and* co-operating chieftainship of those forefathers who went in mutually-friendly command of troops, *and* the complete enclosure of that tribe within the military control of Bûkht-Narsîh[4]. 5. About the disabling of vicious habits and evil deeds, which are entirely connected, and of the heinous demon-worship and mischief which

particulars regarding the siege of Jerusalem by Nebuchadnezzar. From these circumstances we may suspect that Âtûr-farnbag, while collecting materials for his Dînkard, had asked some Jewish friends what information their MSS. contained regarding the old Persians, as the two peoples had been in contact, more or less, ever since the time of the Achaemenian dynasty. If he did so enquire, the Jews would naturally search in the Talmud, in which references to the Persians still survive, though the text is no longer complete. The question is, therefore, whether the MS., whose name has been provisionally read Sîmrâ, can have had any connection with the Talmud. It will be at once evident to any Pahlavi student that Pahl. sî may be read gyê equally well, and that we have no better reason for reading Sîmrâ than for the Gyêmarâ, which has been put into the text, as a suggestion that Âtûr-farnbag was really referring to the Gemarâ of the Jews, the supplement to their commentary upon Scripture. Whether this can be clearly proved remains to be seen, and positive evidence seems scanty.

[1] Or 'congregation.' [2] Or 'including (vandîg).'

[3] Pahl. 'mûnsânô ham-shkûp-vindîg frâz aûbas yehamtûnisnîg.' From which it appears as if there had been a mutual interchange of information between him and his Jewish friends.

[4] The Pahlavi form of Bu'ht-i-nazar, or Nebuchadnezzar.

are owing to them, through the ruler Kaî-Loharâsp[1] being sent, with Bûkht-Narsîh, from the country of Irân to Bêtâ-Makdis[2] of Arûm, and *their* remaining *in* that quarter. 6. And the orthodox belief in the rude particulars *of* religious custom in the mutual deliberation of those of the tribe, the acquaintance with religion of a boor (durû*s*takŏ-i), the difficult arrangements, and the enquirer doubtful of the religion after the many controversial, deliberative, and cause-investigating questions and answers adapted to the importunities of that wordy disciple[3].

7. About how the accepting of this religion *by* the prophets before Zaratû*s*t *occurred*[4], how the pure *and* saintly Zaratû*s*t of the Spîtâmas came[5], and who *will* afterwards come *as* bringers of the same pure *and* good religion *here*after[6]. 8. That is, of the prophets, apostles, and accepters of the religion, *there* were *they* who accepted *it* concisely *and* completely *such* as Gâyômar*d* was, from whom *came* irregularly (durû*s*takŏ) *such* as Masyê and Sîyâmak, Hâôshâng, Tâkhmôrup, Yim, Frê*d*ûn, Mânû*sk*îhar, the Sâmân, the Kayân, and also many other leaders in *those* times[7]. 9. And their acceptance expressly at various times is produced for action, and thereby the adversity of the creatures is removed, benefit

---

[1] The father of Kaî-Vi*s*tâsp (see Bd. XXXI, 28, 29; XXXIV, 7). His expedition to Jerusalem is mentioned in Pahl. Mkh. XXVII, 67, and by some Arab writers.

[2] 'The holy place,' a title of Jerusalem.

[3] Not identified. From this point to Chap. IV, 7, Âtû*r*-farnbag must have used the same authorities as the writer of Dk. VII; but he returns to the Gyêmarâ in Chap. IV, 8.

[4] Dk. VII, i, 7–40. [5] Ibid. 41. [6] Ibid. 42.

[7] See the details in Dk. VII, i, 7–40. §§ 1–8 have been already translated in Grundriss der iranischen Philologie, ii, 93–94.

and prosperity *are* sought, the world is controlled, and the creator and good creations are propitiated.

CHAPTER II.

1. In the pure light *and* equal to the archangels—collected together and reckoned together, since the original creation, *and* completely unmixed—Zaratûs*t* was spiritually fashioned and provided undefectively for the acceptance and propagation of the religion in the world [1]. 2. And when he is sent for the manifestation of restrained saintliness (môkîh) and bodily substance, great glory and radiance become as much discernible in *him* as the same *had* come into the posterity of Yim who are Pôrûshâspô [2], his father, *and* Dûk*d*âûb [3] who is his mother; and also while *he* is *being* born and *for* the duration of life, he produced a radiance, glow, and brilliance from the place of his own abode, that issued intensely and strongly, like the splendour of fire, to distant lands [4].

3. Also *about* the wizards and witches, tyrants, Kîgs, and Karaps, and other miscreants who have produced outrage for him during his birth and childhood, with desire for his destruction; who *have* manifestly come about *his* death *or* disablement, and even so far as *those* who *have come into* the visible assembly *about* the destruction of *his* glory and other *causes of* helplessness [5]. 4. And also including the wolves *and* other wild beasts, to whom *he was*

[1] Dk. VII, ii, 1, 2, 14–21, 36–42, 46, 47; Zs. XIII, 4.
[2] Ibid. 13. [3] Ibid. 3–8; Zs. XIII, 1–3.
[4] Ibid. 56–58; Zs. XIV, 7.
[5] Dk. VII, iii, 5–14; Zs. XVI, 1–7.

cast forth by those of Pôrûshâspô's kinsmen who *were* wizards, *and* the kindred of those frequenting demon-worship, but only as a test [1].

5. *In* like manner *it* is declared *that*, on account of Vohûmanô *being* welcome to him, he laughed outright at birth [2]. 6. His coming for conference *with* Aûha*r*ma*z*d [3], and owing to *his* accepting the religion, Aharman and many demons and fiends have come to him with exhibition of fear, offering of service, and the argument and entreaty of supplicants; and all these have returned from him disapprovingly, defeatedly, and confusedly, through the pure proclamation of his Avesta, the unique perfection of Aûha*r*ma*z*d's will [4], and the indication of a prepared armament (vîrâstŏ-zênîh), a declared reward, a powerful sovereignty, and a way of injury *to* the destroyer.

7. Also the triumph of the sacred beings *in* the end, and the peculiarity *of* the joint control *of* the demons; how, before that, they rushed openly into the world *and* have dwindled, *their* bodily forms *are* shattered [5], and they are so converted into secret decay, that *their* supplicants, deceived and deceivers, became awful disputants through confession of it.

8. And when, through completely accepting the religion from Aûha*r*ma*z*d, he came to the obedient king Kaî-Vi*s*tâsp to attract those of the world, he exhibited glorious actions of many kinds and the

[1] Dk. VII, iii, 15–19; Zs. XVI, 8–11.
[2] Ibid. 2; Zs. XIV, 12, 13.
[3] Ibid. 60–iv, 1; Zs. XXI, 11–XXII, 13.
[4] Dk. VII, iv, 36–41, 61, 62.
[5] Ibid. 42, 44–46, 63.

smiting of demons and fiends; and *he* openly spoke the thoughts of king Vistâsp and many of the multitude *about* hidden matters[1], *thus*: 'A person is possessing life only by destiny, and without his body, *but with* a like destiny, the person possessing life is restored;' *he was* also opposing many wizards, demon-worshippers, demon-consulters, *and* those seduced *by*[2] deceivers who are awful disputants.

9. And this *was* the utterance of those twelve stars whose names *are those* of the twelve *zodiacal* constellations, and the primitive learned of Bâpêl[3], that have come to these, who *are* asking questions of the chief rulers of Khvanîras, *have* to justify *it*, in the controversy, with the spiritual and material customs and rude observances which are diversely manifested, onwards from *the time of* Yim the splendid; and the evidence of it, discernible with him, *was that of* Vohûmanô, Ashavahistô, the fire, and some other good spirits[4].

10. Afterwards, too, the estimating and weighing of the whole utterance of the religion of Aûharmazd *were* held out by him to Vistâsp and those of the world, as very accountably a wonder; and further, too, he remained as *it were* more conflicting with fellow-disputants than his own words opposing the fellow-disputants.

11. Also when, through the effect of glory and the struggle *for being* saved, every class of apostles and prophets and manifestation of tokens and such-like *were*, with certain *and* striking evidence, casting down blessings, even thereupon the obedient king

[1] Dk. VII, iv, 65, 71.

[2] B has 'and demon-separatists (va-shêdâ-gvîdakân).'

[3] Dk. VII, iv, 72.

[4] Ibid. 74, 85; Zs. XXIII, 7.

Kaî-Vistâsp's fear of the adversary of religion, and also other causes, arose, on account of which he *was* then accepting the propagation of the religion [1], when its great glory *and* beauty [2] *were* seen by him. 12. At first, Zarîr [3], Spend-dâd [4], Frashôstar, and Gâmâsp [5], several of the realm *who were* noble, conspicuous, and well-acting, the good *and* princes *of* mankind, beheld visibly the will and desirableness of Aûharmazd and the archangels, and the progressive religion of the creatures, fit for those completely victorious (hûkîragânîg).

13. Lastly, the seizure and capturing (gîrînisnŏ) by the demons *are* beheld *and* watched; *and* they have remained opposing, owing to the number *of* idolators competing wranglingly. 14. And much conflict and slaughter occurred, which arose purely, so that the mingling *of* the religion in the world proceeded [6].

15. *There* are also his pure new bringers and complete controllers of the same religion, Aûshêdar [7], Aûshêdar-mâh [8], and Sôshâns [9]; and through the complete progress of this religion of Aûharmazd, all the good creatures become without disturbance and all-radiant [10].

---

[1] Dk. VII, iv, 87.

[2] K43 has varázŏ; but B, omitting the first letter, has láfô, 'praise.'

[3] A brother and commander-in-chief of Vistâsp, killed in the battle with Argâsp, see Bd. XXXI, 29; YZ. 54–56.

[4] A son of Vistâsp; see Dk. VII, vii, 5; YZ. 82–85.

[5] Two brothers, see Chap. III, 4; Dk. VII, vi, 12; Zs. XXIII, 10.

[6] See Chap. III, 1.

[7] Dk. VII, viii, 55–ix, 13.

[8] Dk. VII, ix, 18–x, 10.

[9] Dk. VII, x, 15–xi, 5.

[10] Dk. VII, xi, 6–11.

CHAPTER III.

1. About that which is manifested as regards the propitiousness, forward intellect, and complete virtue of Zaratûst, it is openly declared that, according to his explaining statements, *there occurred such events* as the victory of Kaî-Vistâsp and the Irânians over Argâsp[1] and an army of Khyôns and other foreigners *of* innumerable kinds, *and* details on that subject; also other assistance of Vistâsp and those of the realm in other necessities.

2. The killing of Zaratûst himself *by* Brâdrô-rêsh[2] the Tûr; the provision of a chariot *by* Srîtô[3] of the Vîsraps; and whatever is on those subjects.

3. Also, specially, matters in the times to come, each consecutively, *when* therein arrive devastators *such* as Alexander[4], and the killer of Akrê-khiradŏ[5], Mahrkûs[6], Dahâk[7], and other devastators; extenders of belief (vîravîsn-vâlân) *such* as the Messiah (Mashikh), Mânih[8], and others; periods *such* as the steel *age*[9], *that* mingled with iron, and others; and organizers, restorers, *and* introducers of religion, *such*

[1] Dk. VII, iv, 77, 83, 84, 87–90; v, 7; this victory occurred in the thirtieth year of the religion, see Zs. XXIII, 8.

[2] Dk. VII, v, 12 n.

[3] Dk. VII, vi, 2–11.

[4] Dk. VII, vii, 7.

[5] Or Aghrêrad (Av. Aghraêratha), killed by his brother Frâsîyâv or Frangrâsîyâk of Tûr, see Bd. XXIX, 5; XXXI, 15, 20–22.

[6] Dk. VII, i, 24; ix, 3.

[7] Ibid. i, 26.

[8] A heretic who flourished A.D. 216–242; see Dk. IX, xxxix, 13 n.

[9] According to Byt. II, 21, 22, the steel age was the time of Khûsrô Anôshêrvân, and that mingled with iron at the end of Zaratûst's millennium.

as A*r*takhshatar[1], Âtû*r*pâ*d*[2], Khûsrôî[3], Pêshyôtan[4], Aûshê*d*ar, Aûshê*d*ar-mâh, Sôshâns[5], and others.

4. The formation of custom, and the indications which *have* come to manifestation and *will* arrive at various periods; and the proclamation of these, too, by *G*âmâsp[6], from the teaching of Zaratû*s*t, is what he wrote, together with the Avesta and Zand, upon oxhides, and it was written *with* gold, and kept in the royal treasury[7]. 5. And it was from it the high-priests of the rulers made many copies; and afterwards, too, it is from it that it happened, both to the less intelligent and the corrupters, that *they* were introducing different opinions *and* different views.

CHAPTER IV.

1. About the selectness and perfection of the race of Irân, that is, how the destroyer and the mingling of defects came into the creation, first into the distribution of the race [of mankind][8] from the children of Sîyâmak[9], *and* good intellect, good disposition,

---

[1] A*r*dashîr Pâpakân (A.D. 226–241), the founder of the Sâsânian dynasty.

[2] Son of Mâraspend, and prime minister of Shahpûhar II (A.D. 309–379).

[3] Anôshêrvân (A.D. 531–578).

[4] A son of Vi*s*tâsp and immortal ruler of Kangde*z*, see Dk. VII, iv, 81.

[5] See Chap. II, 15.

[6] See Chap. II, 12.

[7] This was the original Avesta prepared by order of Vi*s*tâsp, as stated in the last chapter of Dk. III, § 3 (see S. B. E., vol. xxxvii, p. xxxi).

[8] B omits the words in brackets.

[9] Son of Masyê, called Sâmak in Dk. VII, i, 15.

proper affection, proper praise, proper modesty, observance of hope, liberality, truth, generosity, good friendship, *and* other capability, glory, and proper duty are more particularly included for Fravâk[1], and again altered for frontier peoples.

2. Such-like goodness and glory, again, through selection from a promiscuous origin—even till the coming on of various new contaminations, from the demons, among the children of Fravâk—*were* for Hâôshâng and Vâêgere*d*[2], as Hâôshâng through superior glory *was* ruler of the world, and Vâêgere*d* through provincial government (dahyûkânîh) became the cultivator and cherisher of the world; and their well-destined descendants[3] aggrandized the race of the monarchs among the well-born provincial governors (dahyûkân).

3. In union, such-like glory and goodness proceeded, mutually connected, in various ages as settled by the annals (mâ*d*îgân), and the frontiers of Atûr[4] are penetrated; also in various annals *there* were in succession *such men* as Tâkhmôrup, Yim, Frê*d*ûn the Âspîgân, and Airî*k* of Irân, the progenitor of Mânû*s*, Mânû*s*-khvârnar, and Mânû*sk*ihar[5].

4. And, besides including this one, who *was* a monarch of superior glory, and other monarchs *such* as *are* also in the same race[6], the Kayâns[7] *were*

[1] Son of Sîyâmak; he was progenitor of the fifteen undeformed races of mankind (see Bd. XV, 25, 30, 31).

[2] Dk. VII, i, 16–18.

[3] K43 has 'children.'

[4] Probably Assyria; but it is possible to read atval as Ar. a*t*val, and to translate 'ancient frontiers.'

[5] For the foregoing names see Dk. VII, i, 19–30; ii, 70.

[6] Such as Aûzôbô in Dk. VII, i, 31.

[7] From Kaî-Kobâ*d* to Kaî-Khûsrô, as stated in Dk. VII, i, 33–40.

chosen. 5. Even thus, as regards the Kayâns, the annals *have* always to consider him who is monarch as the right *one*, who is a fellow-descendant *of* the lineage, and in whom the glory is residing.

6. The creator Aûha*r*ma*zd* has informed Nêryôsang[1], his own reminder, *that* a similar instance is the supreme Zaratû*s*tship, and the glory of the religion due to the same; also many other reasons, which *are* recountable, *are* declared in the Avesta, indications known only *to* an Irânian person of the best lineage. 7. And this, too, he has said, namely: 'Great glory and goodness of this description *are* appropriatable by the same race, and *are* even now[2] visibly manifest.'

8. About what *are* the requirements of the tribe of those who call *this* really their Gyêmarâ and how *they are* effected by our acquaintance with revelation, that is, *by* much recitation of it; only, several occasions (yâvar 1-*k*and) are necessary in these times. 9. Also action and precaution *are* possible for them, and among the actions and precautions *one* is to assume more especially law and custom, and whatever *was* perverted by us and again made true; and, as to those taught, several persons who *are* intellectual, seeking means, and friends of the soul, *have* come to teach complete delusions to them; also for the same tribe and whomever it is proper to teach, when it is necessary for them, even a worldly

---

[1] The usual messenger of Aûha*r*ma*zd*, see Dk. VII, iv, 84, 85.

[2] B has 'even anew,' by writing kevan backwards, which converts the word into navak. From Chap. I, 7 to this point, the compiler could have found very little of his materials in a Jewish MS., excepting such as had been recently obtained from Persian sources.

priestly authority is guiding for *that* same tribe, because he has come[1].

[1] It would seem that the tribe professed a different religion, but one that bore some resemblance to the Parsi faith in certain essential particulars. The remaining five-sixths of Dk. V are devoted to a miscellaneous collection of religious subjects, resembling a Rivâyat.

SELECTIONS OF *ZÂD*-SPARAM.

SELECTIONS OF ZÂ*D*-SPARAM[1].

CHAPTER XII.

1. About the coming of the religion at a *given* time *being* a resemblance such-like as the birth of a child through two united powers, which are the reception of semen *by* females in procreation, and delivering *it* back to the fathers, and a period of struggling and intermingling, especially by two means: a monarchy with[2] religion of the same tenets (ham-vâ*k*-dênôih), and the existence of similar tenets to *those of* the monarchy *in* the custom *of* the religion. 2. The religion *of* the Maz*d*a-worshippers, when the period of material

---

[1] Zâ*d*-sparam was Dastûr of Sîrkân, about thirty parasangs south of Kirmân, in A. D. 881. At a later date, probably about A. D. 900, he compiled three series of Selections, from religious texts then extant, and these have been preserved by the Parsis in the same MSS. as contain the Dâ*d*istân-î Dînîk (see the Introduction). The first eleven chapters of this first series of Selections have been already translated in S. B. E., vol. v, pp. 155–186, as they refer to some of the subjects detailed in the Bundahis. The remaining chapters are here translated, except the last which refers to the Nasks and Gâthas, and will be found in S. B. E., vol. xxxvii, pp. 401–405. The MS. authorities for the text are K35 and T (see p. 2 and Introduction).

[2] T has 'devoid of.'

organization is being converted again into a spiritual nature, became manifest on the earth, first through Spendarmad[1] *and* afterwards through Aûharmazd, like the reception of a child *by* mothers *and* delivering *it* back to the fathers.

3. The manifestation of the religion through Spendarmad was at that time when Frâsiyâv[2] kept back the water from the country of Irân, and brought the water again; in damsel form she was a speaker for *its* manifestation, *in* reply *to* foreigners, at the house of Mânûskîhar[3], the monarch of the country of Irân. 4. She *was* also dressed, *and* wore radiant clothing which shone out on all sides *for* the length of a Hâsar[4], which is *a distance*, like a Parasang; and, tied on her waist, she wore a golden *sacred* girdle which was the religion of the Mazda-worshippers itself.

5. As to the belt of the religion, it is *that* to which are connected the thirty-three fetters upon the thirty-three sins[5], according to which all sin is divided; so that (kû) the damsels, by whom the tied *sacred* girdle of Spendarmad *was* seen, have become impetuous (taftîgŏ) after that for a tied girdle, on account of *its* seeming beautiful.

6. And this was the motherhood which is supplied through Spendarmad, as a gift, in the year 528

[1] The female archangel who has special charge of the earth and virtuous women (see Dk. VII, ii, 19 n).

[2] See Dk. VII, i, 31; and regarding his irrigation canals, see Bd. XX, 17, 34; XXI, 6.

[3] See Dk. VII, i, 29.

[4] A thousand steps of the two feet, or Roman mile; see Bd. XXVI, 1.

[5] Thirty sins are detailed in Mkh. XXXVI, and thirty-three good works in XXXVII (see S. B. E., vol. xxiv, pp. 71-75).

before Zaratûst came out to *his* conference[1], which is *one of* their statements from the annals of the religion *in* a manuscript of the ancients.

7. The name of Zaratûst is also cited on the earth at 300 years before his conference[2]. 8. For Irân, at the supplication even of the priests in the land, and for the sake of the pacification of a dispute arisen, Aûharmazd produced a great ox, by whom the boundary of Irân next to Tûrân was intimated by pawing with *his* hoofs, and he was kept in a jungle. 9. Whenever contention arose, the boundary was fully made known by that ox, until it was the wish of Kaî-Ûs to take, fully covetously, a portion of the land of Tûrân back *into* Irân, and he saw that the ox is *about* to act very ill-naturedly, because it *was* not besought with *forms* which were prescribed for it, where a boundary was intimated by it[3].

10. *There* were seven brothers, and he who was

---

[1] If this coming to conference with the spirits be 'the coming of the religion,' in the thirtieth year of Vistâsp's reign, then, according to Bundahis chronology, these 528 years will carry us back to twenty-eight years before the accession of Mânûskîhar. As any alteration in the date of Mânûskîhar's accession would disturb the millennial arrangement of Bd. XXXIV, it is probable that some copyist has miswritten the ciphers, and we ought to read 428. This legend appears not to occur elsewhere.

[2] According to Bd. XXXIV, 7, Kaî-Ûs reigned from 360 to 210 years before 'the coming of the religion.' At this point a dislocation of the text occurs in all existing MSS., owing to the misplacement of a loose folio in some unknown copy written before 1530; the contents of this folio, §§ 8–16, are found in the existing MSS. three folios further on (after Chap. XIV, 14), and are here restored to their original position, as determined by the meaning of the text.

[3] T has 'by that ox.' This legend is also told in Dk. VII, ii, 62–66.

the seventh was called Srîtô[1] the Seventh, the largest in body *and* chief in strength, belonging to those instructed in many subjects for Kaî-Ûs, and he was among his princes. 11. Kaî-Ûs summoned *him* into *his* presence and ordered *him* thus: 'Go and kill that ox in the jungle!'

12. Srîtô went, *and* the ox whom he wished to kill expostulated with him, in human words, thus: 'Do not kill me! for though thou canst kill me, he whose guardian spirit is in the Hôm, the death-dispeller, *will* also become manifest on the earth, *he* whose name is Zaratû*s*t of the Spîtâmas[2], and *will* proclaim thy bad action in the world. 13. And the distress in thy soul becomes such as is declared in revelation thus: "As it occurs to him, *so* it *does to* Va*d*ak[3], when they mention his iniquity," and thy death becomes the like and, owing to death, it is mixed up with hers (that is, owing even to hers is the death of Srîtô).'

14. When those words *were* heard by him, Srîtô turned back, *and* went again to Kaî-Ûs; also by his manner, and even apart from this, he stated[4] what the ox *had* spoken with awfulness, *and also* thus:

[1] Srîtô, the seventh son (compare Dk. VII, ii, 64), is not easy to identify. He could not have been Thrita the father of Keresâspa, because this Thrita the Sâmân is said to have been a third son in Pahl. Yas. IX, 30 (Sp.). He may have been Srîtô of the Vîsraps, whose soul visited Vi*s*tâsp in the latter part of his reign, about 350 years later, regarding which a legend is related in Dk. VII, vi, 2–11, and again mentioned in Dk. V, iii, 2; but there is a want of corresponding details for identification.

[2] This is the citation of his name mentioned in § 7.

[3] The mother of Dahâk, whose iniquity is considered as equal to that of the evil spirit, see Dd. LXXII, 5; Dk. IX, x, 3.

[4] T has 'also by his manner he intimated *and* separately stated.'

'I *am* more desirous *than* any one who is in the earth *created by* righteousness, *that* you *should* now order destruction for the ox.'

15. And Kaî-Ûs uttered *his* will, with the conviction of superior wisdom, thus: 'It is not certain whether he whose guardian spirit is in the Hôm, the death-dispeller, is himself, or not; and if he be, and be born [1], *whether* he *will* become manifest, or not;' and he commanded with severity, thus: 'Go and kill it!'

16. *And* Srîtô spoke thus: '*It is* not that I am without strength to kill, because *its* reprieval by me *was* owing to its remonstrance, mentioned to me, that a high-priest is to arise [2].'

17. So *it* is declared thus, *in* another revelation (dênô zagâî) [3], when the Tûrânians *were* backward *in* heart, Kaî-Ûs spoke thus: 'Go out to a certain jungle, in which dwell many chiefs of the witches, and they *will* cut thee up without *any* striving of heart.'

18. And Srîtô went up to the jungle, *where* many witches saw him, who kept their jaws open, and they *spoke* about the handsome *man* thus: 'Slay *and* do not spare!' 19. And compassion *having* gone out of his heart, he went back to the *other* jungle and, with his fist, he broke the back of the ox in three places; and the ox, awfully convulsed (*s*kîftŏ barhamakŏ), kept *up* an outcry.

20. After the slaughter of the ox, owing to its convulsed state which *was* heard by him, the

[1] T omits 'and be born.'

[2] The misplaced folio, which begins with § 8, ends here, but it is not quite certain that a few lines of text are not still missing.

[3] T has 'at another *time* (*b*ên zagâî).'

remembrance of it then became grievous to Srîtô; and he went back to Kaî-Ûs, and informed him how it was, and begged him that he *should* finish off by slaying him[1], because his life was not desirable.

21. Kaî-Ûs spoke thus: '*Shall* I slay thee, for it *was* not designed by thee?'

22. *And* Srîtô spoke thus: 'If thou wilt not slay me, then I *shall* slay thee.'

23. *Again* Kaî-Ûs spoke thus: 'Do not thou slay me, for I am the monarch of the world.'

24. Srîtô continued *his* discontent, until Kaî-Ûs ordered him thus: 'Go out to a certain jungle, because a witch in the shape of a dog is in it, and she will slay thee.'

25. *Then* Srîtô went out to that jungle, and that witch in the shape of a dog *was* seen by him; after he smote the witch, she became two; and he constantly smote *them* till they became a thousand, and the host (gir*d*ŏ) of them slew Srîtô on the spot.

CHAPTER XIII.

1. About the glory of Zaratû*s*t becoming manifest even before *his* birth, *it* is thus declared, that forty-five years before *the time* when Zaratû*s*t came out to his conference[2], when Frênŏ gave birth *to* the mother of Zaratû*s*t[3], whom they called Dûk*d*ak, it

---

[1] T has 'that he *should* command the slaying of him.'

[2] That is, forty-five years before he was thirty years old (see Chap. XXI, 1–14).

[3] It is necessary to translate in this manner, to agree with Dk. VII, ii, 3, but the text, which is ambiguous, runs as follows:— 'amat Frênŏg (Frênŏ-î?) Zaratû*s*t am, zya*s*ân Dûk*d*akŏg ka*r*îtuntô,

came down from the endless light, in the manner of fire, *and* mingled with the fire which was before her; *and* from the fire it mingled with the mother of Zaratûst[1].

2. *For* three nights it was manifest, to all passers-by, as a species of fire *in* the direction of the house, *and* passers *on* the road always saw great radiance. 3. Also when she became fifteen years old, the radiance of that glory which *was* in her, *was* even such *that*, on the path she was walking *along*, its brightness *was* then shed by her[2].

4. About the combination of Zaratûst, *whose* guardian spirit is reverenced; that is, his guardian spirit, in the Hôm, and his glory are given the cow's milk, by his father and mother drinking *it* up[3], *and* *his* spiritual life (ahvô) came into the combination, as was proclaimed *by* his statements in the manuscript about the Guidance of the Ceremonial[4].

5. About the backward connection of Zaratûst with Aûharmazd, through the two who *are* Yim, the best of the worldly existences, and Nêryôsang of the spirits. 6. The enumeration of the lineage of Zaratûst is Zaratûst, *son of* Pôrûshaspô[5], of Purtarâspô,

---

zerkhûntô;' which might also be translated thus: 'when Frênô, the mother of Zaratûst, whom they called Dûkdak, was born.' This Frênô, whether mother or daughter, does not seem to correspond with any Freni mentioned in the Avesta.

[1] See Dk. VII, ii, 2, 3. [2] Ibid. 7, 8.

[3] Ibid. 46, 47.

[4] Not identified, but probably like the Nîrangistân.

[5] This genealogy was, no doubt, derived originally from the same source as that in Dk. VII, ii, 70, but there are several variations, especially in orthography, which are here preserved, unless clearly copyist's blunders. The names marked with an asterisk are written in Pâzand.

of Ahûrva*d*âspô, of Hâê*k*a*d*âspô, of *K*îkhshnû*s*, of Paîtiraspô, of Are*g*a*d*ar*s*î*, of Kharedhar*, of Spîtâmân, of Vaêdî*s*tô, of Ayazem, of Frî*s*, of Ari*g**, of Dûrasrôbô, of Mânû*sk*îhar, of Mânû*s*-khûrnar, of Mânû*s*-khûrnâk, whom Nêryôsang the messenger of Aûha*r*ma*z*d *brought, and* whose mother was Vîzag, *daughter* of Aryag, of Srîtak, of Bîtak, of Frazû*s*ak, of Zû*s*ak, of Fragûzag, of Gûzag, *daughter* of Aîrî*k*, *son* of Frê*d*ûn of the Âspîgâns to the total of ten Âspîgâns, of Yim, of the Vîvang,has, of the Ayang,has, of the Anang,has, of Hôshâng, of Fravâk, of Sîyâmak, of Masîyâ, of Gâyômar*d*.

Chapter XIV.

1. About the wonderful striving of the fiend for the destruction of Zaratû*s*t. 2. When it became near to his birth, the Fever demon, the Pain demon, and the Wind demon of Aharman, each one with 150 demons, have come out to kill Zaratû*s*t, *and* from his spirit they have gone forth to *his* mother. 3. And she is hurried from there by Fever, Pain, and Wind; and at *the distance of* one league (parasang) *there* was a wizard, Impudent (Storkŏ) *by* name, who was the most medical of wizards; in hope of practice he stood up from his seat, *as* she stopped in her progress.

4. A messenger *of* Aûha*r*ma*z*d uttered a cry thus: 'Do not go to a wizard! for they are not healing (bêshazinî*d*âr) for thee; but go back to the house, wash *thy* hands on the morrow with cow's butter held over the fire, also burn (tâpŏ) [1] firewood

[1] T has 'consume (vi*d*ă*z*ŏ).'

and incense for thy own self *and thy* progeny which is in thy womb.' 5. And she acted accordingly and became well[1]; *and* the co-operators of the demon, *and* those of equal power, who *had* not obtained their remedy from her body, are again exposed[2], and spoke thus: 'On account of the existence of fire from all sides we have not succeeded; *it is* a help for every one who is her friend more than opponent; therefore it was not for us, because of the power within her.'

6. The same night as she gave birth, Aharman selected commanders and arrayed his champions (gû*r*d); there are *some* who *are* with one thousand demons, and there are *some* who *are* with two thousand demons; pursuing *and* attacking they have contended. 7. The opposing stand *of* the sacred beings[3], especially of the glory itself at the family[4] fire, was manifest at that birth; and for its splendour and brightness (pa*d*rôkŏ), settled opposite a distant place, they have then found no remedy.

8. At last, Aharman sends Akômanô[5] on, and spoke to him thus: 'Thou canst be very spiritual, who canst be most intimate; thou canst go with deceit into the mind of Zaratû*s*t, and make him turn

---

[1] Compare Dk. VII, ii, 53–55.

[2] T has '*and* all the co-operators *who had* entered her body, *and* those of equal power *who had* reached them, returned helpless from them.'

[3] Thus summarized in Dk. VIII, xiv, 2:—'Also about the arrival of both spirits, the good *one* for developing, and the evil *one* for destroying; the victory *of* the good spirit, and the rearing of Zaratû*s*t.' The 'rearing' is continued in Chaps. XV–XX.

[4] Assuming that [illegible] stands for [illegible] dû*d*ak.

[5] The archdemon of 'evil thought' (Bd. XXVIII, 7) and special opponent of Vohûmanô, the archangel of 'good thought.'

his mind to us who are demons.' 9. And Aûhar-mazd sends Vohûmanô on against him; Akômanô advanced to the front, *and* had come forward to the door, *and* wished to go inside.

10. Vohûmanô schemingly (*k*ârakŏgarîhâ) turned[1] back, and exclaimed to Akômanô thus: 'Go inside!' 11. Akômanô imagined thus: '*There* is nothing to be accomplished by me of what *was* mentioned to me, for Vohûmanô has gone back.' 12. And Vohûmanô went inside, *and* mingled with the reason (vârôm) of Zaratûst, *and* Zaratûst laughed outright[2], for Vohûmanô is a gratifying spirit.

13. Also seven wizards[3] were seated before him, *and* owing to the light in the dwelling, his *having* laughed at birth was conveniently seen, which is opposed to the *habit* of the rest of mankind who cry out at birth *and* are quite terrified.

14. Also, at the same time of birth, he authoritatively accepted the religion from Aûharmazd, as it is stated in revelation, that he spoke at birth thus: 'As is the will of the spiritual lord (ahvô) mayst thou be who art the officiating priest (zôtŏ) (that is, mayst thou be the leader of the creatures)[4].'

15. As Zaratûst, on account of his worldly body, spoke with a worldly voice, Aûharmazd spoke *in* reply to him, on account of the spirits, thus: 'So

[1] Assuming that stŏ stands for vastŏ.

[2] Compare Dk. VII, iii, 2; V, ii, 5. This laughing is not mentioned in Dk. IX, xxiv.

[3] 'Seven midwives' are mentioned in Dk. VII, iii, 2.

[4] This is one form of the Pahlavi Ahunavair (see Dk. IX, xxiv, 4). At this point the text in the MSS. is interrupted by the erroneous insertion of Chap. XII, 8–16, the contents of a loose folio in some former copy, which have been restored to their original position in this translation.

mayst thou be the priestly authority (ra*d* shâe), and so mayst thou be virtuous, owing to whatsoever righteousness *occurs;* and I confidently proclaim *thee* righteous (that is, I am thy controller)[1].'

16. Another day, Pôrûshaspô went and enquired of the wizards who kept in front at the place, thus: 'What is the *cause* when infants cry out at birth, beyond that *which occurs* when they laugh outright[2]?' 17. And they replied thus: 'Because *those who* are made to cry *have* seen mortality as *their* end, *and those* having laughed *have* seen their own righteousness.'

CHAPTER XV.

1. About the brothers who *were* a band of opponents of Zaratûs*t*. 2. The Karaps and Aûsikhshes[3] *were* brothers' sons, and have become the devastation (gâstâragîh) of the Irânians; the devastators of the Irânians (Êrânân) *were* from Kôkharê*d*[4], and Kôkharê*d* *was* born from Aêshm and Mânûs*a*k, the sister of Mânûs*k*îhar[5]. 3. At the place where Zaratûs*t* *was* born, five brothers have been, whose names were Brâ*d*-rûkhsh, Brâ*d*-rôyis*n*, Brâ*d*-rêsh the Tûr, Hazân, and Vadast[6]. 4. Their

---

[1] Compare Dk. IX, xxiv, 4. [2] Compare Dk. VII, iii, 24, 25.

[3] Av. 'Karapâ Usikhsh-*k*â' of Yas. XLIV, 20 c; the Kavâ, a third class of pre-Zoroastrian priests, is also mentioned ibid. 20 d. Compare Dk. VII, ii, 9 n.

[4] Av. Ka*h*v*a*redha, Yas. LX, 6, 7 (Sp.) where it is translated by kâstâr, 'diminisher, devastator,' of whom it is here said to be the father; see also Yt. III, 9, 12, 16.

[5] Compare the legend of the descent of the ape and bear from a demon and Yimak, sister of Yim, in Bd. XXIII, 1.

[6] As these names do not occur in the Avesta, their pronunciation

brotherhood of five—of which the middle *one was* Brâ*d*-rêsh the Tûr, who became more of an adversary of Zaratû*s*t—*was* a semblance *of* the brotherhood of five who *were* sons of Pôrûshaspô, of whom the middle *one* was Zaratû*s*t.

5. Of the four brothers *of* Zaratû*s*t, the names of the two before Zaratû*s*t *were* Ratû*s*tar and Rangû*s*tar, and of the two after *him* No*d*arîgâ and Nîvê*d*is[1]. 6. The middle position of Zaratû*s*t is for the reason that he is so produced at that time, as an intermedium of the early narrators and the later narrators, that three millenniums came before him and three after. 7. So that he *has* prescribed to the creatures in what manner he would teach the ancients as to what *had* occurred, and *in* what manner *it* is also to be done as regards what *will* occur; as is stated in the Gâthas[2] thus: 'Both those I ask of thee, *O* Aûhar*m*a*zd*! even whatever *has* happened till now, *and* whatever shall happen henceforth?'

CHAPTER XVI.

1. About the trials (aûzmâyi*s*nŏ) which occurred

has to be guessed so as to give a probable meaning to the Pahlavi spelling. The writing of the last name is complicated; it is written [Pahlavi] and [Pahlavi] in the two MS. authorities, which forms can be most obviously read Vasam and Saman, but Saman can also be read as the Zvâri*s* yad*â*=dast, 'a hand;' this leads to the conclusion that the original name underlies the form Vadast, and this is confirmed by the name of the Karap Vaêdvôi*s*t written at full length in Dk. VII, iv, 21–24. See ibid. ii, 9 n.

[1] These brothers seem unmentioned elsewhere, and the existence of the elder two would imply another mother. The pronunciation of the names is guessed.

[2] Pahl. Yas. XXXI, 14 a.

to him whose practice *was* lawful, and the signs of prophecy *that* are seen therein, *it* is thus declared, namely; 'Another day, when *the child had* been born, Pôrûshaspô called one of those five brothers of the race of Karaps, and spoke thus: "Fully observe the marks *and* specks of my son Zaratûst."'

2. *The Karap* went *and* sat down before Zaratûst, and the head of Zaratûst *was* thereupon severely twisted by him, in order that he should be killed; *but* he, being fearless, watched the wizards whose terror *was* distressing[1]. 3. As *it was* in those ten nights for hospitality, Aûharmazd sent Spendarmad, Arêdvisûr, and Ardâî-fravard[2] down to the earth, by way of female *care;* thereupon no variation occurred to *the child*, and, further, the hand of that Karap *was* withered[3], and that wizard demanded the life[4] of Zaratûst from Pôrûshaspô for the harm from him, which sprang *upon* him*self* from his own action.

4. *At* the same time Pôrûshaspô took Zaratûst, and gave him to the Karap, that he might do with him according to his own will. 5. He seized him and threw him out, at the feet of the oxen who were going on a path to the water; the leader of that drove of oxen stood still in *his* vicinity, and 150 oxen, which walked behind it, *were* kept away from him thereby; *and* Pôrûshaspô took *him*, and carried him back to the house[5].

6. Also the second day, *the Karap* threw *him* out

---

[1] Assuming that vôshîg stands for vêshîg=bêshîg.

[2] The three female spirits that represent the earth, pure water, and guardian spirits, respectively.

[3] Compare Dk. VII, iii, 4–7.

[4] Assuming that the MS. dênô stands for *g*ân.

[5] Compare Dk. VII, iii, 11, 12.

at the feet of the horses; and the leader of the horses stood still in the vicinity of Zaratûst, and 150 horses, which walked behind it, *were* kept away from him thereby; *and* Pôrûshaspô took *him*, and carried him back to the house [1].

7. Also the third day, firewood is gathered together by *the Karap*, and Zaratûst is deposited on *it* by him, the fire is stirred up by him, yet *with* the same result (ham-bûn-i*k*), the *child* is not burnt by it, and those marks, which existed *and were* made upon him, *were* a preservation from it [2].

8. And the fourth day, he is thrown by *the Karap* into the lair (âshyânakŏ) of a wolf; the wolf was not in the lair, *and* when it wished to go back to the den (sûràkŏ), it stopped when it came in front of some radiance, *in* the manner of a mother, at the place *where its* cub was. 9. In the night, Vohûmanô *and* Srôsh the righteous brought a woolly (kûrû-sakŏ) sheep *with* udder *full* of milk into the den, and it gave milk to Zaratûst, in digestible draughts (guvârakŏ guvârakŏ), until day*light* [3].

10. In the dawn, the mother of Zaratûst went to that place, in the expectation that it *would* be necessary to bring a skeleton out of the den, and the woolly *sheep* came out *and* ran away; his mother supposed that it was the wolf, and she spoke thus: 'Thou *hast* devoured to repletion; mayst thou endure for ever without it!' 11. She went farther, *and* when she saw Zaratûst quite safe, she then took him up and spoke thus: 'I *will* not give *thee* to any one during life, not though both the provinces of Râgh and Nô*d*ar *should* arrive here together [4].'

[1] Compare Dk. VII, iii, 13, 14.
[2] Ibid. 9, 10.
[3] Ibid. 15–17; V, ii, 4.
[4] Ibid. 18, 19.

12. Because these *princes were* among the spiritual from two provinces which *are* in Âtûr-pâdakân, such as *are* at sixty leagues (parasang) from Kîst; Zaratûst arose from Râgh, and Vistâsp from Nôdar. 13. And of these two provinces, Râgh was according to the name of Êrikŏ, *son* of Dûrêsrôbô, *son* of Mânûskîhar[1], from whom arose the race of Zaratûst: and Nôdar *was* according to the name of Nôdar, *son* of Mânûskîhar, from whom arose the race of Vistâsp.

Chapter XVII.

1. These were his tokens at birth:—One day, one of those five brothers of the Karaps saw Zaratûst, and he looked a long while upwards, downwards, *and* on all sides around[2].

2. Pôrûshaspô enquired thus: 'What *was* there when thou lookedst upwards, what when *thou lookedst* downwards, *and* what when thou lookedst on all sides?'

3. And he replied thus, namely: 'When I looked upwards, it *was* for this reason, when I saw that our souls[3] *that* go up to the sky, *will* go up to the best

---

[1] Compare Chap. XIII, 6; Dk. VII, ii, 70.

[2] Compare Dk. VII, iii, 27–30.

[3] Assuming that the MS. gadâ, 'glory, or destiny,' has lost an initial n, with which it was originally nismâ=Chald. נִשְׁמָא 'the soul;' as the copyists have not been aware of the existence of this Zvâris equivalent for rûbân, 'the soul,' for some centuries, it has been altered into gadâ, by the omission of its first letter, in nearly all but the very oldest existing MSS., such as K20 and M6 in Bd. XV, 3–5, and even there the medial m is really missing, though apparently existing in the final â; the irregularity of using s for sh is common in Pahlavi.

existence[1], owing to the words of this soul of mankind. 4. When I looked downwards, I saw that, owing to the action of this *one*, the demon and fiend, the wizard and witch become buried below the earth, *and* fall paralyzed back to hell. 5. And when I looked on all sides, I saw that the words of this *one will* extend through the whole earth; and when *they have* become as the law of the seven regions, each person is kept clothed *with* a robe (kapâh) of seven skins, in which the glory of the seven archangels *has* arisen.'

6. And Brâ*d*-rûkhsh the Tûr went forth; when he went to the right side (arakŏ), Zaratû*s*t hastened away to the left, and when he went to the left side, Zaratû*s*t hastened to the right, and he is thereby concealed from Brâ*d*-rûkhsh the Tûr, *who* has not met with him.

Chapter XVIII.

1. About his diverse want of participation (gvî*d* akhvê*s*îh) with *his* parents this also is declared, that the demons, at an assembly of wizards, produced an outcry *for* a conference (ham-vâ*k*ô lâyi*s*nŏ) thus: 'That son of Pôrûshaspô is senseless and foolish *and* secretly corrupted; no one, man *or* woman, *will* consider *or* accept *him as* exalted.'

2. The tidings came to Pôrûshaspô, and Pôrûshaspô spoke unto Zaratû*s*t thus: 'I thought that I *had* begotten a son who *would* become a priest, a warrior, and a husbandman, and now thou

[1] The ordinary heaven, see Dd. XX, 3.

wouldst be foolish and secretly corrupted; thou shouldst proceed to the Karaps, so that they may cure *thee*.'

3. Zaratûst gave answer thus: 'I *am he* that is thy son, a priest, warrior, and husbandman.' 4. And, by command of Pôrûshaspô he harnessed two horses to a chariot (var*d*înŏ), and he went with Pôrûshaspô.

5. When they came to the place according to the decision of Pôrûshaspô, into the presence of one Karap of those said five brethren, that wizard took a cup and made water, and spoke thus: 'This he should drink who is a son of thine, so that he *may* become well;' and he acted with this conviction, that so he would change to the same nature as theirs.

6. Zaratûst spoke to Pôrûshaspô thus: 'Thou mayst give *it* back to him who is thy protector *and* high-priest;' and he arose (âkhê*g*î*d*)[1] and went back to *their* place.

7. On the way, Zaratûst gave *their* two horses water, on account of *their* thirst; and he thought thus: 'Unprofitable was my going to the residence of the Karaps, except *in* this manner, when, through giving water to the horses, my soul *was* then expanded.'

CHAPTER XIX.

1. About his interfering talk (andarg-gôbisnŏîh) with the iniquitous, this also is declared, that one

[1] T has 'he saluted (nîyâyî*d*).' This legend has not yet been found elsewhere.

day Dûrêsrôbô[1] the Karap, as *it were* from the same five brethren, came out to the house of Pôrûshaspô; *and* Pôrûshaspô placed a bowl (*g*âmakŏ) of mare's milk before *him*, and spoke to him thus: 'Consecrate *it*.'

2. Zaratûst expostulated with Pôrûshaspô thus: 'I *will* consecrate *it*.' 3. Pôrûshaspô spoke thus: 'He should consecrate, and the grace is to be offered up by you[2];' *and* as many as three times *they* mutually disputed.

4. *Then* up stood Zaratûst, and his right foot struck at the bowl and emptied it, and he spoke thus: 'I reverence righteousness, I reverence the righteous *and* the poor, men *and* women; do thou, *O* Pôrûshaspô! prepare a portion for him in whom *there* is worthiness.'

5. And Dûrêsrôbô spoke unto Zaratûst thus: 'As *some* of my portion *of* daily *food was* first thrown away by thee, it is I who *will* bring *it* on both thy lives, and *will* utterly destroy thee.' 6. Zaratûst spoke interruptingly[3] thus: 'With complete mindfulness I *will* look upon thee with both eyes, and *will* utterly destroy thee.'

7. And, for a long time, they constantly looked, one at the other, with unshrinking gaze; *but* the divine nature of Zaratûst is victorious over the witchcraft of that *wizard*, *and* Dûrêsrôbô is further disturbed; he also asked for *his* horse *and* spoke thus: 'On account of this *boy*, *it* is impossible for me to stay.'

---

[1] So spelt in Zs., but Dûrâsrôbô in Dk.; also the former has always Pôrûshaspô, but the latter Pôrûshâspô. Compare the same legend in Dk. VII, iii, 34-45.

[2] Pahl. 'val*â* aê *yazêdŏ*, *a*fê*d* vâ*g* dahisnŏ.'

[3] Or 'inwardly.'

8. He sat upon the horse, *and* when he had gone a little *way*, he fell off from the horse, through severe distress, and died; and the children of his children's children have died upon the same spot[1].

CHAPTER XX.

1. About the righteousness of his desires *it* is thus declared, that when he became fifteen years old, the sons of Pôrûshaspô demanded a portion from *their* father, and their portions are allotted out by him. 2. Among the clothes *there* was a girdle, the width of which *was* four finger-*breadths;* and of the four[2] portions around and the girdle, which it was possible to bring forth, Zaratûst selected *the latter* and tied *it* on him*self*. 3. This was owing to the precepts (parvânakân) of Vohûmanô who came into his reason at birth; as to whatever is not the custom *his* mind *was* now quite closed, and in that which is the custom *it was* impetuously exercised by him.

4. About *his* compassionate disposition and the streams of the Arag province[3], this also is declared,

---

[1] Probably meaning that he died childless.

[2] The MSS. have 'three,' but there were five sons (Chap. XV, 5), and the numbers are written in ciphers which are very easily corrupted.

[3] Pahl. 'Aragistân ôdhâvô (T dhâ)' = 'udhâ-î Arangîstânô' of P. Vd. I, 77 (Sp.); compare Av. 'upa aodhaêshu Rang,hayau,' of Vd. I, 19; Yt. XII, 18. In the Irânian Bd. XX, 8 we are told that 'the Arang river is that of which *it* is said that it comes out from Albûrz in the land of Sûrak, which they call also Sham (Shâm); and it passes on through the land of Êgiptôs, which they call also Misr, and there they call it the swift river Êgipitôis.' It is

that *there* was a river, *and* from them the body of a naked woman floated, for the reason that, on account of the strength and swiftness of the river, a woman, except when she was quite naked while she *was* in it, was not able to pass; and an old person, such as he who is of seventy years *and* is called in revelation a Hânô [1], for want of power (*a*pâ*d*îyâvandîh râî), was not able to go back through it by his own strength. 5. Zaratûs*t* came on to the bank of the water, *and* of women *and* old people seven persons had come, and are passed on by him, *in* the manner of a bridge [2]; it was an emblem of the *spiritual* performers [3] of bridging work, that is, of those providing a passage to heaven.

6. About his liberal disposition *it* is declared, that the fodder of Pôrûshaspô, which was stored for the beasts *of burden*, *was* not *only* for the beasts of Pôrûshaspô in a scarcity, but *also* for distribution among the beasts of others, which, owing to their hunger on account of the scarcity, then constantly ate off the tails of each other; *and it was* given to them plentifully.

7. About his abandoning worldly desire, *and* his laying hold of righteousness of way, this, too, is declared, that when he became twenty years old, without the consent (*b*ên akâmakîh) of *his* father and mother, he wandered forth *and* departed from

one of the two mythical rivers which were supposed to bound the Irânian world, and seems to represent the Aras as a northern and the Nile as a western boundary. Arang often becomes Arag in Pahlavi, just as sang becomes sag.

[1] Av. hanô in Vd. III, 19, 20; &c.

[2] Probably holding each other's hands.

[3] The sacred beings who assist the righteous souls to pass over the *K*invad bridge.

their house, and openly enquired thus: 'Who is most desirous of righteousness *and* most nourishing the poor?' 8. And they spoke thus: 'He who is the youngest (kêhistô) son of Aûrvaîtô-dih[1] the Tûr, who every day gives an iron caldron (*g*âmak), which is the height of a horse, full of bread and milk *and* other food, unto the poor.' 9. Zaratûst went on to that place, and with his co-operation, for the nourishment of the poor, some of the chief men performed duty by carrying forth food for the poor.

10. About his compassion, not only upon mankind, but also his other creatures, this, too, is declared, that a bitch *was* seen by him, which had given birth to five[2] puppies, and it was three days then that she *had* not obtained food[3]. 11. Whomever she saw, she then advanced her mouth towards him, and became as it were prostrated; Zaratûst provided a remedy, *by* swiftly bringing up bread for her, *but* when *he was* bringing it she had expired.

12. About his own desire for the good quality[4] of a wife, on account also of the will of *his* parents, *and his* not mingling his own seed before a suitable obtainment, this, too, is declared, that when his father sought a wife for him, Zaratûst argued with the bride (nêshâ) thus: 'Show me thy face, so that I may find out (barkhâm) its kind of appearance, *and* this, too, whether its appearance *be* undesirable, or shall not be gratifying;' and the bride turned away her face from him. 13. And Zaratûst spoke thus:

[1] See Dk. VII, iv, 7 n.

[2] T has 'seven,' but this difference may have arisen from an erroneous mode of writing the ciphers in T.

[3] T has 'a bone for food.'

[4] T has 'good child-bearing.'

'Whoever takes away a sight from me, does not practise respect for me.'

14. About his *having* accepted progress even from the iniquitous, *that* listened sinfully desirous, who accepted so much advantageousness as *was* manifest, this, too, is declared, that he came into an assembly who were well known in the place for much knowledge, and he enquired of them thus: 'What is most favourable for the soul?' 15. And they spoke thus: 'To nourish the poor, to give fodder to cattle, to bring firewood to the fire, to pour Hôm-juice into water, and[1] to worship many demons with words, with the words which are called revelation (dênô).' 16. Then Zaratûst nourished the poor, foddered the cattle, brought firewood to the fire, and squeezed Hôm into water, *but* never are any demons whatever worshipped with words *by* Zaratûst.

Chapter XXI.

1. About his coming to thirty years of age *it is* thus declared, that *on* the lapse of thirty years onwards from *his* appearance, *on* the day Anêrân of the month Spendarmad[2], he had proceeded in that direction *in* which *there* occurred the *so*-called festival of spring (*g*as*n*ŏ-î vahâr)[3], forty-five days beyond

[1] T inserts 'not' here, which is clearly wrong, and must have been introduced by some copyist who did not observe that the assembly, though learned, was sinful; and that the object of the anecdote is to exhibit Zaratûst's ability to distinguish between good works and sin, when still untaught by the sacred beings.

[2] On the last day of the twelfth Parsi month.

[3] The Maidhyôzaremaya season-festival, held on the fifteenth day of the second Parsi month.

new-year's day, *at* a place become specially noted, where people went, from many quarters, out to the place of festival (*g*a*s*nŏ*k*âr).

2. When Zaratû*s*t, for the sake of going off to the festival place, halted on the way in walking, he chanced upon a solitary (aêvatâk) plain, and he saw, in a vision, that mankind and a much-adorned worldly *existence were* kept away to the north, so that all the people in the earth have become fully manifest in the north. 3. And he at the head (pavan têkh) of them *was* Mê*d*yômâh, son of Ârâstâî[1], *even* as Ârâstâî was brother of Pôrûshaspô[2]; Mê*d*yômâh *was* the leader of all mankind *who* have gone out to the presence of Zaratû*s*t, and he became *their* guide, so that first Mê*d*yômâh *and* afterwards the whole material existence are attracted.

4. And about his coming out to the conference, *on* the lapse of those forty-five days, *at* the place of festival *at* dawn *on* the day Dadvô[3]-pavan-Mit*r*ô of the month A*r*davahi*s*tô. 5. And Zaratû*s*t, for the purpose of squeezing the Hôm, went forth to the bank of the water of the Dâîtîh, because it is the river[4] of the conference for the supremacy (patîh) of Zaratû*s*t, *and* is the water of *Â*v*â*n[5] which has consisted of four channels (bêtâ). 6. Zaratû*s*t also

[1] See Yt. XIII, 95.

[2] So Mê*d*yômâh was first cousin of Zaratû*s*t, and became his first convert; see also Chap. XXIII, 1.

[3] The Pahlavi letters represent Av. dadhv*a*u, 'creator'; compare the Khvârizmian name دذو of the fifteenth day of the month in Sachau's Albîrûnî, p. 57, l. 35. The date here given is the fifteenth of the second month, as in § 1.

[4] Assuming that ru*d* stands for rû*d*.

[5] Probably Anâhita, the female spirit of pure water, mentioned by her title Arêdvisûr in Chap. XVI, 3.

passed on through it; and its first *channel* was up to the ankle[1], the second up to the knee, the third up to the parting of the two thighs, and the fourth up to the neck. 7. This was an indicator that his religion comes four times to supremacy; the manifestations of which are through Zaratûst, Aûshêdar, Aûshêdar-mâh, and Sôshâns[2].

8. When he came up from the water, and put on his clothes, he then saw the archangel Vohûmanô[3] in the form (âyûînakŏ) of a man, handsome, brilliant, and elegant, who wore his hair curve-tailed[4], because the curved tail is an indication of duality; *who* had put on *and* wore a dress like silk, than which *there* was no making anything superior, for it was light itself; and his height was nine *times* as much as *that of* Zaratûst.

9. He also enquired of Zaratûst[5] thus: 'Who mayst thou be, and from whom of them mayst thou be? also what is mostly thy desire, and the endeavour in thy existence?' 10. And he replied thus: 'I am Zaratûst of the Spîtâmas; among the existences righteousness is more *my* desire, and my wish is that I *may* become aware *of* the will of the sacred beings, and *may* practise so much righteousness as they exhibit to me in the pure existence.'

11. And Vohûmanô directed Zaratûst[6] thus: 'Do

[1] Literally 'up to the leg (zang).'

[2] The past and future apostles of Zoroastrianism. For the last three, see Dk. VII, ix–xi.

[3] Compare Dk. VII, iii, 51–54.

[4] Assuming that vagdumak is a variant of the usual gagdûmak. The scorpion (vagdum) would be a sign of duality, as, being a noxious creature, it was produced by the evil spirit Aharman.

[5] Compare Dk. VII, iii, 55–59.

[6] Compare ibid. iii, 60–62.

thou proceed to an assembly of the spirits!' 12. As much as Vohûmanô walked on in nine steps, Zaratûst *did* in ninety steps, and when he had gone ninety steps farther than him, he saw the assembly of the seven archangels. 13. When he came within twenty-four feet of the archangels, he then did not see his own shadow on the ground, on account of the great brilliancy of the archangels; the position of the assembly was in Irân, and in the direction of the districts on the bank of the water of the Dâitîh. 14. Zaratûst offered homage, and spoke thus: 'Homage to Aûharmazd, and homage to the archangels!' *and* he went forward *and* sat down in the seat of the enquirers.

15. As to the asking of questions by Zaratûst, he enquired of Aûharmazd thus: 'In the embodied world which is the first of the perfect ones, which the second, *and* which the third?' 16. And Aûharmazd replied thus: 'The first perfection is good thoughts, the second good words, *and* the third good deeds.'

17. Zaratûst also enquired thus: 'Which *thing* is good, which is better[1], and which is the best of all habits?' 18. *And* Aûharmazd replied thus: 'The title[2] of the archangels is good, the sight of them is better, and carrying out their commands is the best of all habits.'

19. Afterwards he demonstrated the duality of the original evolutions (bûn gastânŏ)[3], and the divergence in each control, *and* spoke thus: 'Of those spirits, he who *was* wicked preferred the

---

[1] Both MSS. have 'worse' here.

[2] This title, ameshaspenta, is 'immortal benefactor.'

[3] The two prime movers in creation.

practice which is iniquitous (Aharman's desire was *for* the practice which is iniquitous), *and* the spirit of righteousness, the propitious (Aûharmazd) prefers righteousness [1].' 20. Specially he demonstrated the divergence in each control of the exhibitors of light, and he spoke thus: 'Neither our thoughts [2], nor desires, nor words, nor deeds, nor religion, nor spiritual faculties *agree* [3]; *he* who is loving light, his place is with the luminaries; *and he* who *is loving* darkness is with the dark ones [4].'

21. On the same day also, his omniscient wisdom appeared three times: as regards the same first questions, it pointed out the sky in great light and splendour, and in its exhibition *of* the prevention *of* darkness, at the sight of which *it becomes* an opposing existence as regards that darkness. 22. And it exhibited its own appearance proportionally *to* the sky, when it kept its head at the summit of the sky, *its* feet at the bottom of the sky, and *its* hands reached to both sides of the sky; the sky also kept *it* covered, in the manner of a garment.

23. The six archangels [5] were manifest by their similar stature (ham-basnîh), in such manner that it is obvious each one successively is apparently one finger's *breadth* shorter than the other. 24. The archangels exhibited three kinds *of* achievement

[1] Quoted from Pahl. Yas. XXX, 5 ab. The words in parentheses are glosses inserted by the Pahlavi translator.

[2] Both MSS. have 'spirits' by inserting a stroke in the middle of the Pahlavi word.

[3] An imperfect quotation, omitting glosses, from Pahl. Yas. XLIV, 2 cde (Sp.).

[4] A similar idea is expressed in Vd. XIX, 30, but the Pahlavi version of half of it is lost.

[5] Apart from Aûharmazd, their president.

(pasâkhtan)[1] for the religion; first, *by* means of fires, and Zaratûst walked three steps on *them*, with *the words*, 'good thoughts, good words, and good deeds,' and *was* not burnt; and secondly, hot metal is poured on to *his* chest, cooled thereby, and, grasping *it* with *his* hand, he held *it* for the archangels. 25. Aûharmazd spoke thus: 'After *the establishment of* the pure religion, when a dispute occurs in the religion, those who are thy disciples *will* pour *it* on to a spiritual lord, they *will* take *it* up with the hand, *and will* thoroughly believe in him who is over the whole embodied existence.' 26. The third *was* cutting with a knife, *and* the vital parts (ahvôn) becoming visible, which are inside the abdomen, *with* a flowing forth of blood; and, after the hands are rubbed over *it*, it became healed. 27. And this is pointed out, namely: 'Thy and thy correligionists' accepting of the pure religion is, as to the steadfast *in* other religions, such that, through such-like burning of fire, pouring of hot metal, and through an operation with a sharp instrument, *there* is no perversion from the good religion.'

CHAPTER XXII.

1. About the seven questionings (7-frasnŏih), with reference to religion, of the seven archangels, *which* occurred in seven places[2].

2. For the occurrence of the first questioning[3], that of Aûharmazd, the person of Zaratûst, who *was*

---

[1] By way of ordeal, a relic of the old faith in incantation.

[2] Compare Dk. VIII, xiv, 5, 6, 9.

[3] This has been narrated in the preceding chapter.

the upholder of Aûharmazd, came out to a conference on the bank of the water of Dâîtîh [1].

3. For the occurrence of the second, *which* is Vohûmanô's, five animals out of the five species [2] which are the worldly tokens of Vohûmanô, have come with Zaratûst to a conference on Hûgar and Aûsind [3]; and on that day also, before their coming out to the conference, *their* tongues are fully liberated *and* spoke with human words. 4. And among the rest [4] is a fish of one species, Arzuvâ [5] *by* name; of those in burrows (khanŏîgânŏ) *are* the white ermine *and* white marten; of the flying creatures (vâyandagân) *is* the Karsipt [6], a bird like a species of water-fowl; of the wide-travellers (farâkhvŏ-raftârânŏ) is the hare which is showing wild beasts the way to the water; and of those suitable for grazing (karakŏ-argânîgân) is the white ass-goat; with human words they also accepted the religion from Aûharmazd. 5. With the chieftainship of the five species they are intrusted, so that the like animals also, with their own voices, *and* as much as their knowledge is capable, shall recount the powerfulness *of* the religion.

---

[1] See Dk. VII, iii, 51, 54.

[2] These species, which are named in § 4, are those mentioned in the Avesta, Visp. I, 1.

[3] Av. Hukairya of Yt. XII, 24, and Us-hindu of Yt. VIII, 32, described in Bd. XII, 5, 6, as two neighbouring mountains, for the pure water of Arêdvisûr falls from the summit of Hûgar to Aûsind which stands in the circumambient ocean.

[4] The remainder of K 35, the MS. brought by Westergaard from Kirmân, is lost; but an old copy of it (BK, see the Introduction) exists in Bombay, which supplies the missing text, as an authority independent of T.

[5] See Bd. XIV, 26; apparently the same as the Ariz, or Kar, the chief of fish, ibid. XVIII, 3, 5; XXIV, 13.

[6] See Bd. XIV, 23; XIX, 16; XXIV, 11.

6. And freedom from assault, exemption from persecution, and proper maintenance of the five species of animals, *were* prescribed by him [1] to Zaratûst with seemingly very awful admonition.

7. For the occurrence of the third questioning, which is A*rd*avahi*s*tô's, the spirits of the fires have come out with Zaratû*s*t to a conference at the Tô*g*ân water [2]; and, in that questioning, care for the proper maintenance of the Varahrân fire [3], and the propitiation of all fires, is explained to him.

8. For the occurrence of the fourth questioning, which is Shatvê*r*'s, the spirits of the metals have come with Zaratû*s*t to a conference at Sarâî [4], a settlement on the Mîvân [4]; *and he was* fully admonished about various proper preservations of the metals, *and as to* not producing warlike accoutrements of gold.

9. For the occurrence of the fifth questioning, which is Spenda*r*ma*d*'s, the spirits of the regions, frontiers, stations (aûstâmân), settlements (rû*d*astâkân), and districts, as many as were desirable, have come out with Zaratû*s*t to a conference *where* there is a spring (khânîgô-aê) which comes out from the Asnavad mountain [5], *and* goes into the Dâitîh, like those of Satavês who is blowing the Pâîrîgs [6]. 10. And *Zaratûst was* also thus ad-

[1] By Vohûmanô, as the protector of useful animals.

[2] Possibly the Te*g*end river, the Zend or Zôndak of Bd. XX, 7, 15.

[3] The Bahrâm, or sacred fire at places of worship.

[4] Names not clearly identified, and readings uncertain.

[5] In Âtû*r*-pâtakân, and the Gû*s*nasp, fire was established upon it (see Bd. XII, 2, 26; XVII, 7).

[6] Pahl. 'Satavês-î Pâîrîg damânŏ ânŏ *k*îgûn.' Referring probably to Yt. VIII, 8, 9. Satavês is the *southern* chieftain of the stars, as correctly stated in the Irânian Bûndahi*s* (compare Bd. II, 7; XIII, 12); and the Pâîrîgs are meteors.

monished by her, about the care and propitiation of the earth: that each district is *to be* intrusted *to* a faithful testifier (gôkâs-î vâvar), each settlement *to* a judge acquainted with the law, *each* station *to* an officiating priest (magôpatŏ) of just intentions, *and* each frontier *to* a pure priestly authority (ra*d*ŏ); over all is proclaimed the councillor of the spirits, the supreme priest (magôpatânŏ magôpatŏ), and through him the sovereignty of Aûha*r*ma*zd* is provided.

11. For the occurrence of the sixth questioning, which is Khû*r*da*d*'s, the spirits of seas *and* rivers have come with Zaratû*s*t to a conference at the Asnavad mountain[1], and he *was* told about the care and propitiation of water.

12. For the occurrence of the seventh questioning, which is Amû*r*da*d*'s, the spirits of plants have come out with Zaratû*s*t to a conference on the precipitous bank of the Darega[2], on the bank (bâr) of the water of Dâîtîh, and different places; and he *was* informed about the care *and* propitiation of plants.

13. The seven questionings are explained within the length of these winters, which are *of* five months, *and* within ten years[3].

---

[1] See § 9.

[2] Pahl. 'pavan Daregîn zbâr' = Av. 'Dregya paiti zbarahi' of Vd. XIX, 4; a mythical river in Aîrân-vêg, where Pôrûshaspô resided (Bd. XX, 32).

[3] The Pahlavi is rather vague, but it is clear that Zaratû*s*t starts for his conference at thirty years of age (Chap. XXI, 1), returns from it ten years later (Chap. XXIII, 1), and the conversion of Vi*s*tâsp occupies two years longer (Chap. XXIII, 5), occurring when Zaratû*s*t was forty-two years old and thirty-five years before his passing away at the age of seventy-seven (Chap. XXIII, 9).

At this point another dislocation of text occurs in all existing

CHAPTER XXIII.

1. On the completion of revelation, that is, at the end of the ten years, Mê*d*yômâh, son of Ârâstâî, became faithful to Zaratû*s*t.

2. Afterwards, on *having* obtained *his* requests [1], he came back to the conference of Aûha*r*ma*zd*, and he spoke thus: 'In ten years *only* one man *has been* attracted by me.' 3. *And* Aûha*r*ma*zd* spoke thus: '*There will* be days when so few *are* not attracted by you, who *are* themselves the occasion of the resurrection of the world; when, apart from Dahâk [2], the beneficence of the formation of the renovation *of the universe* attracts every one besides, and the impenitence of Dahâk is destroyed.'

4. When he came out from the presence of Aûha*r*ma*zd*, with the same paradox, he thereby indicated his religion *as* complete to Spenda*r*ma*d* through *his* intelligence.

5. In the two years after that [3], the Kavîgs *and*

MSS., owing to the accidental interpolation of three loose folios of another text, between this chapter and the next, in some unknown copy written before 1530. In the MSS. the text is written continuously, without division into chapters. But the connection of this chapter with the next one, which is here restored to its proper position, is clearly shown by the reference to the 'ten years' of conference, with which this chapter ends, and the next one begins. The accidentally interpolated text is here classified as Chaps. XXIV and XXV, but its real connections have not yet been traced.

[1] That is, the replies of the archangels to his enquiries.

[2] See Dk. VII, i, 26. He was chained by Frê*d*ûn in Mount Dimâvand, to escape in the latter days, to be slain by Keresâsp, and to be specially punished at the resurrection (Bd. XII, 31; XXX, 16; Byt. III, 55–61).

[3] See Dk. VII, iv, 2.

Karaps of Vistâsp, *in* the manner of opponents (hamêstarânîh), propounded thirty-three enquiries (khvâstakŏ)[1] to him, so that *by* command of Vistâsp he became the explainer of those thirty-three enquiries. 6. Of the thirty-three habits[2] of iniquity, come for opposition to the religion of the sacred beings; of the declaration, by revelation, of those thirty-three indications of fetters[3]; *and* of the restraint of the thirty-three iniquitous practices by the thirty-three best good works, *there are* statements in revelation. 7. Including the acceptance of the religion *by* Vistâsp from Zaratûst, after the re-demonstration of its judicially multiform prophecy and spiritual character, which are looked into through the evidence of three speakers about *them*, the archangels who, with worldly manifestation, have become apparent unto Vistâsp and *his* councillors *and* mighty ones; *they* are Vohûmanô, Ardavahistô, and the Bûrzîn-Mitrô fire[4].

8. About the reward which *existed* before the beneficence of Zaratûst, and *its* being seen how, through guidance by Aûharmazd, *it* is demonstrated by him to those of the world, so that Mêdyômâh is attracted in the tenth year in the forest of reedy hollows (kanyâstânŏ[5] vêsakŏ) which is the haunt of swine of the wild-boar *species* (khazûrâ-î varâzŏ gâs); in the twentieth year the Kavig who is son

[1] See Dk. VII, iv, 67.

[2] Reading sôn = Pers. sân; but the MSS. have dênô, 'religions.' The thirty sins and thirty-three good works, detailed in Mkh. XXXVI, XXXVII, are certainly referred to at the end of this section.

[3] Compare Chap. XII, 5, and Dk. VII, iv, 67.

[4] See Dk. VII, iv, 74.

[5] Hybrid Zvâris of Pers. nayistân.

of Kûndah[1] is attracted; in the thirtieth year the Khyôns[2] arrive, who make an incursion (var*d*akŏ) into the countries of Irân, owing to the Kavîgs, those who *are* more of their own race; and in the fortieth year Vohûnêm, son of Avarô*s*tar[3], is born.

9. In the forty-seventh year Zaratû*s*t passes away, who attains seventy-seven years and forty days in the month A*rd*avahi*s*tô, *on* the day Khûr[4]; *and* for eight rectified (vêhi*k*akŏ) months, till the month Dadvô and day Khûr, he should be brought *forward* as to be reverenced.

10. *In* the same month A*rd*avahi*s*tô, in the sixty-third[5] year, Frashô*s*tar[6] passed away, and in the sixty-fourth *year* *G*âmâsp[7], *the same* as became the priest of priests after Zaratû*s*t; in the seventy-third year Hangâûrûsh, son of *G*âmâsp[8]; in the eightieth year Asmôk-khanvatô[9], and *also* in the eightieth

---

[1] Or Kûnîh which is the name of a demon (see Sg. XVI, 13, 16, 18, 19); but such an identification is uncertain.

[2] Av. *Hv*yaona of Yt. IX, 30, 31; XVII, 50, 51. Compare Dk. VII, iv, 77, 83, 84, 87–90; v, 7.

[3] Av. gen. 'Vohu-nemang,hô Avâraostrôis' of Yt. XIII, 104.

[4] The eleventh day of the second month.

[5] T has 43d, and the date is lost in the other MS. authority. But 43d is highly improbable for two reasons: first, it would make this date the only one out of chronological order in the series here given; secondly, it would render it inconsistent with the statement, in Dk. VII, vi, 12, that two priests came, from other regions, to ask Frashô*s*tar about the religion, fifty-seven years after it had been accepted by Zaratû*s*t. By substituting 63d (the Pahlavi cipher most likely to be corrupted into 43d) both these inconsistencies are removed.

[6] See Dk. VII, vi, 12; V, ii, 12.

[7] See Dk. V, ii, 12; iii, 4.

[8] Av. gen. 'Hang,haurushô *G*âmâspanahê' of Yt. XIII, 104.

[9] Av. gen. 'Asmô-*hv*anvatô' of Yt. XIII, 96, and Westergaard's Yt. XXII, 37.

year Kabed-ûs-spâê[1], who is called also Akht the wizard, is killed.

11. Of the six great upholders of the religion there are the two daughters of Zaratûst, whose names are Frênŏ and Srîtŏ[2], *with* Aharûbŏ-stôtô, *son* of Mê*d*yômâh[3], and another three, who *are* renowned for their religion for a hundred years, who are Vohûnêm[4] that is born in the fortieth year of the religion, *S*ênô[5] is *afterwards* born and passes away in the two-hundredth year, *and* as to his hundred-discipledom[6], it exists day and night till the three-hundredth year. 12. Afterwards the religion is disturbed and the monarchy is contested (*g*angî-aîtŏ).

13. About the three customs (dâ*d*ŏ) which Zaratûst prescribed as the best:—The first of them is this: 'Do not go without others, except with magisterial authority (apatkâr ra*d*îhâ);' the second is: 'Though they shall proceed unlawfully as to you, consider *your* actions lawfully beforehand;' *and* the third is: 'Next-of-kin marriage, for the

[1] As kabed is Zvâris for 'many,' we may assume that kabed-ûs =Av. nom. pourus which usually becomes pouru in compounds; so that the compound name, or title, in the text, probably represents Av. Pouruspâdha (Yt. X, 109, 111), 'having many troops,' a suitable title for Akht the wizard (Av. Akhtya of Yt. V, 82) who is said, in Gf. I, 2, to have invaded a district with an army of seven myriads. He was killed, in Zoroastrian fashion, by the recital of a religious formula.

[2] There was a third daughter, Pôru*k*îst (see Bd. XXXII, 5), but she may not have survived her father.

[3] Av. gen. 'Ashastvô Maidhyôi-m*a*ung,hôis' of Yt. XIII, 106.

[4] See § 8.

[5] He was born in the 100th year; see Dk. VII, vii, 6.

[6] This seems to be the sixth upholder of the religion, the third of those lasting about a century.

sake of the pure progress of *your* race, is the best *of* the actions of the living, which *are* provided for the proper begetting of children[1].'

CHAPTER XXIV.

1. About the five dispositions of priests, and the ten admonitions with which all instruction as to religion is connected[2].

2. Of those five dispositions the first is innocence.

3. The second is discrimination among[3] thoughts, words, and deeds; [to fully distinguish the particulars of destruction from indestructiveness, *such* as

---

[1] This chapter ends the first series of Selections of Zâ*d*-sparam, and is immediately followed in the MSS. by a second series. It is evident from the extent of this chapter, as compared with the amount of text contained in the three misplaced folios (see p. 162, n. 3), that this chapter could have occupied only about one folio and a half in the dislocated MS., so that the second series must have commenced on the same folio as contained the end of this chapter, and that Chaps. XXIV, XXV cannot have belonged to this series. The three misplaced folios contain two distinct texts; the first (Chap. XXIV) is an Irânian version of the Five Dispositions of priests and the Ten Admonitions, and is here translated; the second (Chap. XXV) contains some details about the Nasks and Gâthas, and has been already translated in S.B.E., vol. xxxvii, pp. 401–405.

[2] This Irânian version of the Dispositions and Admonitions is more complete than the Indian version, which, like the Bundahis, was brought from Irân five or six centuries ago, and is found in two MSS. (Pt. and J) written in India about 500 years ago, and now in the libraries of Dastûrs Dr. Peshotan and Dr. Jâmâsp, respectively. Passages which occur only in the Irânian version are here enclosed in brackets, and other differences between the two versions are mentioned in the notes.

[3] The Indian version has 'of.'

noxious creatures from cattle; and of production from unproductiveness, *such* as the righteous *and* worthy from the wicked *and* unworthy].

4. The third is authoritativeness, because that priestly master is always wiser and speaking more correctly who is taught wisely and teaches with more correct words.

5. The fourth is to[1] [understand *and* consider the ceremonial as the ceremonial of Aûharmazd, *and* the essentials with all goodness, beneficence, *and* authority; to be steadfast in his religion, and to consider the indications of protection (sâyag)[2] which are established for his religion. 6. To maintain the reverence of the luminaries prayerfully, *also* the reverence of the emanations[3] *from* the six[4] *archangels*, be they fire, be they earth, *or* be they of bodily form, and of the creatures *which* are formed by them; also the pure cleansing from dead matter, menstruation, bodily refuse, and other hurtfulness; this is in order that they *may* be characterised, and thereby constituted, *as* better-principled, more sensible[5], and purer, and they *may* become less faulty. 7. The reverence of mankind is to consider authoritatively about knowledge *and* property; the reverence of cattle is *about* fodder, little hardship, and moderate maintenance; the reverence of plants is *about* sowing and ripening for the food of the worthy. 8. The ceremonial which is glorifying all

[1] Ind. vers. has only: 'to celebrate the ceremonial of the sacred beings with the correct words, inward prayers, and complete mastery of the text (narm-nasgîhâ) in the ritual.' It omits §§ 6–8 altogether.

[2] T has 'limit (kûstak).'

[3] T has 'issue.'

[4] T has 'seven.'

[5] Or 'more fragrant;' hû-bôdtar has both meanings.

the sacred beings, praises the luminaries *and* worldly creations improperly, and is antagonistic to them, because complete glorification is proper through complete recitation of the ritual; and the ceremonial of any one whatever is his own proper duty professionally, so long as it is possible to keep proceeding with very little sinfulness].

9. The fifth is to struggle prayerfully [1], day and night, with *your* own fiend [2], *and all* life long not to depart from steadfastness, nor allow *your* proper duty [3] *to go* out of *your* hands.

10. And the first of those ten admonitions is to proceed with good repute, for the sake of occasioning approving remarks *as to* [4] the good repute of *your* own guardian *and* teacher, high-priest *and* master [5].

11. The second is to become awfully refraining from evil repute, for the sake of evil repute not occurring *to* relations and guardians.

12. The third is not to beat *your* own teacher with a snatched-up stick, and not to bring scandal upon his name, for the sake of annoying him, by *uttering* that which *was* not heard from *your* own teacher.

13. The fourth is *that* whatever is taught liberally by *your* own teacher, *you have* to deliver back to the worthy, for the sake of not extorting a declaration of renown from the righteous [6].

14. The fifth is *that* the reward of doers of good

[1] Ind. vers. has: 'to remain in diligence intelligently.'

[2] Ind. vers. has: 'opponent.'

[3] Ind. vers. has: 'steadfastness in religion, and to be diligent in *your* proper duty.' But it omits the rest of the sentence.

[4] Ind. vers. has: 'for the sake of the appropriateness of.'

[5] Or 'father.'

[6] T has: 'not extracting the purity of the righteous.'

works *and* the punishment of criminals *have to be* established by law, for the sake of progress[1].

15. The sixth is to keep the way of the good open to *your* house, for the sake of making[2] righteousness welcome in *your* own abode.

16. The seventh is *that*, for the sake of not developing the fiend insensibly in *your* reason, *you are* not to keep *it* with the religion of the good[3], nor to remain in impenitence of sin.

17. The eighth[4] is *that*, for the sake of severing the fiend from the reason, *you have* to force malice *away* from *your* thoughts, and to become quickly repentant of sin.

18. The ninth is to fully understand the forward movement[5] of the religion, also to keep the advancing of the religion further forwards, and to seek *your* share of duty therein; and on a backward movement, when adversity happens to the religion, to have the religion back again, and to keep *your* body in the continence (makavadîh) of religion.

19. The tenth is *that there is* to be a period of obedience (Srôshdârîh) towards the ruler and priestly authority, the high-priesthood of the religious[6].

---

[1] Ind. vers. adds: 'of religion.'

[2] Ind. vers. inserts: 'a token of;' and T has: 'making the righteousness of the sacred beings in writing welcome.'

[3] Ind. vers. has: 'not to maintain malice with the good,' which is more probable, and kênŏ, 'malice,' is easily corrupted into dênô, 'religion,' in Pahlavi writing.

[4] This eighth admonition is omitted in the Irânian MSS.

[5] Ind. vers. adds: 'and backward movement.'

[6] Chapter XXV, about the three divisions of revelation, is translated in S. B. E., vol. xxxvii, pp. 401–405.

INDEX.

OBSERVATIONS.

1. The references, in this index, are to books, chapters, and sections; the chapters being denoted by the larger ciphers.

2. Though different forms of the same name may occur in the text, only one form is usually given in the index, to which the references to all forms are attached; except when the forms differ so much as to be widely separated in the index.

3. Pâzand forms are printed in italics, as their orthography is usually corrupt. In all such italicised names any letters which would elsewhere be italic are printed in roman type.

4. Abbreviations used are:—Av. for Avesta, Dk. for Dînka*rd*, Int. for Introduction, m. for mountain, meas. for measure, MS. for manuscript, n. for footnote, Pahl. for Pahlavi, patron. for patronymic, r. for river, Zs. for Selections of Zâ*d*-sparam.

INDEX.

ERRATUM.

P. 20, l. 4. The name of the district of Alâk should probably be read Arâk, as the province is called Râgh in Zs. XVI, 13.

TRANSLITERATION OF ORIENTAL ALPHABETS ADOPTED FOR THE TRANSLATIONS OF THE SACRED BOOKS OF THE EAST.

CONSONANTS.	MISSIONARY ALPHABET. I Class.	II Class.	III Class.	Sanskrit.	Zend.	Pehlevi.	Persian.	Arabic.	Hebrew.	Chinese.
Gutturales.										
1 Tenuis	k	...	....	क	𐬐	[illegible]	ک	ك	כּ	k
2 „ aspirata	kh	...	....	ख	𐬑	[illegible]	...	...	כ	kh
3 Media	g	...	....	ग	𐬔	[illegible]	گ	...	גּ	...
4 „ aspirata	gh	...	....	घ	𐬖	[illegible]	...	...	ג	...
5 Gutturo-labialis	q	...	....	...	....	...	ق	ق	ק	...
6 Nasalis	ṅ (ng)	...	....	ङ	{𐬢 (ng) / 𐬣 (N)}	...	...	...	...	...
7 Spiritus asper	h	...	....	ह	𐬵 (𐬓 *hv*)	[illegible]	ه	ه	ה	h, hs
8 „ lenis	'	...	....	...	....	...	ا	ا	א	...
9 „ asper faucalis	ʻh	...	....	...	....	...	ح	ح	ח	...
10 „ lenis faucalis	ʼh	...	....	...	....	...	ع	ع	ע	...
11 „ asper fricatus	...	*ʻh*	....	...	....	...	خ	خ	ח	...
12 „ lenis fricatus	...	*ʼh*	....	...	....	...	...	...	...	...
Gutturales modificatae (palatales, &c.)										
13 Tenuis	...	*k*	....	च	𐬗	[illegible]	چ	...	...	*k*
14 „ aspirata	...	*kh*	....	छ	....	...	...	...	...	*kh*
15 Media	...	*g*	....	ज	𐬘	[illegible]	ج	ج	...	...
16 „ aspirata	...	*gh*	....	झ	....	...	غ	غ	...	...
17 „ Nasalis	...	*ñ*	....	ञ	....	...	...	...	...	...

CONSONANTS (*continued*).	MISSIONARY ALPHABET. I Class.	II Class.	III Class.	Sanskrit.	Zend.	Pehlevi.	Persian.	Arabic.	Hebrew.	Chinese.
18 Semivocalis	y	. . .	. . . .	य	𐬫 𐬌 init.	[illegible]	ي	ي	י	y
19 Spiritus asper	. . .	($\acute{y}$)	. . . .	. . .	. . . .	. . .	. . .	. . .	. . .	. . .
20 ,, lenis	. . .	($\grave{y}$)	. . . .	. . .	. . . .	. . .	. . .	. . .	. . .	. . .
21 ,, asper assibilatus . .	. . .	*s*	. . . .	श	𐬱	[illegible]	ش	ش	. . .	. . .
22 ,, lenis assibilatus . .	. . .	*z*	. . . .	. . .	𐬲	[illegible]	ژ	. . .	. . .	*z*
Dentales.										
23 Tenuis	t	. . .	. . . .	त	𐬙	[illegible]	ت	ت	תּ	t
24 ,, aspirata	th	. . .	. . . .	थ	𐬚	. . .	. . .	. . .	ת	th
25 ,, assibilata	. . .	. . .	TH	. . .	. . . .	. . .	ث	ث	. . .	. . .
26 Media	d	. . .	. . . .	द	𐬛	[illegible]	د	د	דּ	. . .
27 ,, aspirata	dh	. . .	. . . .	ध	𐬜	. . .	. . .	. . .	ד	. . .
28 ,, assibilata	. . .	. . .	DH	. . .	. . . .	. . .	ذ	ذ	. . .	. . .
29 Nasalis	n	. . .	. . . .	न	𐬥	[illegible]	ن	ن	נ	n
30 Semivocalis	l	. . .	. . . .	ल	. . . .	[illegible]	ل	ل	ל	l
31 ,, mollis 1	. . .	*l*	. . . .	ळ	. . . .	. . .	. . .	. . .	. . .	. . .
32 ,, mollis 2	. . .	. . .	L	. . .	. . . .	. . .	. . .	. . .	. . .	. . .
33 Spiritus asper 1	s	. . .	. . . .	स	𐬯	[illegible]	س(ث)	س	שׂ	s
34 ,, asper 2	. . .	. . .	s (ʃ)	. . .	. . . .	. . .	. . .	. . .	ס	. . .
35 ,, lenis	z	. . .	. . . .	. . .	𐬰	[illegible]	ز (ذ)	ز	ז	z
36 ,, asperrimus 1	. . .	. . .	z (ʒ)	. . .	. . . .	. . .	ص	ص	צ	ʒ, ʒh
37 ,, asperrimus 2	. . .	. . .	ẓ (ʒ)	. . .	. . . .	. . .	ض	. . .	. . .	. . .

Dentales modificatae (linguales, &c.)										
38 Tenuis	. . .	*t*	. . . .	ट	. . . .	. . .	ط	ط	ט	. . .
39 „ aspirata	. . .	*th*	. . . .	ठ	. . . .	. . .	ظ	ظ	. . .	. . .
40 Media	. . .	*d*	. . . .	ड	[illegible]	[illegible]	. . .	. . .	. . .	. . .
41 „ aspirata	. . .	*dh*	. . . .	ढ	. . . .	. . .	. . .	ض	. . .	. . .
42 Nasalis	. . .	*n*	. . . .	ण	[illegible]	. . .	. . .	. . .	. . .	. . .
43 Semivocalis	r	. . .	. . . .	र	[illegible]	[illegible]	ر	ر	ר	. . .
44 „ fricata	. . .	*r*	. . . .	. . .	. . . .	. . .	. . .	. . .	. . .	*r*
45 „ diacritica	. . .	. . .	R	. . .	. . . .	. . .	. . .	. . .	. . .	. . .
46 Spiritus asper	sh	. . .	. . . .	ष	[illegible]	[illegible]	. . .	. . .	. . .	sh
47 „ lenis	zh	. . .	. . . .	. . .	. . . .	. . .	. . .	. . .	. . .	. . .
Labiales.										
48 Tenuis	p	. . .	. . . .	प	[illegible]	[illegible]	پ	. . .	פּ	p
49 „ aspirata	ph	. . .	. . . .	फ	. . . .	. . .	. . .	. . .	פ	ph
50 Media	b	. . .	. . . .	ब	[illegible]	[illegible]	ب	ب	בּ	. . .
51 „ aspirata	bh	. . .	. . . .	भ	. . . .	. . .	. . .	. . .	ב	. . .
52 Tenuissima	. . .	*p*	. . . .	. . .	. . . .	. . .	. . .	. . .	. . .	. . .
53 Nasalis	m	. . .	. . . .	म	[illegible]	[illegible]	م	م	מ	m
54 Semivocalis	w	. . .	. . . .	. . .	[illegible]	. . .	. . .	. . .	. . .	w
55 „ aspirata	hw	. . .	. . . .	. . .	. . . .	. . .	. . .	. . .	. . .	. . .
56 Spiritus asper	f	. . .	. . . .	. . .	[illegible]	[illegible]	ف	ف	. . .	f
57 „ lenis	v	. . .	. . . .	व	»	[illegible]	و	و	ו	. . .
58 Anusvâra	. . .	*m*	. . . .	ं	[illegible] ã	. . .	. . .	. . .	. . .	. . .
59 Visarga	. . .	*h*	. . . .	ः	. . . .	. . .	. . .	. . .	. . .	. . .

VOWELS.	MISSIONARY ALPHABET. I Class.	II Class.	III Class.	Sanskrit.	Zend.	Pehlevi.	Persian.	Arabic.	Hebrew.	Chinese.
1 Neutralis	0	...	....	...	....	...	...	...	ְ	ă
2 Laryngo-palatalis	ĕ	...	....	...	....	...	...	...	...	...
3 ,, labialis	ŏ	...	....	...	....	𐭠 fin.	...	...	...	...
4 Gutturalis brevis	a	...	....	अ	𐬀	𐭠 init.	َ	َ	ַ	a
5 ,, longa	â	(a)	....	आ	𐬁	𐭠	َا	َا	ָ	â
6 Palatalis brevis	i	...	....	इ	𐬌	...	ِ	ِ	ִ	i
7 ,, longa	î	(i)	....	ई	𐬍	𐭩	ِي	ِي	ִי	î
8 Dentalis brevis	*li*	...	....	ऌ	....	...	...	...	...	...
9 ,, longa	*lî*	...	....	ॡ	....	...	...	...	...	...
10 Lingualis brevis	*ri*	...	....	ऋ	....	...	...	...	...	...
11 ,, longa	*rî*	...	....	ॠ	....	...	..	..	...	...
12 Labialis brevis	u	...	....	उ	𐬎	...	ُ	ُ	ֻ	u
13 ,, longa	û	(u)	....	ऊ	𐬏	𐭥	ُو	ُو	וּ	û
14 Gutturo-palatalis brevis	e	...	....	...	𐬈 (e) 𐬆 (e)	...	...	...	ֶ	e
15 ,, longa	ê (ai)	(e)	....	ए	𐬉, 𐬇	𐭩	..	..	ֵ	ê
16 Diphthongus gutturo-palatalis	âi	(ai)	....	ऐ	....	...	َي	َي	...	âi
17 ,, ,,	ei (ĕi)	...	....	...	....	...	...	...	...	ei, êi
18 ,, ,,	oi (ŏu)	...	....	...	....	...	...	...	...	...
19 Gutturo-labialis brevis	o	...	....	...	𐬊	...	...	...	ָ	o
20 ,, longa	ô (au)	(o)	....	ओ	𐬋	𐭥	..	..	וֹ	...
21 Diphthongus gutturo-labialis	âu	(au)	....	औ	𐬈𐬎 (*au*)	...	َو	َو	...	âu
22 ,, ,,	eu (ĕu)	...	....	...	....	...	...	...	...	...
23 ,, ,,	ou (ŏu)	...	....	...	....	...	...	...	...	...
24 Gutturalis fracta	ä	...	....	...	....	...	...	...	...	...
25 Palatalis fracta	ï	...	....	...	....	...	...	...	...	...
26 Labialis fracta	ü	...	....	...	....	...	...	...	...	ü
27 Gutturo-labialis fracta	ö	...	....	...	....	...	...	...	...	...

A CATALOGUE

OF

Clarendon Press Publications.

Contents.

14/4/97.

Clarendon Press, Oxford.

I. LITERATURE AND PHILOLOGY.

SECTION I.

DICTIONARIES, GRAMMARS, &c.

ANGLO-SAXON. An Anglo-Saxon Dictionary, based on the MS. Collections of the late JOSEPH BOSWORTH, D.D., Professor of Anglo-Saxon, Oxford. Edited and enlarged by Prof. T. N. TOLLER, M.A.

Parts I–III. A–SÁR. 4to, stiff covers, 15*s*. each.

Part IV. Sect. I. SÁR–SWÍÐRIAN. 8*s*. 6*d*.

—— The Student's Dictionary of Anglo-Saxon. By H. SWEET, M.A., Ph.D., LL.D., small 4to, 8*s*. 6*d*. *net*.

ARABIC. A Practical Arabic Grammar. Compiled by A. O. GREEN, Lieut.-Colonel, R.E.

Part I. *Third Edition. Enlarged.* Crown 8vo, 7*s*. 6*d*.

Part II. *Third Edition. Enlarged and Revised.* 10*s*. 6*d*.

BENGALI. Grammar of the Bengali Language; Literary and Colloquial. By JOHN BEAMES. Crown 8vo, cloth, 7*s*. 6*d*.; cut flush, 6*s*.

BURMESE. A Burmese Reader. By R. F. St. Andrew St. John, Hon. M.A. Crown 8vo, 10s. 6d.

CELTIC. Ancient Cornish Drama. Edited and translated by E. Norris, with a Sketch of Cornish Grammar, an Ancient Cornish Vocabulary, &c. 2 vols. 8vo, 1l. 1s.

The Sketch of Cornish Grammar separately, stitched, 2s. 6d.

CHINESE. A Handbook of the Chinese Language. By James Summers. 8vo, half-bound, 1l. 8s.

ENGLISH. **A NEW ENGLISH DICTIONARY, on Historical Principles**: founded mainly on the materials collected by the Philological Society. Imperial 4to.

					£	s.	d.
Vol.	I.	A, B	Edited by Dr. Murray	Half-morocco	2	12	6
Vol.	II.	C	Edited by Dr. Murray	Half-morocco	2	12	6

*** See also page 6.

FINNISH. A Finnish Grammar. By C. N. E. Eliot, M.A. Crown 8vo, roan, 10s. 6d.

GOTHIC. A Primer of the Gothic Language; with Grammar, Notes, and Glossary. By Joseph Wright, Ph.D. Extra fcap. 8vo, cloth, 4s. 6d.

GREEK. A Greek-English Lexicon, by H. G. Liddell, D.D., and Robert Scott, D.D. *Seventh Edition, Revised and Augmented throughout.* 4to, 1l. 16s.

—— An Intermediate Greek-English Lexicon, founded upon the Seventh Edition of the above. Small 4to, 12s. 6d.

—— A Greek-English Lexicon, abridged from Liddell and Scott's 4to edition, chiefly for the use of Schools. *Twenty-fifth Edition.* Square 12mo, 7s. 6d.

—— **A Concordance to the Septuagint** and the other Greek Versions of the Old Testament (including the Apocryphal Books). By the late Edwin Hatch, M.A., and Henry Redpath, M.A. In six Parts. Imperial 4to, *each* 21s.

GREEK (*continued*). A copious Greek-English Vocabulary, compiled from the best authorities. 24mo, 3*s*.

—— **Etymologicon Magnum.** Ad Codd. mss. recensuit et notis variorum instruxit T. GAISFORD, S.T.P. 1848. fol. 1*l*. 12*s*.

—— **Suidae Lexicon.** Ad Codd. mss. recensuit T. GAISFORD, S.T.P. Tomi III. 1834. fol. 2*l*. 2*s*.

HEBREW. A Hebrew and English Lexicon of the Old Testament, with an Appendix containing the Biblical Aramaic, based on the Thesaurus and Lexicon of GESENIUS, by FRANCIS BROWN, D.D., S. R. DRIVER, D.D., and C. A. BRIGGS, D.D. Parts I—V. Small 4to, 2*s*. 6*d*. *each*. Part VI. [*In the Press.*]

—— The Book of Hebrew Roots, by ABU 'L-WALÎD MARWÂN IBN JANÂH, otherwise called RABBÎ YÔNÂH. Now first edited, with an Appendix, by AD. NEUBAUER. 4to, 2*l*. 7*s*. 6*d*.

—— A Treatise on the use of the Tenses in Hebrew. By S. R. DRIVER, D.D. *Third Edition.* Crown 8vo, 7*s*. 6*d*.

HINDŪSTĀNĪ. A Hindūstānī Grammar. By A. O. GREEN, Lieut.-Colonel, R.E.

Part I. Crown 8vo, cloth, price 8*s*. 6*d*. Part II. 7*s*. 6*d*.

ICELANDIC. An Icelandic-English Dictionary, based on the MS. collections of the late RICHARD CLEASBY. Enlarged and completed by G. VIGFÚSSON, M.A. 4to, 3*l*. 7*s*.

—— A List of English Words the Etymology of which is illustrated by comparison with Icelandic. Prepared in the form of an Appendix to the above. By W. W. SKEAT, Litt.D. Stitched, 2*s*.

—— An Icelandic Primer, with Grammar, Notes, and Glossary. By HENRY SWEET, M.A., Ph.D. *Second Edition.* Extra fcap. 8vo, 3*s*. 6*d*.

—— An Icelandic Prose Reader, with Notes, Grammar, and Glossary, by Dr. GUÐBRAND VIGFÚSSON and F. YORK POWELL, M.A. Extra fcap. 8vo, 10*s*. 6*d*.

LATIN. A Latin Dictionary, founded on Andrews' edition of Freund's Latin Dictionary, revised, enlarged, and in great part rewritten by CHARLTON T. LEWIS, Ph.D., and CHARLES SHORT, LL.D. 4to, 1*l*. 5*s*.

LATIN (*continued*). A School Latin Dictionary. By CHARLTON T. LEWIS, Ph.D. Small 4to, 18s.

—— An Elementary Latin Dictionary. By CHARLTON T. LEWIS, Ph.D. Square 8vo, 7s. 6d.

—— Scheller's Dictionary of the Latin Language, revised and translated into English by J. E. RIDDLE, M.A. 1835. fol. 1l. 1s.

—— Contributions to Latin Lexicography. By HENRY NETTLESHIP, M.A. 8vo, 21s.

MELANESIAN. The Melanesian Languages. By ROBERT H. CODRINGTON, D.D., of the Melanesian Mission. 8vo, 18s.

RUSSIAN. A Grammar of the Russian Language. By W. R. MORFILL, M.A. Crown 8vo, 6s.

SANSKRIT. A Practical Grammar of the Sanskrit Language, arranged with reference to the Classical Languages of Europe, for the use of English Students, by Sir M. MONIER-WILLIAMS, D.C.L. *Fourth Edition.* 8vo, 15s.

—— A Sanskrit-English Dictionary, Etymologically and Philologically arranged, with special reference to Greek, Latin, German, Anglo-Saxon, English, and other cognate Indo-European Languages. By Sir M. MONIER-WILLIAMS, D.C.L. 4to, 4l. 14s. 6d.

—— Nalopákhyánam. Story of Nala, an Episode of the Mahá-Bhárata: the Sanskrit text, with a copious Vocabulary, and an improved version of Dean MILMAN'S Translation, by Sir M. MONIER-WILLIAMS, D.C.L. *Second Edition, Revised and Improved.* 8vo, 15s.

—— Sakuntalā. A Sanskrit Drama, in Seven Acts. Edited by Sir M. MONIER-WILLIAMS, D.C.L. *Second Edition.* 8vo, 21s.

SWAHILI. English-Swahili Dictionary. By A. C. MADAN, M.A. Extra fcap. 8vo, 7s. 6d. *net.*

SYRIAC. Thesaurus Syriacus: collegerunt Quatremère, Bernstein, Lorsbach, Arnoldi, Agrell, Field, Roediger: edidit R. PAYNE SMITH, S.T.P.

Vol. I, containing Fasciculi I–V, sm. fol., 5l. 5s.

The First Five Fasciculi may also be had separately.

Fasc. VI, 1l. 1s.; VII, 1l. 11s. 6d.; VIII, 1l. 16s.; IX, 1l. 5s.

—— Compendious Syriac Dictionary. Founded upon the above, and edited by J. PAYNE SMITH (Mrs. MARGOLIOUTH). Part I, 8s. 6d. *net.*

TAMIL. First Lessons in Tamil. By G. U. POPE, D.D. *Fifth Edition.* Crown 8vo, 7*s.* 6*d.*

—— The First Catechism of Tamil Grammar. By G. U. POPE, D.D., with an English Translation by D. S. HERRICK, B.A. Crown 8vo, 3*s.*

BIBLIOGRAPHICAL WORKS.

Cotton's Typographical Gazetteer. 1831. 8vo, 12*s.* 6*d.*

—— Typographical Gazetteer. Second Series. 1866. 8vo, 12*s.* 6*d.*

Dowling (J. G.). Notitia Scriptorum SS. Patrum aliorumque vet. Eccles. Mon. quae in Collectionibus Anecdotorum post annum Christi MDCC. in lucem editis continentur. 8vo, 4*s.* 6*d.*

Ebert's Bibliographical Dictionary, translated from the German. 4 vols. 1837. 8vo, 1*l.* 10*s.*

The Early Oxford Press. A Bibliography of Printing and Publishing at Oxford, '1468'–1640. With Notes, Appendices, and Illustrations. By FALCONER MADAN, M.A. Demy 8vo, cloth, 18*s.*

SECTION II.

ANGLO-SAXON AND ENGLISH.

HELPS TO THE STUDY OF THE LANGUAGE AND LITERATURE.

A NEW ENGLISH DICTIONARY on Historical Principles, founded mainly on the materials collected by the Philological Society. Imperial 4to.

PRESENT STATE OF THE WORK.

Vol.	Letter	Editor	Part / Binding	£	s.	d.
Vol. I.	A, B	Edited by Dr. Murray	Half-morocco	2	12	6
Vol. II.	C	Edited by Dr. Murray	Half-morocco	2	12	6
Vol. III.	D	Edited by Dr. Murray	D–Depravation	0	8	6
			Depravative–Distrustful	0	12	6
			Distrustfully–Doom	0	2	6
		(The remainder of the Letter D *is far advanced.)*				
	E	Edited by Henry Bradley	E–Every	0	12	6
			Everybody–Ezod	0	5	0
Vol. IV.	F	Edited by Henry Bradley	F–Field	0	7	6
			Field–Fish	0	2	6
			Fish–Flexuose	0	2	6
			Flexuosity–Foister	0	2	6
		(The remainder of the Letter F *is far advanced.)*				
	G	To be edited by Henry Bradley.	*In Preparation.*			

*** One Section at least, consisting of Sixty-four Pages, is now published Quarterly at Half-a-Crown.

The Dictionary is also, as heretofore, issued in the original Parts, of which the following are already published:—

Series	Part	Contents		£	s.	d.
Series I.	Parts I–VII.	A–Crouching	*each*	0	12	6
,,	Part VIII.	Crouchmas–Depravation		0	12	6
,	Part IX.	Depravative–Distrustful		0	12	6
Series II.	Part I.	E–Every		0	12	6
,,	Part II.	Everybody–Field		0	12	6

Bosworth and Toller. An Anglo-Saxon Dictionary, based on the MS. collections of the late JOSEPH BOSWORTH, D.D. Edited and enlarged by Prof. T. N. TOLLER, M.A. Parts I-III. A-SÁR. 4to, stiff covers, 15*s*. each. Part IV. Sect. I. SÁR-SWÍÐRIAN. 8*s*. 6*d*.

Earle. A Book for the Beginner in Anglo-Saxon. By JOHN EARLE, M.A. *Third Edition.* Extra fcap. 8vo, 2*s*. 6*d*.

—— The Philology of the English Tongue. *Fifth Edition, Newly Revised.* Extra fcap. 8vo, 8*s*. 6*d*.

Mayhew. Synopsis of Old English Phonology. By A. L. MAYHEW, M.A. Extra fcap. 8vo, bevelled boards, 8*s*. 6*d*.

Mayhew and Skeat. A Concise Dictionary of Middle English, from A.D. 1150 to 1580. By A. L. MAYHEW, M.A., and W. W. SKEAT, Litt.D. Crown 8vo, half-roan, 7*s*. 6*d*.

Skeat. An Etymological Dictionary of the English Language, arranged on an Historical Basis. By W. W. SKEAT, Litt.D. *Second Edition.* 4to, 2*l*. 4*s*.

A Supplement to the First Edition of the above. 4to, 2*s*. 6*d*.

—— A Concise Etymological Dictionary of the English Language. *Sixth Edition.* Crown 8vo, 5*s*. 6*d*.

—— Principles of English Etymology. First Series. *The Native Element. Second Edition.* Crown 8vo, 10*s*. 6*d*.

—— Principles of English Etymology. Second Series. *The Foreign Element.* Crown 8vo, 10*s*. 6*d*.

—— A Primer of English Etymology. *Second and Revised Edition.* Extra fcap. 8vo, stiff covers, 1*s*. 6*d*.

—— A Student's Pastime: being a select series of Articles reprinted from 'Notes and Queries.' Crown 8vo, 7*s*. 6*d*. *net.*

—— Twelve Facsimiles of Old English Manuscripts, with Transcriptions and an Introduction. 4to, paper covers, 7*s*. 6*d*.

Stratmann. A Middle English Dictionary, containing Words used by English Writers from the Twelfth to the Fifteenth Century. By FRANCIS HENRY STRATMANN. *A New Edition*, Re-arranged, Revised, and Enlarged by HENRY BRADLEY, M.A. Small 4to, half-morocco, 1*l*. 11*s*. 6*d*.

Sweet. A New English Grammar, Logical and Historical. Part I. Introduction, Phonology, and Accidence. By HENRY SWEET, M.A. Crown 8vo, 10*s*. 6*d*.

—— A Short Historical English Grammar. Extra fcap. 8vo, 4*s*. 6*d*.

—— A Primer of Historical English Grammar. Extra fcap. 8vo, 2*s*.

—— History of English Sounds from the Earliest Period. With full Word-Lists. 8vo, 14*s*.

—— The Student's Dictionary of Anglo-Saxon. Small 4to, 8*s*. 6*d*. *net*.

—— An Anglo-Saxon Primer, with Grammar, Notes, and Glossary. *Seventh Edition*. Extra fcap. 8vo, 2*s*. 6*d*.

—— An Anglo-Saxon Reader. In Prose and Verse. With Grammatical Introduction, Notes, and Glossary. *Seventh Edition, Revised and Enlarged*. Crown 8vo. 9*s*. 6*d*.

—— A Second Anglo-Saxon Reader. Extra fcap. 8vo, 4*s*. 6*d*.

—— Old English Reading Primers:

I. Selected Homilies of Ælfric. *Second Edition*, 2*s*.

II. Extracts from Alfred's Orosius. *Second Edition*, 2*s*.

—— First Middle English Primer, with Grammar and Glossary. *Second Edition*. Extra fcap. 8vo, 2*s*. 6*d*.

—— Second Middle English Primer. Extracts from Chaucer, with Grammar and Glossary. *Second Edition*. Extra fcap. 8vo, 2*s*. 6*d*.

—— Elementarbuch des Gesprochenen Englisch. Grammatik, Texte und Glossar. *Third Edition*. Extra fcap. 8vo, stiff covers, 2*s*. 6*d*.

—— A Primer of Spoken English. *Second Edition, Revised*. Extra fcap. 8vo, 3*s*. 6*d*.

—— An Icelandic Primer, with Grammar, Notes and Glossary. *Second Edition*. Extra fcap. 8vo, 3*s*. 6*d*.

—— A Primer of Phonetics. Extra fcap. 8vo, 3*s*. 6*d*.

—— A Manual of Current Shorthand, Orthographic and Phonetic. Crown 8vo, 4*s*. 6*d*.

Tancock. An Elementary English Grammar and Exercise Book. By O. W. TANCOCK, M.A. *Third Edition.* Extra fcap. 8vo, 1s. 6d.

—— An English Grammar and Reading Book, for Lower Forms in Classical Schools. *Fourth Edition.* Extra fcap. 8vo, 3s. 6d.

Saxon Chronicles. Two of the Saxon Chronicles Parallel; with Supplementary Extracts from the others. A Revised Text. Edited, with Introduction, Notes, Appendices, and Glossary, by C. PLUMMER, M.A., and J. EARLE, M.A. Vol. I. Text, Appendices, and Glossary. 10s. 6d.

—— —— (787–1001 A.D.) Crown 8vo, stiff covers, 3s.

Specimens of Early English. A New and Revised Edition. With Introduction, Notes, and Glossarial Index.

Part I. From Old English Homilies to King Horn (A.D. 1150 to A.D. 1300). By R. MORRIS, LL.D. *Second Edition.* Extra fcap. 8vo, 9s.

Part II. From Robert of Gloucester to Gower (A.D. 1298 to A.D. 1393). By R. MORRIS, LL.D., and W. W. SKEAT, Litt.D. *Third Edition, Revised.* Extra fcap. 8vo, 7s. 6d.

Specimens of English Literature, from the 'Ploughman's Crede' to the 'Shepheardes Calender' (A.D. 1394 to A.D. 1579). With Introduction, Notes, and Glossarial Index. By W. W. SKEAT, Litt.D. *Fifth Edition.* Extra fcap. 8vo, 7s. 6d.

Typical Selections from the best English Writers, with Introductory Notices. In 2 vols. *Second Edition.* Extra fcap. 8vo, 3s. 6d. each.

Vol. I. Latimer to Berkeley. Vol. II. Pope to Macaulay.

A SERIES OF ENGLISH CLASSICS.

The Deeds of Beowulf. An English Epic of the Eighth Century done into Modern Prose. With an Introduction and Notes, by JOHN EARLE, M.A. Crown 8vo, 8*s.* 6*d.*

The Gospel of St. Luke in Anglo-Saxon. Edited from the MSS. With Introduction, Notes, and Glossary. By JAMES W. BRIGHT, Ph.D. Extra fcap. 8vo, 5*s.*

The Ormulum, with the Notes and Glossary of Dr. R. M. WHITE. Edited by R. HOLT, M.A. 2 vols. Extra fcap. 8vo, 1*l.* 1*s.*

CHAUCER.

The Complete Works of Geoffrey Chaucer. Edited, from numerous Manuscripts, by W. W. SKEAT, Litt.D. In Six Volumes, demy 8vo, with Portrait and Facsimiles. Price 4*l.* 16*s.*, or 16*s.* each volume.

Chaucerian and other Pieces. Edited from numerous Manuscripts, by W. W. SKEAT, Litt.D. Price to Subscribers, 12*s.* [*Nearly ready.*

The Prologue to the Canterbury Tales. (School Edition.) Edited by W. W. SKEAT, Litt.D. Extra fcap. 8vo, 1*s.*

The Prologue, the Knightes Tale, The Nonne Preestes Tale; from the Canterbury Tales. Edited by R. MORRIS, LL.D. A New Edition, with Collations and Additional Notes by W. W. SKEAT, Litt.D. Extra fcap. 8vo, 2*s.* 6*d.*

The Prioresses Tale; Sir Thopas; The Monkes Tale; The Clerkes Tale; The Squieres Tale, &c. Edited by W. W. SKEAT, Litt.D. *Fifth Edition.* Extra fcap. 8vo, 4*s.* 6*d.*

The Tale of the Man of Lawe; The Pardoneres Tale; The Second Nonnes Tale; The Chanouns Yemannes Tale. By W. W. SKEAT, Litt.D. *New Edition.* Extra fcap. 8vo, 4*s.* 6*d.*

Minor Poems. Edited by W. W. SKEAT, Litt.D. *Second Edition.* Crown 8vo, 10*s.* 6*d.*

The Hous of Fame. Edited by W. W. SKEAT, Litt.D. Crown 8vo, paper boards, 2*s.*

The Legend of Good Women. Edited by W. W. SKEAT, Litt.D. Crown 8vo, 6*s.*

CHAUCER (*continued*).

The Student's Chaucer. Being a complete Edition of his Works, edited from numerous MSS., with Introduction and Glossary, by W. W. SKEAT, Litt.D. In one vol., crown 8vo, cloth, 7*s*. 6*d*.

The Oxford Chaucer. On India Paper, cloth extra, 9*s*. 6*d*.

LANGLAND (W.).

The Vision of William concerning Piers the Plowman, in three Parallel Texts; together with Richard the Redeless. By WILLIAM LANGLAND (about 1362–1399 A.D.). Edited from numerous Manuscripts, with Preface, Notes, and a Glossary, by W. W. SKEAT, Litt.D. 2 vols. 8vo, 1*l*. 11*s*. 6*d*.

—— The Vision of William concerning Piers the Plowman, by WILLIAM LANGLAND. Edited, with Notes, by W. W. SKEAT, Litt.D. *Sixth Edition.* Extra fcap. 8vo, 4*s*. 6*d*.

Gamelyn, The Tale of. Edited, with Notes, Glossary, &c., by W. W. SKEAT, Litt.D. *Second Edition, Revised.* Extra fcap. 8vo, stiff covers, 1*s*. 6*d*.

Wycliffe.

The Books of Job, Psalms, Proverbs, Ecclesiastes, and the Song of Solomon: according to the Wycliffite Version made by NICHOLAS DE HEREFORD, about A.D. 1381, and Revised by JOHN PURVEY, about A.D. 1388. With Introduction and Glossary by W. W. SKEAT, Litt.D. Extra fcap. 8vo, 3*s*. 6*d*.

The New Testament in English, according to the Version by JOHN WYCLIFFE, about A.D. 1380, and Revised by JOHN PURVEY, about A.D. 1388. With Introduction and Glossary by W. W. SKEAT, Litt.D. Extra fcap. 8vo, 6*s*.

Minot (Laurence). Poems. Edited, with Introduction and Notes, by JOSEPH HALL, M.A. *Second Edition.* Extra fcap. 8vo, 4*s*. 6*d*.

Spenser's Faery Queene. Books I and II. Designed chiefly for the use of Schools. With Introduction and Notes by G. W. KITCHIN, D.D., and Glossary by A. L. MAYHEW, M.A. Extra fcap. 8vo, 2*s*. 6*d*. each.

Hooker. Ecclesiastical Polity, Book I. Edited by R. W. CHURCH, M.A. Extra fcap. 8vo, 2*s*. [See also p. 65.]

OLD ENGLISH DRAMA.

York Plays. The Plays performed by the Crafts or Mysteries of York, on the day of Corpus Christi, in the 14th, 15th, and 16th centuries; now first printed from the unique manuscript in the library of Lord Ashburnham. Edited, with Introduction and Glossary, by LUCY TOULMIN SMITH. 8vo, 1*l.* 1*s.*

English Miracle Plays, Moralities, and Interludes. Specimens of the Pre-Elizabethan Drama. Edited, with an Introduction, Notes, and Glossary, by ALFRED W. POLLARD, M.A. *Second Edition.* Crown 8vo, 7*s.* 6*d.*

The Pilgrimage to Parnassus, with the Two Parts of the Return from Parnassus. Three Comedies performed in St. John's College, Cambridge, A.D. MDXCVII–MDCI. Edited from MSS. by W. D. MACRAY, M.A., F.S.A. Medium 8vo, bevelled boards, gilt top, 8*s.* 6*d.*

Marlowe's Edward II. With Introduction, Notes, &c. By O. W. TANCOCK, M.A. *Second Edition.* Extra fcap. 8vo, stiff covers, 2*s.*; cloth, 3*s.*

Marlowe and Greene. Marlowe's Tragical History of Dr. Faustus, and Greene's Honourable History of Friar Bacon and Friar Bungay. Edited by A. W. WARD, Litt. D. *New and Enlarged Edition.* Crown 8vo, 6*s.* 6*d.*

SHAKESPEARE. Select Plays. Extra fcap. 8vo, stiff covers.

Edited by W. G. CLARK, M.A., and W. ALDIS WRIGHT, D.C.L.

The Merchant of Venice. 1*s.* — Macbeth. 1*s.* 6*d.*
Richard the Second. 1*s.* 6*d.* — Hamlet. 2*s.*

Edited by W. ALDIS WRIGHT, D.C.L.

The Tempest. 1*s.* 6*d.* — Midsummer Night's Dream. 1*s.* 6*d.*
As You Like It. 1*s.* 6*d.* — Coriolanus. 2*s.* 6*d.*
Julius Caesar. 2*s.* — Henry the Fifth. 2*s.*
Richard the Third. 2*s.* 6*d.* — Twelfth Night. 1*s.* 6*d.*
King Lear. 1*s.* 6*d.* — King John. 1*s.* 6*d.*
Henry the Eighth. 2*s.* — Much Ado about Nothing. 1*s.* 6*d.*

Shakespeare as a Dramatic Artist; a popular Illustration of the Principles of Scientific Criticism. By R. G. MOULTON, M.A. *Third Edition, Enlarged.* Crown 8vo, 7*s.* 6*d.*

Bacon.

Advancement of Learning. Edited by W. ALDIS WRIGHT, D.C.L. *Third Edition.* Extra fcap. 8vo, 4*s.* 6*d.*

The Essays. Edited, with Introduction and Illustrative Notes, by S. H. REYNOLDS, M.A. 8vo, half-bound, 12*s.* 6*d.*

MILTON.

Areopagitica. With Introduction and Notes. By JOHN W. HALES, M.A. *Third Edition.* Extra fcap. 8vo, 3*s.*

Poems. Edited by R. C. BROWNE, M.A. In two Volumes. *New Edition, Revised.* Extra fcap. 8vo, 6*s.* 6*d.*

Sold separately, Vol. I, 4*s.*; Vol. II, 3*s.*

In paper covers:

Lycidas, 3*d.* Comus, 6*d.*

Edited with Notes, by O. ELTON, B.A.

Lycidas, 6*d.* L'Allegro, 4*d.* Il Penseroso, 4*d.* Comus, 1*s.*

Paradise Lost. Book I. Edited by H. C. BEECHING, M.A. Extra fcap. 8vo, stiff covers, 1*s.* 6*d.*; in Parchment, 3*s.* 6*d.*

Paradise Lost. Book II. Edited by E. K. CHAMBERS, B.A. Extra fcap. 8vo, 1*s.* 6*d.*

Books I and II combined, 2*s.* 6*d.*

Samson Agonistes. Edited, with Introduction and Notes, by J. CHURTON COLLINS, M.A. Extra fcap. 8vo, stiff covers, 1*s.*

Milton's Prosody. By ROBERT BRIDGES. Extra fcap. 8vo, stiff covers, 1*s.* 6*d.*

Bunyan.

The Pilgrim's Progress, Grace Abounding, Relation of the Imprisonment of Mr. JOHN BUNYAN. Edited, with Biographical Introduction and Notes, by E. VENABLES, M.A. Extra fcap. 8vo, cloth, 3*s.* 6*d.*

The Holy War, and The Heavenly Footman. Edited by MABEL PEACOCK. Extra fcap. 8vo, 3*s.* 6*d.*

Fuller. Wise Words and Quaint Counsels of Thomas Fuller. Selected by AUGUSTUS JESSOPP, D.D. Crown 8vo, 6*s.*

Clarendon.

History of the Rebellion. Book VI. Edited by T. ARNOLD, M.A. *Second Edition.* Crown 8vo, 5s.

Characters and Episodes of the Great Rebellion. Selections from Clarendon. Edited by G. BOYLE, M.A., Dean of Salisbury. Crown 8vo, gilt top, 7s. 6d. [See also p. 67.]

Dryden. Select Poems. (Stanzas on the Death of Oliver Cromwell; Astraea Redux; Annus Mirabilis; Absalom and Achitophel; Religio Laici; The Hind and the Panther.) Edited by W. D. CHRISTIE, M.A. *Fifth Edition.* Revised by C. H. FIRTH, M.A. Extra fcap. 8vo, 3s. 6d.

—— An Essay of Dramatic Poesy. Edited, with Notes, by THOMAS ARNOLD, M.A. *Second Edition.* Extra fcap. 8vo, 3s. 6d.

Locke. Conduct of the Understanding. Edited, with Introduction, Notes, &c., by T. FOWLER, D.D. *Third Edition.* Extra fcap. 8vo, 2s. 6d.

Addison. Selections from Papers in the Spectator. With Notes. By T. ARNOLD, M.A. Extra fcap. 8vo, 4s. 6d.

Steele. Selections from the Tatler, Spectator, and Guardian. Edited by AUSTIN DOBSON. *Second Edition.* Crown 8vo, 7s. 6d.

Swift. Selections from his Works. Edited, with Life, Introductions, and Notes, by HENRY CRAIK. Two Vols. Crown 8vo, cloth extra, 15s.

Each volume may be had separately, price 7s. 6d.

Pope. Select Works. With Introduction and Notes. By MARK PATTISON, B.D.

Essay on Man. *Sixth Edition.* Extra fcap. 8vo, 1s. 6d.

Satires and Epistles. *Fourth Edition.* Extra fcap. 8vo, 2s.

Parnell. The Hermit. Paper covers, 2d.

Thomson. The Seasons, and The Castle of Indolence. Edited by J. LOGIE ROBERTSON, M.A. Extra fcap. 8vo, 4s. 6d.

—— The Castle of Indolence. By the same Editor. Extra fcap. 8vo, 1s. 6d.

Gray. Selected Poems. Edited by EDMUND GOSSE, M.A. Extra fcap. 8vo. In Parchment, 3s.

Gray. *The same*, together with Supplementary Notes for Schools, by FOSTER WATSON, M.A. Stiff covers, 1*s*. 6*d*.

—— Elegy, and Ode on Eton College. Paper covers, 2*d*.

Chesterfield. Lord Chesterfield's Worldly Wisdom. Selections from his Letters and Characters. Edited by G. BIRKBECK HILL, D.C.L. Crown 8vo, 6*s*.

Goldsmith.

Selected Poems. Edited, with Introduction and Notes, by AUSTIN DOBSON. Extra fcap. 8vo, 3*s*. 6*d*.

The Traveller. Edited by G. BIRKBECK HILL, D.C.L. Stiff covers, 1*s*.

The Deserted Village. Paper covers, 2*d*.

JOHNSON.

Rasselas. Edited, with Introduction and Notes, by G. BIRKBECK HILL, D.C.L. Extra fcap. 8vo, bevelled boards, 3*s*. 6*d*.; in Parchment, 4*s*. 6*d*.

Rasselas; Lives of Dryden and Pope. Edited by ALFRED MILNES, M.A. (London). Extra fcap. 8vo, 4*s*. 6*d*.; or Lives of DRYDEN and POPE only, stiff covers, 2*s*. 6*d*.

Life of Milton. Edited by C. H. FIRTH, M.A. Extra fcap. 8vo, cloth, 2*s*. 6*d*.; stiff covers, 1*s*. 6*d*.

Wit and Wisdom of Samuel Johnson. Edited by G. BIRKBECK HILL, D.C.L. Crown 8vo, 7*s*. 6*d*.

Vanity of Human Wishes. With Notes, by E. J. PAYNE, M.A. Paper covers, 4*d*.

Boswell's Letters of Samuel Johnson, LL.D. Collected and Edited by G. BIRKBECK HILL, D.C.L. 2 vols. Medium 8vo, half-roan, 28*s*.

Boswell's Life of Johnson. With the Journal of a Tour to the Hebrides. Edited by G. BIRKBECK HILL, D.C.L., Pembroke College. 6 vols. Medium 8vo, half-bound, 3*l*. 3*s*.

Cowper. Edited, with Life, Introductions, and Notes, by H. T. GRIFFITH, B.A.

I. The Didactic Poems of 1782, with Selections from the Minor Pieces, A.D. 1779–1783. Extra fcap. 8vo, 3*s*.

II. The Task, with Tirocinium, and Selections from the Minor Poems, A.D. 1784–1799. *Third Edition.* Extra fcap. 8vo, 3*s*.

Burke. Select Works. Edited, with Introduction and Notes, by E. J. PAYNE, M.A.

I. Thoughts on the Present Discontents; the two Speeches on America. *Second Edition.* Extra fcap. 8vo, 4*s*. 6*d*.

II. Reflections on the French Revolution. *Second Edition.* Extra fcap. 8vo, 5*s*.

III. Four Letters on the Proposals for Peace with the Regicide Directory of France. *Second Edition.* Extra fcap. 8vo, 5*s*.

Burns. Selected Poems. Edited, with Introduction, Notes, and a Glossary, by J. LOGIE ROBERTSON, M.A. Crown 8vo, 6*s*.

Keats. Hyperion, Book I. With Notes by W. T. ARNOLD, B.A. Paper covers, 4*d*.

Byron. Childe Harold. With Introduction and Notes, by H. F. TOZER, M.A. *Third Edition.* Extra fcap. 8vo, 3*s*. 6*d*.; in Parchment, 5*s*.

Scott. Lady of the Lake. Edited, with Preface and Notes, by W. MINTO, M.A. Extra fcap. 8vo, 3*s*. 6*d*.

—— Lay of the Last Minstrel. By the same Editor. With Map. *Second Edition.* Extra fcap. 8vo, 2*s*.; in Parchment, 3*s*. 6*d*.

—— Lay of the Last Minstrel. Introduction and Canto I, with Preface and Notes, by the same Editor. 6*d*.

—— Lord of the Isles. Edited, with Introduction and Notes, by THOMAS BAYNE. Extra fcap. 8vo, 3*s*. 6*d*.

—— Marmion. Edited, with Introduction and Notes, by T. BAYNE. Extra fcap. 8vo, 3*s*. 6*d*.

—— The Talisman. Edited by H. B. GEORGE, M.A. Extra fcap. 8vo, stiff covers, 2*s*.

Shelley. Adonais. Edited, with Introduction and Notes, by W. M. ROSSETTI. Crown 8vo, 5*s*.

Campbell. Gertrude of Wyoming. Edited, with Introduction and Notes, by H. MACAULAY FITZGIBBON, M.A. *Second Edition.* Extra fcap. 8vo, 1*s*.

Wordsworth. The White Doe of Rylstone, &c. Edited by WILLIAM KNIGHT, LL.D. Extra fcap. 8vo, 2*s*. 6*d*.

Palgrave. The Treasury of Sacred Song. With Notes Explanatory and Biographical. By F. T. PALGRAVE, M.A. *Thirteenth Thousand.* Extra fcap. 8vo, 4*s*. 6*d*.

SECTION III.

EUROPEAN LANGUAGES, MEDIAEVAL AND MODERN.

(1) FRENCH, ITALIAN, AND SPANISH.

Brachet's Etymological Dictionary of the French Language. Translated by G. W. KITCHIN, D.D. *Third Edition.* Crown 8vo, 7*s*. 6*d*.

—— Historical Grammar of the French Language. Translated by G. W. KITCHIN, D.D. *Seventh Edition.* Extra fcap. 8vo, 3*s*. 6*d*.

Brachet and Toynbee. A Historical Grammar of the French Language. From the French of Auguste Brachet. Rewritten and Enlarged by PAGET TOYNBEE, M.A. Crown 8vo, 7*s*. 6*d*.

Saintsbury. Primer of French Literature. By GEORGE SAINTSBURY, M.A. *Fourth Edition, Revised.* Extra fcap. 8vo, 2*s*.

—— Short History of French Literature. *Fourth Edition.* Crown 8vo, 10*s*. 6*d*.

—— Specimens of French Literature, from Villon to Hugo. *Second Edition.* Crown 8vo, 9*s*.

Cest Daucasin et de Nicolete. Reproduced in Photofacsimile and Type-transliteration from the unique MS. in the Bibliothèque Nationale at Paris, by the care of F. W. BOURDILLON, M.A. Small quarto, half-vellum, 24*s*. *net*.

Song of Dermot and the Earl. An Old French Poem. Edited, with Translation, Notes, &c., by G. H. ORPEN. Extra fcap. 8vo, 8*s*. 6*d*.

Toynbee. Specimens of Old French (ix–xv centuries). With Introduction, Notes, and Glossary. By PAGET TOYNBEE, M.A. Crown 8vo, 16*s*.

Beaumarchais' Le Barbier de Séville. Edited, with Introduction and Notes, by AUSTIN DOBSON. Extra fcap. 8vo, 2*s*. 6*d*.

Corneille's Horace. Edited, with Introduction and Notes, by GEORGE SAINTSBURY, M.A. Extra fcap. 8vo, 2*s*. 6*d*.

Molière's Les Précieuses Ridicules. Edited, with Introduction and Notes, by ANDREW LANG, M.A. *Second Edition.* Extra fcap. 8vo, 1*s*. 6*d*.

Musset's On ne badine pas avec l'Amour, and Fantasio. Edited, with Prolegomena, Notes, &c., by W. H. POLLOCK. Extra fcap. 8vo, 2*s*.

Racine's Esther. Edited, with Introduction and Notes, by GEORGE SAINTSBURY, M.A. Extra fcap. 8vo, 2*s*.

Voltaire's Mérope. Edited, with Introduction and Notes, by GEORGE SAINTSBURY, M.A. Extra fcap. 8vo, 2*s*.

*** *The above six Plays may be had in ornamental case, and bound in Imitation Parchment, price* 12*s*. 6*d*.

Molière. Le Misanthrope. Edited by H. W. G. MARKHEIM, M.A. Extra fcap. 8vo, 3*s*. 6*d*.

MASSON'S FRENCH CLASSICS.

Edited by Gustave Masson, B.A.

Corneille's Cinna. With Notes, Glossary, &c. Extra fcap. 8vo, 2*s*.; stiff covers, 1*s*. 6*d*.

Louis XIV and his Contemporaries; as described in Extracts from the best Memoirs of the Seventeenth Century. With English Notes, Genealogical Tables, &c. Extra fcap. 8vo, 2*s*. 6*d*.

Maistre, Xavier de, &c. Voyage autour de ma Chambre, by XAVIER DE MAISTRE; Ourika, by MADAME DE DURAS; Le Vieux Tailleur, by MM. ERCKMANN-CHATRIAN; La Veillée de Vincennes, by ALFRED DE VIGNY; Les Jumeaux de l'Hôtel Corneille, by EDMOND ABOUT; Mésaventures d'un Écolier, by RODOLPHE TÖPFFER. *Third Edition, Revised.* Extra fcap. 8vo, 2*s*. 6*d*.

—— Voyage autour de ma Chambre. Limp, 1*s*. 6*d*.

Molière's Les Fourberies de Scapin. With Voltaire's Life of Molière. Extra fcap. 8vo, stiff covers, 1*s*. 6*d*.

—— Les Femmes Savantes. With Notes, Glossary, &c. Extra fcap. 8vo, cloth, 2*s*.; stiff covers, 1*s*. 6*d*.

Regnard's Le Joueur, and **Brueys and Palaprat's** Le Grondeur. Extra fcap. 8vo, 2*s*. 6*d*.

Sévigné, Madame de, and her chief Contemporaries. Selections from their Correspondence. Extra fcap. 8vo, 3*s*.

Blouët. L'Éloquence de la Chaire et de la Tribune Françaises. Edited by PAUL BLOUËT, B.A. Vol. I. Sacred Oratory. Extra fcap. 8vo, 2*s*. 6*d*.

Gautier, Théophile. Scenes of Travel. Selected and Edited by GEORGE SAINTSBURY, M.A. *Second Edition.* Extra fcap. 8vo, 2*s*.

Perrault's Popular Tales. Edited from the Original Editions, with Introduction, &c., by A. LANG, M.A. Extra fcap. 8vo, 5*s*. 6*d*.

Quinet's Lettres à sa Mère. Selected and Edited by GEORGE SAINTSBURY, M.A. Extra fcap. 8vo, 2*s*.

Sainte-Beuve. Selections from the Causeries du Lundi. Edited by GEORGE SAINTSBURY, M.A. Extra fcap. 8vo, 2*s*.

A Primer of Italian Literature. By F. J. SNELL, M.A. Extra fcap. 8vo, 3*s*. 6*d*.

Dante. Tutte Le Opere di Dante Alighieri, nuovamente rivedute nel testo dal Dr. E. MOORE. Crown 8vo, 7*s*. 6*d*.

Also, an India Paper edition, cloth extra, 9*s*. 6*d*.; and Miniature edition, 3 vols., in case, 10*s*. 6*d*.

—— Studies in Dante. Series I. Scripture and Classical Authors in Dante. By E. MOORE, D.D. 8vo, cloth, 10*s*. 6*d*. *net*.

Dante. Selections from the Inferno. With Introduction and Notes. By H. B. COTTERILL, B.A. Extra fcap. 8vo, 4*s.* 6*d.*

Tasso. La Gerusalemme Liberata. Cantos i, ii. With Introduction and Notes. By the same Editor. Extra fcap. 8vo, 2*s.* 6*d.*

Cervantes. The Adventure of the Wooden Horse, and Sancho Panza's Governorship. Edited, with Introduction, Life and Notes, by CLOVIS BÉVENOT, M.A. Extra fcap. 8vo, 2*s.* 6*d.*

(2) GERMAN AND GOTHIC.

Max Müller. The German Classics, from the Fourth to the Nineteenth Century. With Biographical Notices, Translations into Modern German, and Notes. By the Right Hon. F. MAX MÜLLER, M.A. A New Edition, Revised, Enlarged, and Adapted to WILHELM SCHERER'S 'History of German Literature,' by F. LICHTENSTEIN. 2 vols. Crown 8vo, 21*s.*

Scherer. A History of German Literature by WILHELM SCHERER. Translated from the Third German Edition by Mrs. F. C. CONYBEARE. Edited by the Right Hon. F. MAX MÜLLER. 2 vols. 8vo, 21*s.*

Or, separately, 10*s.* 6*d.* each volume.

—— A History of German Literature, from the Accession of Frederick the Great to the Death of Goethe. By the same. Crown 8vo, 5*s.*

Wright. An Old High German Primer. With Grammar, Notes, and Glossary. By JOSEPH WRIGHT, Ph.D. Extra fcap. 8vo, 3*s.* 6*d.*

—— A Middle High German Primer. With Grammar, Notes, and Glossary. By the same Author. Extra fcap. 8vo, 3*s.* 6*d.*

—— A Primer of the Gothic Language. With Grammar, Notes, and Glossary. By the same Author. Extra fcap. 8vo, 4*s.* 6*d.*

LANGE'S GERMAN COURSE.

By HERMANN LANGE, Lecturer on French and German at the Manchester Technical School, and Lecturer on German at the Manchester Athenaeum.

I. **Germans at Home**; a Practical Introduction to German Conversation, with an Appendix containing the Essentials of German Grammar. *Third Edition.* 8vo, 2*s.* 6*d.*

II. **Grammar of the German Language.** 8vo, 3*s.* 6*d.*

III. **German Manual**; a German Grammar, Reading Book, and a Handbook of German Conversation. *Second Edition.* 8vo, 7*s.* 6*d.*

IV. **German Composition**; A Theoretical and Practical Guide to the Art of Translating English Prose into German. *Third Edition.* 8vo, 4*s.* 6*d.*

*** *A Key to the above,* price 5*s. net.*

German Spelling; A Synopsis of the Changes which it has undergone through the Government Regulations of 1880. 6*d.*

BUCHHEIM'S GERMAN CLASSICS.

Edited, with Biographical, Historical, and Critical Introductions, Arguments (to the Dramas), and Complete Commentaries, by C. A. BUCHHEIM, *Phil. Doc., Professor in King's College, London.*

Becker (the Historian). Friedrich der Grosse. Edited, with Notes, an Historical Introduction, and a Map. *Third Edition.* 3*s.* 6*d.*

Goethe:

(*a*) Egmont. A Tragedy. *Fourth Edition.* 3*s.*

(*b*) Dichtung und Wahrheit. The first four books. 4*s.* 6*d.*

(*c*) Iphigenie auf Tauris. A Drama. *Fourth Edition, revised.* 3*s.*

Halm: Griseldis. 3*s.*

Heine:

(*a*) Prosa: being Selections from his Prose Writings. *Second Edition.* 4*s.* 6*d.*

(*b*) Harzreise. With Map. *Third Edition.* 2*s.* 6*d.*

BUCHHEIM'S GERMAN CLASSICS (continued).

Lessing:

(*a*) Nathan der Weise. *Second Edition.* 4*s*. 6*d*.

(*b*) Minna von Barnhelm. A Comedy. *Seventh Edition.* 3*s*. 6*d*.

Schiller:

(*a*) Wilhelm Tell. A Drama. Large Edition. With Map. *Seventh Edition.* 3*s*. 6*d*.

(*b*) Wilhelm Tell. School Edition. With Map. *Fourth Edition.* 2*s*.

(*c*) Historische Skizzen. With Map. *Fifth Edition.* 2*s*. 6*d*.

(*d*) Jungfrau von Orleans. *Second Edition.* 4*s*. 6*d*.

(*e*) Maria Stuart. 3*s*. 6*d*.

Modern German Reader. A Graduated Collection of Extracts from Modern German Authors. Edited by C. A. BUCHHEIM, Phil. Doc.

Part I. **Prose Extracts.** With English Notes, a Grammatical Appendix, and a complete Vocabulary. *Seventh Edition.* 2*s*. 6*d*.

Part II. **Extracts in Prose and Poetry.** With English Notes and an Index. *Second Edition.* 2*s*. 6*d*.

German Poetry for Beginners. Edited, with English Notes and a complete Vocabulary, by EMMA S. BUCHHEIM. Extra fcap. 8vo, 2*s*.

Elementary German Prose Composition. With Notes, Vocabulary, &c. By the same Editor. Cloth, 2*s*.; stiff covers, 1*s*. 6*d*.

Short German Plays, for Reading and Acting. With Notes and Vocabulary. By the same Editor. Extra fcap. 8vo, cloth, 3*s*.

Chamisso. Peter Schlemihl's Wundersame Geschichte. Edited, with Notes and a complete Vocabulary, by EMMA S. BUCHHEIM. *Fourth Thousand.* Extra fcap. 8vo, 2*s*.

Hoffmann (Franz). Heute mir Morgen dir. Edited, with Notes, by J. H. MAUDE, M.A. Extra fcap. 8vo, 2*s*.

Lessing. The Laokoon; with English Notes by A. HAMANN, Phil. Doc., M.A. Revised, with an Introduction, by L. E. UPCOTT, M.A. Extra fcap. 8vo, 4*s*. 6*d*.

Niebuhr: Griechische Heroen-Geschichten (Tales of Greek Heroes). With English Notes and Vocabulary, by EMMA S. BUCHHEIM. Second Revised Edition. Extra fcap. 8vo, cloth, 2*s*.; stiff covers, 1*s*. 6*d*. Edition A. *Text in German Type.* Edition B. *Text in Roman Type.*

Riehl's Seines Vaters Sohn *and* Gespensterkampf. Edited, with Notes, by H. T. GERRANS, M.A. Extra fcap. 8vo, 2*s*.

Schiller's Wilhelm Tell. Translated into English Verse by E. MASSIE, M.A. Extra fcap. 8vo, 5*s*.

(3) SCANDINAVIAN.

Cleasby and Vigfússon. An Icelandic-English Dictionary. 4to, 3*l*. 7*s*.

Sargent. Grammar of the Dano-Norwegian Language. By J. Y. SARGENT, M.A. Crown 8vo, 7*s*. 6*d*.

Sweet. Icelandic Primer, with Grammar, Notes, and Glossary. By HENRY SWEET, M.A. *Second Edition.* Extra fcap. 8vo, 3*s*. 6*d*.

Vigfússon. Sturlunga Saga, including the Islendinga Saga of Lawman STURLA THORDSSON and other works. Edited by GUDBRAND VIGFÚSSON, M.A. In 2 vols. 8vo, 2*l*. 2*s*.

Vigfússon and Powell. Icelandic Prose Reader, with Notes, Grammar, and Glossary. By G. VIGFÚSSON, M.A., and F. YORK POWELL, M.A. Extra fcap. 8vo, 10*s*. 6*d*.

—— Corpvs Poeticvm Boreale. The Poetry of the Old Northern Tongue, from the Earliest Times to the Thirteenth Century. Edited, classified and translated by GUDBRAND VIGFÚSSON, M.A., and F. YORK POWELL, M.A. 2 vols. 8vo, 2*l*. 2*s*.

SECTION IV.

CLASSICAL LANGUAGES.

(1) LATIN.

STANDARD WORKS AND EDITIONS.

Ellis (Robinson). The Fables of Phaedrus. *1s. net.*

King and **Cookson.** The Principles of Sound and Inflexion, as illustrated in the Greek and Latin Languages. By J. E. KING, M.A., and CHRISTOPHER COOKSON, M.A. 8vo, *18s.*

Lewis and **Short.** A Latin Dictionary, founded on Andrews' edition of Freund's Latin Dictionary, revised, enlarged, and in great part rewritten by CHARLTON T. LEWIS, Ph.D., and CHARLES SHORT, LL.D. 4to, *1l. 5s.*

Lindsay. The Latin Language: An Historical Account of Latin Sounds, Stems, and Flexions. By W. M. LINDSAY, M.A. Demy 8vo, *21s.*

Merry. Selected Fragments of Roman Poetry. Edited, with Introduction and Notes, by W. W. MERRY, D.D. Crown 8vo, *6s. 6d.*

Nettleship. Contributions to Latin Lexicography. By HENRY NETTLESHIP, M.A. 8vo, *21s.*

—— Lectures and Essays on Subjects connected with Latin Scholarship and Literature. Crown 8vo, *7s. 6d.*

—— Lectures and Essays. *Second Series.* Edited by F. HAVERFIELD, M.A. With Portrait and Memoir. Crown 8vo, *7s. 6d.*

—— The Roman Satura. 8vo, sewed, *1s.*

—— Ancient Lives of Vergil. 8vo, sewed, *2s.*

Papillon. Manual of Comparative Philology. By T. L. PAPILLON, M.A. *Third Edition.* Crown 8vo, *6s.*

Pinder. Selections from the less known Latin Poets. By NORTH PINDER, M.A. 8vo, 15*s.*

Rushforth. Latin Historical Inscriptions, illustrating the History of the Early Empire. By G. McN. RUSHFORTH, M.A. 8vo, 10*s. net.*

Sellar. Roman Poets of the Republic. By W. Y. SELLAR, M.A. *Third Edition.* Crown 8vo, 10*s.*

—— Roman Poets of the Augustan Age. VIRGIL. *Second Edition.* Crown 8vo, 9*s.*

—— —— HORACE and the ELEGIAC POETS. With a Memoir of the Author by ANDREW LANG, M.A., and a Portrait. 8vo, cloth, 14*s.*

Wordsworth. Fragments and Specimens of Early Latin. With Introductions and Notes. By J. WORDSWORTH, D.D. 8vo, 18*s.*

Avianus. The Fables. Edited, with Prolegomena, Critical Apparatus, Commentary, &c., by R. ELLIS, M.A., LL.D. 8vo, 8*s.* 6*d.*

Catulli Veronensis Liber. Iterum recognovit, apparatum criticum prolegomena appendices addidit, ROBINSON ELLIS, A.M. 8vo, 16*s.*

Catullus, a Commentary on. By ROBINSON ELLIS, M.A. *Second Edition.* 8vo, 18*s.*

Cicero. De Oratore Libri Tres. With Introduction and Notes. By A. S. WILKINS, Litt.D. 8vo, 18*s.*

Also separately—

Book I, *Third Edition.* 7*s.* 6*d.* Book II, *Second Edition.* 5*s.* Book III, 6*s.*

—— Philippic Orations. With Notes. By J. R. KING, M.A. *Second Edition.* 8vo, 10*s.* 6*d.*

—— Pro Milone. Edited, with Introduction and Commentary, by A. C. CLARK, M.A. 8vo, 8*s.* 6*d.*

—— Select Letters. With English Introductions, Notes, and Appendices. By ALBERT WATSON, M.A. *Fourth Edition.* 8vo, 18*s.*

Horace. With a Commentary. Vol. I. The Odes, Carmen Seculare, and Epodes. By E. C. WICKHAM, D.D. *Third Edition.* 8vo, 12*s.*

—— Vol. II. The Satires, Epistles, and De Arte Poetica. By the same Editor. 8vo, 12*s.*

Livy, Book I. With Introduction, Historical Examination, and Notes. By J. R. SEELEY, M.A. *Third Edition.* 8vo, 6*s.*

Manilius. Noctes Manilianae; sive Dissertationes in Astronomica Manilii. Accedvnt Coniectvrae in Germanici Aratea. Scripsit R. ELLIS. Crown 8vo, 6*s.*

Nonius Marcellus: De Conpendiosa Doctrina I–III. Edited with Introduction and Critical Apparatus by the late J. H. ONIONS, M.A. 8vo, 10*s.* 6*d.*

Ovid. P. Ovidii Nasonis Ibis. Ex Novis Codicibus edidit, Scholia Vetera Commentarium cum Prolegomenis Appendice Indice addidit, R. ELLIS, A.M. 8vo, 10*s.* 6*d.*

—— P. Ovidi Nasonis Tristium Libri V. Recensuit S. G. OWEN, A.M. 8vo, 16*s.*

Persius. The Satires. With a Translation and Commentary. By JOHN CONINGTON, M.A. Edited by HENRY NETTLESHIP, M.A. *Third Edition.* 8vo, 8*s.* 6*d.*

Plautus. Rudens. Edited, with Critical and Explanatory Notes, by E. A. SONNENSCHEIN, M.A. 8vo, 8*s.* 6*d.*

Quintilian. Institutionis Oratoriae Liber X. Edited by W. PETERSON, M.A. 8vo, 12*s.* 6*d.*

Scriptores Latini rei Metricae. Ed. T. GAISFORD, S.T.P. 8vo, 5*s.*

Tacitus. The Annals. Books I–VI. Edited, with Introduction and Notes, by H. FURNEAUX, M.A. *Second Edition.* 8vo, 18*s.*

—— Books XI–XVI. By the same Editor. 8vo, 20*s.*

—— De Germania. With Introduction, Notes, and Map. By the same Editor. 8vo, 6*s.* 6*d.*

—— Dialogus De Oratoribus. A Revised Text, with Introductory Essays and Critical and Explanatory Notes. By W. PETERSON, M.A., LL.D. 8vo, 10*s.* 6*d.*

LATIN EDUCATIONAL WORKS.

GRAMMARS, EXERCISE BOOKS, ETC.

Allen.

Rudimenta Latina. Comprising Accidence, and Exercises of a very Elementary Character, for the use of Beginners. By JOHN BARROW ALLEN, M.A. Extra fcap. 8vo, 2s.

An Elementary Latin Grammar. By the same Author. *One Hundred and Thirty-seventh Thousand.* Extra fcap. 8vo, 2s. 6d.

A First Latin Exercise Book. By the same Author. *Seventh Edition.* Extra fcap. 8vo, 2s. 6d.

A Second Latin Exercise Book. By the same Author. *Second Edition.* Extra fcap. 8vo, 3s. 6d.

*** A Key to First and Second Latin Exercise Books, in one volume, price 5s. *net.* Supplied *to Teachers only,* on application to the Secretary, Clarendon Press.

An Introduction to Latin Syntax. By W. S. GIBSON, M.A. Extra fcap. 8vo, 2s.

First Latin Reader. By T. J. NUNNS, M.A. *Third Edition.* Extra fcap. 8vo, 2s.

A Latin Prose Primer. By J. Y. SARGENT, M.A. Extra fcap. 8vo, 2s. 6d.

Passages for Translation into Latin. Selected by J. Y. SARGENT, M.A. *Seventh Edition.* Extra fcap. 8vo, 2s. 6d.

*** A Key to the above, price 5s. *net.* Supplied *to Teachers only,* on application to the Secretary, Clarendon Press.

Latin Prose Composition. By G. G. RAMSAY, M.A., LL.D. Extra fcap. 8vo.

Vol. I. *Syntax, Exercises with Notes, &c. Fourth Edition.* 4s. 6d.

Or in two Parts, 2s. 6d. each, viz.

Part I, *The Simple Sentence.* Part II, *The Compound Sentence.*

*** A Key to the above, price 5s. *net.* Supplied *to Teachers only,* on application to the Secretary, Clarendon Press.

Vol. II. *Passages of Graduated Difficulty for Translation into Latin, together with an Introduction on Continuous Prose. Third Edition.* 4s. 6d.

Latin Prose Versions. Contributed by various Scholars. Edited by GEORGE G. RAMSAY, M.A., LL.D., Litt.D. Extra fcap. 8vo, 5*s*.

Hints and Helps for Latin Elegiacs. By H. LEE-WARNER, M.A. Extra fcap. 8vo, 3*s*. 6*d*.

*** A Key to the above, price 4*s*. 6*d*. *net*. Supplied *to Teachers only*, on application to the Secretary, Clarendon Press.

Reddenda Minora; or, Easy Passages, Latin and Greek, for Unseen Translation. For the use of Lower Forms. Composed and selected by C. S. JERRAM, M.A. *Sixth Edition. Revised and Enlarged.* Extra fcap. 8vo, 1*s*. 6*d*.

Anglice Reddenda; or, Extracts, Latin and Greek, for Unseen Translation. By C. S. JERRAM, M.A. *Fourth Edition.* Extra fcap. 8vo, 2*s*. 6*d*.

—— *Second Series.* By the same Editor. 3*s*.

—— *Third Series.* By the same Editor. 3*s*.

Models and Exercises in Unseen Translation. By H. F. FOX, M.A., and T. M. BROMLEY, M.A. *Revised Edition.* Extra fcap. 8vo, 5*s*. 6*d*.

*** A Key to Passages quoted in the above, price 6*d*. Supplied *to Teachers only*, on application to the Secretary, Clarendon Press.

An Elementary Latin Dictionary. By CHARLTON T. LEWIS, Ph.D. Square 8vo, 7*s*. 6*d*.

A School Latin Dictionary. By the same. 4to, 18*s*.

An Introduction to the Comparative Grammar of Greek and Latin. By J. E. KING, M.A., and C. COOKSON, M.A. Cr. 8vo, 5*s*. 6*d*.

A Short Historical Latin Grammar. By W. M. LINDSAY, M.A. Crown 8vo, 5*s*. 6*d*.

LATIN CLASSICS FOR SCHOOLS.

Caesar. The Commentaries (for Schools). With Notes and Maps. By CHARLES E. MOBERLY, M.A.

The Gallic War. *Second Edition.* Extra fcap. 8vo.

—— Books I and II, 2*s*.; III–V, 2*s*. 6*d*.; VI–VIII, 3*s*. 6*d*.

—— Books I–III, *stiff cover*, 2*s*.

The Civil War. Extra fcap. 8vo, 3*s*. 6*d*.

Catulli Veronensis Carmina Selecta, secundum recognitionem ROBINSON ELLIS, A.M. Extra fcap. 8vo, 3*s.* 6*d.*

Cicero. Selection of Interesting and Descriptive Passages. With Notes. By HENRY WALFORD, M.A. In three Parts. *Third Edition.* Extra fcap. 8vo, 4*s.* 6*d.* Each Part separately, 1*s.* 6*d.*

Part I. Anecdotes from Grecian and Roman History.
Part II. Omens and Dreams: Beauties of Nature.
Part III. Rome's Rule of her Provinces.

—— De Amicitia. With Introduction and Notes. By ST. GEORGE STOCK, M.A. Extra fcap. 8vo, 3*s.*

—— De Senectute. Edited, with Introduction and Notes, by L. HUXLEY, M.A. Extra fcap. 8vo, 2*s.*

—— pro Cluentio. With Introduction and Notes. By W. RAMSAY, M.A. Edited by G. G. RAMSAY, M.A. *Second Edition.* Extra fcap. 8vo, 3*s.* 6*d.*

—— pro Marcello, pro Ligario, pro Rege Deiotaro. With Introduction and Notes. By W. Y. FAUSSET, M.A. Extra fcap. 8vo, 2*s.* 6*d.*

—— pro Milone. With Notes, &c. By A. B. POYNTON, M.A. Extra fcap. 8vo, 2*s.* 6*d.*

—— pro Roscio. With Notes. By ST. GEORGE STOCK, M.A. Extra fcap. 8vo, 3*s.* 6*d.*

—— Select Orations (for Schools). In Verrem Actio Prima. De Imperio Gn. Pompeii. Pro Archia. Philippica IX. With Introduction and Notes by J. R. KING, M.A. *Second Edition.* Extra fcap. 8vo, 2*s.* 6*d.*

—— In Q. Caecilium Divinatio, and In C. Verrem Actio Prima. With Introduction and Notes, by J. R. KING, M.A. Extra fcap. 8vo, limp, 1*s.* 6*d.*

—— Speeches against Catilina. With Introduction and Notes, by E. A. UPCOTT, M.A. *Second Edition.* Extra fcap. 8vo, 2*s.* 6*d.*

—— Selected Letters (for Schools). With Notes. By the late C. E. PRICHARD, M.A., and E. R. BERNARD, M.A. *Second Edition.* Extra fcap. 8vo, 3*s.*

—— Select Letters. Text. By ALBERT WATSON, M.A. *Second Edition.* Extra fcap. 8vo, 4*s.*

Cornelius Nepos. With Notes. By Oscar Browning, M.A. *Third Edition.* Revised by W. R. Inge, M.A. Extra fcap. 8vo, 3*s.*

Horace. With a Commentary. (In a size suitable for the use of Schools.) Vol. I. The Odes, Carmen Seculare, and Epodes. By E. C. Wickham, D.D. *Second Edition.* Extra fcap. 8vo, 6*s.*

—— Odes, Book I. By the same Editor. Extra fcap. 8vo, 2*s.*

—— Selected Odes. With Notes for the use of a Fifth Form. By the same Editor. Extra fcap. 8vo, 2*s.*

Juvenal. Thirteen Satires. Edited, with Introduction and Notes, by C. H. Pearson, M.A., and Herbert A. Strong, M.A., LL.D. *Second Edition.* Crown 8vo, 9*s.*

Livy. Books V–VII. With Introduction and Notes. By A. R. Cluer, B.A. *Second Edition.* Revised by P. E. Matheson, M.A. Extra fcap. 8vo, 5*s.*

—— Book V. By the same Editors. Extra fcap. 8vo, 2*s.* 6*d.*

—— Book VII. By the same Editors. Extra fcap. 8vo, 2*s.*

—— Books XXI–XXIII. With Introduction and Notes. By M. T. Tatham, M.A. *Second Edition, Enlarged.* Extra fcap. 8vo, 5*s.*

—— Book XXI. By the same Editor. Extra fcap. 8vo, 2*s.* 6*d.*

—— Book XXII. With Introduction, Notes, and Maps. By the same Editor. Extra fcap. 8vo, 2*s.* 6*d.*

—— Selections (for Schools). With Notes and Maps. By H. Lee-Warner, M.A. Extra fcap. 8vo. In Parts, limp, each 1*s.* 6*d.*

Part I. The Caudine Disaster. New Edition.

Part II. Hannibal's Campaign in Italy. New Edition.

Part III. The Macedonian War.

Ovid. Selections for the use of Schools. With Introductions and Notes, and an Appendix on the Roman Calendar. By W. Ramsay, M.A. Edited by G. G. Ramsay, M.A. *Third Edition.* Extra fcap. 8vo, 5*s.* 6*d.*

—— Tristia. Book I. The Text revised, with an Introduction and Notes. By S. G. Owen, B.A. *Second Edition.* Extra fcap. 8vo, 3*s.* 6*d.*

Ovid. Tristia. Book III. With Introduction and Notes. By the same Editor. Extra fcap. 8vo, *2s.*

Plautus. Captivi. Edited by WALLACE M. LINDSAY, M.A. Extra fcap. 8vo, *2s. 6d.*

—— Trinummus. With Notes and Introductions. (Intended for the Higher Forms of Public Schools.) By C. E. FREEMAN, M.A., and A. SLOMAN, M.A. Extra fcap. 8vo, *3s.*

Pliny. Selected Letters (for Schools). With Notes. By C. E. PRICHARD, M.A., and E. R. BERNARD, M.A. *Third Edition.* Extra fcap. 8vo, *3s.*

Quintilian. Institutionis Oratoriae Liber X. By W. PETERSON, M.A. Extra fcap. 8vo, *3s. 6d.*

Sallust. With Introduction and Notes. By W. W. CAPES, M.A. *Second Edition.* Extra fcap. 8vo, *4s. 6d.*

Tacitus. The Annals. *Text only.* Crown 8vo, *6s.*

—— The Annals. Books I–IV. Edited, with Introduction and Notes (for the use of Schools and Junior Students), by H. FURNEAUX, M.A. Extra fcap. 8vo, *5s.*

—— The Annals. Book I. With Introduction and Notes, by the same Editor. Extra fcap. 8vo, limp, *2s.*

Terence. Andria. With Notes and Introductions. By C. E. FREEMAN, M.A., and A. SLOMAN, M.A. Extra fcap. 8vo, *3s.*

—— Adelphi. With Notes and Introductions. By A. SLOMAN, M.A. Extra fcap. 8vo, *3s.*

—— Phormio. With Notes and Introductions. By A. SLOMAN, M.A. Extra fcap. 8vo, *3s.*

Tibullus and **Propertius.** Selections. Edited by G. G. RAMSAY, M.A. *Second Edition.* Extra fcap. 8vo, *6s.*

Virgil. With an Introduction and Notes. By T. L. PAPILLON, M.A., and A. E. HAIGH, M.A. 2 vols. Crown 8vo, cloth, *6s.* each; or, stiff covers, *3s. 6d.* each.

—— Aeneid. Books I–III; IV–VI; VII–IX; X–XII. By the same Editors. Crown 8vo, stiff covers, *2s. each.*

—— Bucolics and Georgics. By the same Editors. Crown 8vo, stiff covers, *2s. 6d.*

Virgil. The Complete Works of Virgil. Edited by T. L. PAPILLON, M.A., and A. E. HAIGH, M.A. Including the Minor Works, with numerous Emendations by Professor ROBINSON ELLIS. 32mo. On Writing Paper for MS. Notes, 5*s.*; *on Oxford India Paper, cloth elegant,* 6*s.*

—— Bucolics. Edited by C. S. JERRAM, M.A. Extra fcap. 8vo, 2*s.* 6*d.*

—— Georgics, Books I, II. By the same Editor. Extra fcap. 8vo, 2*s.* 6*d.*

—— Georgics, Books III, IV. By the same Editor. Extra fcap. 8vo, 2*s.* 6*d.*

—— Aeneid I. With Introduction and Notes. By the same Editor. Extra fcap. 8vo, limp, 1*s.* 6*d.*

—— Aeneid IX. Edited, with Introduction and Notes, by A. E. HAIGH, M.A. Extra fcap. 8vo, limp, 1*s.* 6*d.* In two Parts, 2*s.*

(2) GREEK.

STANDARD WORKS AND EDITIONS.

Allen. Notes on Abbreviations in Greek Manuscripts. By T. W. ALLEN, M.A., Queen's College, Oxford. Royal 8vo, 5*s.*

Chandler. A Practical Introduction to Greek Accentuation. By H. W. CHANDLER, M.A. *Second Edition.* 10*s.* 6*d.*

Farnell. The Cults of the Greek States. By L. R. FARNELL, M.A. 8vo. Vols. I and II, with 61 Plates and over 100 Illustrations, *cloth,* 1*l.* 12*s. net.*

Vol. III (completing the work), *in the Press.*

Grenfell. An Alexandrian Erotic Fragment and other Greek Papyri, chiefly Ptolemaic. Edited by B. P. GRENFELL, M.A. Small 4to, 8*s.* 6*d. net.*

Grenfell and Hunt. New Classical Fragments and other Greek and Latin Papyri. Edited by B. P. GRENFELL, M..A, and A. S. HUNT, M.A. With Plates, 12*s.* 6*d. net.*

Grenfell and Mahaffy. Revenue Laws of Ptolemy Philadelphus. 2 vols. Text and Plates. 1*l.* 11*s.* 6*d. net.*

Haigh. The Attic Theatre. A Description of the Stage and Theatre of the Athenians, and of the Dramatic Performances at Athens. By A. E. HAIGH, M.A. 8vo, 12*s.* 6*d.*

Haigh. The Tragic Drama of the Greeks. With Illustrations. By A. E. HAIGH, M.A. 8vo, 12*s.* 6*d.*

Head. Historia Numorum: A Manual of Greek Numismatics. By BARCLAY V. HEAD, D.C.L. Royal 8vo, half-bound, 2*l.* 2*s.*

Hicks. A Manual of Greek Historical Inscriptions. By E. L. HICKS, M.A. 8vo, 10*s.* 6*d.*

King and Cookson. The Principles of Sound and Inflexion, as illustrated in the Greek and Latin Languages. By J. E. KING, M.A., and CHRISTOPHER COOKSON, M.A. 8vo, 18*s.*

Liddell and Scott. A Greek-English Lexicon, by H. G. LIDDELL, D.D., and ROBERT SCOTT, D.D. *Seventh Edition, Revised and Augmented throughout.* 4to, 1*l.* 16*s.*

Monro. Modes of Ancient Greek Music. By D. B. MONRO, M.A., Provost of Oriel College. 8vo, 8*s.* 6*d.* *net.*

Papillon. Manual of Comparative Philology. By T. L. PAPILLON, M.A. *Third Edition.* Crown 8vo, 6*s.*

Paton and Hicks. The Inscriptions of Cos. By W. R. PATON and E. L. HICKS. Royal 8vo, linen, with Map, 28*s.*

Smyth. The Sounds and Inflections of the Greek Dialects (Ionic). By HERBERT WEIR SMYTH, Ph.D. 8vo, 24*s.*

Thompson. A Glossary of Greek Birds. By D'Arcy W. THOMPSON, M.A. 8vo, buckram, 10*s.* *net.*

Veitch. Greek Verbs, Irregular and Defective. By W. VEITCH, LL.D. *Fourth Edition.* Crown 8vo, 10*s.* 6*d.*

Aeschinem et **Isocratem**, Scholia Graeca in. Edidit G. DINDORFIUS. 1852. 8vo, 4*s.*

Aeschyli quae supersunt in Codice Laurentiano quoad effici potuit et ad cognitionem necesse est visum typis descripta edidit R. MERKEL. Small folio, 1*l.* 1*s.*

Aeschylus: Tragoediae et Fragmenta, ex recensione GUIL. DINDORFII. *Second Edition.* 1851. 8vo, 5*s.* 6*d.*

—— Annotationes GUIL. DINDORFII. Partes II. 1841. 8vo, 10*s.*

Anecdota Graeca Oxoniensia. Edidit J. A. CRAMER, S.T.P. Tomi IV. 1835. 8vo, 1*l.* 2*s.*

—— Graeca e Codd. MSS. Bibliothecae Regiae Parisiensis. Edidit J. A. CRAMER, S.T.P. Tomi IV. 1839. 8vo, 1*l.* 2*s.*

Apsinis et **Longini** Rhetorica. E Codicibus MSS. recensuit JOH. BAKIUS. 1849. 8vo, 3*s*.

Aristophanes. A Complete Concordance to the Comedies and Fragments. By HENRY DUNBAR, M.D. 4to, 1*l*. 1*s*.

—— J. Caravellae Index in Aristophanem. 8vo, 3*s*.

—— Comoediae et Fragmenta, ex recensione GUIL. DINDORFII. Tomi II. 1835. 8vo, 11*s*.

—— Annotationes GUIL. DINDORFII. Partes II. 8vo, 11*s*.

—— Scholia Graeca ex Codicibus aucta et emendata a GUIL. DINDORFIO. Partes III. 1838. 8vo, 1*l*.

ARISTOTLE.

—— Ex recensione IMMANUELIS BEKKERI. Accedunt Indices Sylburgiani. Tomi XI. 1837. 8vo, 2*l*. 10*s*.

The volumes (except vols. I and IX) may be had separately, price 5*s*. 6*d*. each.

—— **Ethica Nicomachea,** recognovit breviquc Adnotatione critica instruxit I. BYWATER. 8vo, 6*s*.

—— **The same,** on 4to paper, for Marginal Notes, 10*s*. 6*d*.

Also in Crown 8vo, *paper cover*, 3*s*. 6*d*.

—— Contributions to the Textual Criticism of Aristotle's Nicomachean Ethics. By INGRAM BYWATER. Stiff cover, 2*s*. 6*d*.

—— Notes on the Nicomachean Ethics of Aristotle. By J. A. STEWART, M.A. 2 vols. 8vo, 32*s*.

—— **The Politics,** with Introductions, Notes, &c., by W. L. NEWMAN, M.A., Fellow of Balliol College, Oxford. Vols. I and II. Medium 8vo, 28*s*.

—— **The Politics,** translated into English, with Introduction, Marginal Analysis, Notes, and Indices, by B. JOWETT, M.A. Medium 8vo. 2 vols. 21*s*.

—— **Aristotelian Studies.** I. On the Structure of the Seventh Book of the Nicomachean Ethics. By J. C. WILSON, M.A. 8vo, stiff covers, 5*s*.

—— The English Manuscripts of the **Nicomachean Ethics,** described in relation to Bekker's Manuscripts and other Sources. By J. A. STEWART, M.A. (Anecdota Oxon.) Small 4to, 3*s*. 6*d*.

—— On the History of the process by which the **Aristotelian** Writings arrived at their present form. By R. SHUTE, M.A. 8vo, 7*s*. 6*d*.

Aristotle. Physics. Book VII. Collation of various MSS.; with Introduction by R. SHUTE, M.A. (Anecdota Oxon.) Small 4to, 2s.

Choerobosci Dictata in Theodosii Canones, necnon Epimerismi in Psalmos. E Codicibus MSS. edidit THOMAS GAISFORD, S.T.P. Tomi III. 8vo, 15s.

Demosthenes. Ex recensione GUIL. DINDORFII. Tomi IX. 8vo, 2l. 6s.

Separately—

Textus, 1l. 1s. Annotationes, 15s. Scholia, 10s.

Demosthenes and Aeschines. The Orations of Demosthenes and Aeschines on the Crown. With Introductory Essays and Notes. By G. A. SIMCOX, M.A., and W. H. SIMCOX, M.A. 8vo, 12s.

Euripides. Tragoediae et Fragmenta, ex recensione GUIL. DINDORFII. Tomi II. 1833. 8vo, 10s.

—— Annotationes GUIL. DINDORFII. Partes II. 8vo, 10s.

—— Scholia Graeca, ex Codicibus aucta et emendata a GUIL. DINDORFIO. Tomi IV. 8vo, 1l. 16s.

—— Alcestis, ex recensione G. DINDORFII. 8vo, 2s. 6d.

Harpocrationis Lexicon. Ex recensione G. DINDORFII. Tomi II. 8vo, 10s. 6d.

Hephaestionis Enchiridion, Terentianus Maurus, Proclus, &c. Edidit T. GAISFORD, S.T.P. Tomi II. 10s.

Heracliti Ephesii Reliquiae. Recensuit I. BYWATER, M.A. Appendicis loco additae sunt Diogenis Laertii Vita Heracliti, Particulae Hippocratei De Diaeta Lib. I, Epistolae Heracliteae. 8vo, 6s.

Herodotus. Books V and VI. Terpsichore and Erato. Edited, with Notes and Appendices, by EVELYN ABBOTT, M.A., LL.D. 8vo, with two Maps, 10s. 6d.

HOMER.

—— A Complete Concordance to the Odyssey and Hymns of Homer; to which is added a Concordance to the Parallel Passages in the Iliad, Odyssey, and Hymns. By HENRY DUNBAR, M.D. 4to, 1l. 1s.

—— Seberi Index in Homerum. 1780. 8vo, 6s. 6d.

—— A Grammar of the Homeric Dialect. By D. B. MONRO, M.A. *Second Edition.* 8vo, 14s.

Homeri Opera et Reliquiae. Recensuit D. B. MONRO, M.A. Crown 8vo, India Paper Edition, 10s. 6d. *net.*

—— **Ilias,** cum brevi Annotatione C. G. HEYNII. Accedunt Scholia minora. Tomi II. 8vo, 15s.

—— **Ilias,** ex rec. GUIL. DINDORFII. 8vo, 5s. 6d.

HOMER (*continued*).

—— Scholia Graeca in Iliadem. Edited by W. DINDORF, after a new collation of the Venetian MSS. by D. B. MONRO, M.A., Provost of Oriel College. 4 vols. 8vo, 2*l.* 10*s.*

—— Scholia Graeca in Iliadem Townleyana. Recensuit ERNESTUS MAASS. 2 vols. 8vo, 1*l.* 16*s.*

—— **Odyssea**, ex rec. G. DINDORFII. 8vo, 5*s.* 6*d.*

—— Scholia Graeca in Odysseam. Edidit GUIL. DINDORFIUS. Tomi II. 8vo, 15*s.* 6*d.*

—— Odyssey. Books I–XII. Edited with English Notes, Appendices, &c. By W. W. MERRY, D.D., and the late JAMES RIDDELL, M.A. *Second Edition.* 8vo, 16*s.*

—— **Hymni Homerici.** Codicibus denuo collatis recensuit ALFREDUS GOODWIN. Small folio. With four Plates. 21*s. net.*

Oratores Attici, ex recensione BEKKERI:

I. Antiphon, Andocides, et Lysias. 8vo, 7*s.*

II. Isocrates. 8vo, 7*s.*

III. Isaeus, Aeschines, Lycurgus, Dinarchus, &c. 8vo, 7*s.*

Paroemiographi Graeci, quorum pars nunc primum ex Codd. MSS. vulgatur. Edidit T. GAISFORD, S.T.P. 8vo, 5*s.* 6*d.*

PLATO.

—— **Apology**, with a revised Text and English Notes, and a Digest of Platonic Idioms, by JAMES RIDDELL, M.A. 8vo, 8*s.* 6*d.*

—— **Philebus**, with a revised Text and English Notes, by EDWARD POSTE, M.A. 8vo, 7*s.* 6*d.*

—— **Republic**; The Greek Text. Edited, with Notes and Essays, by the late B. JOWETT, M.A., and LEWIS CAMPBELL, M.A., LL.D. In Three Volumes. Medium 8vo, cloth, 2*l.* 2*s.*

—— **Sophistes** and **Politicus**, with a revised Text and English Notes, by L. CAMPBELL, M.A. 8vo, 10*s.* 6*d.*

—— **Theaetetus**, with a revised Text and English Notes, by L. CAMPBELL, M.A. *Second Edition.* 8vo, 10*s.* 6*d.*

—— **The Dialogues**, translated into English, with Analyses and Introductions, by B. JOWETT, M.A. *Third Edition.* 5 vols. medium 8vo, 4*l.* 4*s.* In half-morocco, 5*l.*

—— **The Republic**, translated into English, with Analysis and Introduction, by B. JOWETT, M.A. *Third Edition.* Medium 8vo, 12*s.* 6*d.*; half-roan, 14*s.*

—— A Subject-Index to the Dialogues of Plato. By EVELYN ABBOTT, M.A. 8vo, cloth, 2*s.* 6*d.*

Plotinus. Edidit F. CREUZER. Tomi III. 4to, 1*l.* 8*s.*

Plutarchi Moralia, id est, Opera, exceptis Vitis, reliqua. Edidit DANIEL WYTTENBACH. Accedit Index Graecitatis. Tomi VIII. Partes XV. 1795–1830. 8vo, cloth, 3*l.* 10*s.*

Polybius. Selections. Edited by J. L. STRACHAN-DAVIDSON, M.A. With Maps. Medium 8vo, buckram, 21*s.*

Sophocles.

—— The Plays and Fragments. With English Notes and Introductions, by LEWIS CAMPBELL, M.A. 2 vols.

Vol. I. Oedipus Tyrannus. Oedipus Coloneus. Antigone. 8vo, 16*s.*

Vol. II. Ajax. Electra. Trachiniae. Philoctetes. Fragments. 8vo, 16*s.*

—— Tragoediae et Fragmenta, ex recensione et cum commentariis GUIL. DINDORFII. *Third Edition.* 2 vols. Fcap. 8vo, 1*l.* 1*s.*

Each Play separately, limp, 2*s.* 6*d.*

—— Tragoediae et Fragmenta cum Annotationibus GUIL. DINDORFII. Tomi II. 8vo, 10*s.*

The Text, Vol. I, 5*s.* 6*d.* The Notes, Vol. II, 4*s.* 6*d.*

Stobaei Florilegium. Ad MSS. fidem emendavit et supplevit T. GAISFORD, S.T.P. Tomi IV. 8vo, 1*l.*

—— Eclogarum Physicarum et Ethicarum libri duo. Accedit Hieroclis Commentarius in aurea carmina Pythagoreorum. Ad MSS. Codd. recensuit T. GAISFORD, S.T.P. Tomi II. 8vo, 11*s.*

Strabo, Selections from. With an Introduction on Strabo's Life and Works. By H. F. TOZER, M.A., F.R.G.S. With Maps and Plans. 8vo, cloth, 12*s.*

Thucydides. Book I. Edited with Introduction, Notes, and Maps, by W. H. FORBES, M.A. 8vo, 8*s.* 6*d.*

Thucydides. Translated into English, with Introduction, Marginal Analysis, Notes, and Indices. By B. JOWETT, M.A. 2 vols. Medium 8vo, 1*l.* 12*s.*

Xenophon. Ex rec. et cum annotatt. L. DINDORFII.

I. Historia Graeca. *Second Edition.* 8vo, 10*s.* 6*d.*

II. Expeditio Cyri. *Second Edition.* 8vo, 10*s.* 6*d.*

III. Institutio Cyri. 8vo, 10*s.* 6*d.*

IV. Memorabilia Socratis. 8vo, 7*s.* 6*d.*

V. Opuscula Politica Equestria et Venatica cum Arriani Libello de Venatione. 8vo, 10*s.* 6*d.*

GREEK EDUCATIONAL WORKS.

Grammars, Exercise Books, &c.

Chandler. The Elements of Greek Accentuation: abridged from his larger work by H. W. Chandler, M.A. Extra fcap. 8vo, 2*s*. 6*d*.

King and **Cookson.** An Introduction to the Comparative Grammar of Greek and Latin. By J. E. King, M.A., and C. Cookson, M.A. Extra fcap. 8vo, 5*s*. 6*d*.

Liddell and **Scott.** An Intermediate Greek-English Lexicon, founded upon the Seventh Edition of Liddell and Scott's Greek Lexicon. Small 4to, 12*s*. 6*d*.

Liddell and **Scott.** A Greek-English Lexicon, abridged from Liddell and Scott's 4to edition. Square 12mo, 7*s*. 6*d*.

Miller. A Greek Testament Primer. An Easy Grammar and Reading Book for the use of Students beginning Greek. By the Rev. E. Miller, M.A. *Second Edition.* Extra fcap. 8vo, paper covers, 2*s*.; cloth, 3*s*. 6*d*.

Moulton. The Ancient Classical Drama. A Study in Literary Evolution. Intended for Readers in English and in the Original. By R. G. Moulton, M.A. Crown 8vo, 8*s*. 6*d*.

Wordsworth. A Greek Primer, for the use of beginners in that Language. By the Right Rev. Charles Wordsworth, D.C.L. *Eighty-third Thousand.* Extra fcap. 8vo, 1*s*. 6*d*.

—— Graecae Grammaticae Rudimenta in usum Scholarum. Auctore Carolo Wordsworth, D.C.L. *Nineteenth Edition.* 12mo, 4*s*.

A Primer of Greek Prose Composition. By J. Y. Sargent, M.A. Extra fcap. 8vo, 3*s*. 6*d*.

*** A Key to the above, price 5*s*. *net*. Supplied *to Teachers only*, on application to the Secretary, Clarendon Press.

Passages for Translation into Greek Prose. By J. Young Sargent, M.A. Extra fcap. 8vo, 3*s*.

Exemplaria Graeca. Being Greek Renderings of Selected 'Passages for Translation into Greek Prose.' By the same Author. Extra fcap. 8vo, 3*s*.

Models and Materials for Greek Iambic Verse. By J. Y. Sargent, M.A. Extra fcap. 8vo, 4*s*. 6*d*.

Graece Reddenda. By C. S. Jerram, M.A. Extra fcap. 8vo, 2*s*. 6*d*.

Reddenda Minora; or, Easy Passages, Latin and Greek, for Unseen Translation. By the same Author. *Third Edition.* Extra fcap. 8vo, 1*s*. 6*d*.

Anglice Reddenda; or, Extracts, Latin and Greek, for Unseen Translation. By the same Author. Extra fcap. 8vo, 2*s*. 6*d*.

Anglice Reddenda. *Second Series.* By the same Author. Extra fcap. 8vo, 3*s*.

Anglice Reddenda. *Third Series.* For the use of Middle and Higher Forms. By the same Author. Extra fcap. 8vo, 3*s*.

Models and Exercises in Unseen Translation. By H. F. Fox, M.A., and T. M. Bromley, M.A. Extra fcap. 8vo, 5*s*. 6*d*.

*** A Key to Passages quoted in the above, price 6*d*. Supplied *to Teachers only*, on application to the Secretary, Clarendon Press.

Golden Treasury of Ancient Greek Poetry. By R. S. Wright, M.A. *Second Edition.* Revised by Evelyn Abbott, M.A., LL.D. Extra fcap. 8vo, 10*s*. 6*d*.

Golden Treasury of Greek Prose, being a Collection of the finest passages in the principal Greek Prose Writers, with Introductory Notices and Notes. By R. S. Wright, M.A., and J. E. L. Shadwell, M.A. Extra fcap. 8vo, 4*s*. 6*d*.

Greek Readers.

Easy Greek Reader. By Evelyn Abbott, M.A. In one or two Parts. Extra fcap. 8vo, 3*s*.

First Greek Reader. By W. G. Rushbrooke, M.L. *Third Edition.* Extra fcap. 8vo, 2*s*. 6*d*.

Second Greek Reader. By A. M. Bell, M.A. *Second Edition.* Extra fcap. 8vo, 3*s*.

Specimens of Greek Dialects; being a **Fourth Greek Reader.** With Introductions, &c. By W. W. Merry, D.D. Extra fcap. 8vo, 4*s*. 6*d*.

Selections from Homer and the Greek Dramatists; being a Fifth Greek Reader. With Explanatory Notes and Introductions to the Study of Greek Epic and Dramatic Poetry. By Evelyn Abbott, M.A. Extra fcap. 8vo, 4*s*. 6*d*.

Greek Classics for Schools.

Aeschylus. In Single Plays. Extra fcap. 8vo.

Agamemnon. With Introduction and Notes, by Arthur Sidgwick, M.A. *Fourth Edition.* 3*s*.

Choephoroi. By the same Editor. 3*s*.

Eumenides. By the same Editor. *New Edition.* 3*s*.

Prometheus Bound. With Introduction and Notes, by A. O. Prickard, M.A. *Second Edition.* 2*s*.

Aristophanes. In Single Plays. Edited, with English Notes, Introductions, &c., by W. W. Merry, D.D. Extra fcap. 8vo.

The Acharnians. *Fourth Edition*, 3*s*.

The Birds. 3*s*. 6*d*.

The Clouds. *Third Edition*, 3*s*.

The Frogs. *Third Edition*, 3*s*.

The Knights. *Second Edition*, 3*s*.

The Wasps. 3*s*. 6*d*.

Cebes. Tabula. With Introduction and Notes. By C. S. Jerram, M.A. Extra fcap. 8vo, 2*s*. 6*d*.

Demosthenes. Orations against Philip. With Introduction and Notes, by Evelyn Abbott, M.A., and P. E. Matheson, M.A.

Vol. I. Philippic I. Olynthiacs I–III. *Third Edition.* Extra fcap. 8vo, 3*s*.

Vol. II. De Pace, Philippic II, De Chersoneso, Philippic III. Extra fcap. 8vo, 4*s*. 6*d*.

—— **Philippics** only, reprinted from the above. 2*s*. 6*d*.

Euripides. In Single Plays. Edited with Introduction and Notes. Extra fcap. 8vo.

Alcestis. By C. S. JERRAM, M.A. *Fifth Edition.* 2s. 6d.

Bacchae. By A. H. CRUICKSHANK, M.A. 3s. 6d.

Cyclops. By W. E. LONG, M.A. 2s. 6d.

Hecuba. By C. H. RUSSELL, M.A. 2s. 6d.

Helena. By C. S. JERRAM, M.A. 3s.

Heracleidae. By C. S. JERRAM, M.A. 3s.

Ion. By C. S. JERRAM, M.A. 3s.

Iphigenia in Tauris. *New Edition, Revised.* By C. S. JERRAM, M.A. 3s.

Medea. By C. B. HEBERDEN, M.A. *Second Edition.* 2s.

Herodotus. Book IX. Edited, with Notes, by EVELYN ABBOTT, M.A. Extra fcap. 8vo, 3s.

Herodotus. Selections. Edited, with Introduction and Notes, by W. W. MERRY, D.D. Extra fcap. 8vo, 2s. 6d.

Homer.

For Beginners. Iliad, Book III. By M. T. TATHAM, M.A. Extra fcap. 8vo, 1s. 6d.

Iliad, Books I–XII. With an Introduction and a brief Homeric Grammar, and Notes. By D. B. MONRO, M.A. *Fourth Edition.* Extra fcap. 8vo, 6s.

Iliad, Books XIII–XXIV. With Notes. By the same Editor. *Third Edition.* Extra fcap. 8vo, 6s.

Iliad, Book I. By the same Editor. *Third Edition.* Extra fcap. 8vo, 1s. 6d.

Iliad, Book XXI. With Introduction and Notes. By HERBERT HAILSTONE, M.A. Extra fcap. 8vo, 1s. 6d.

Odyssey, Books I–XII. By W. W. MERRY, D.D. *Fiftieth Thousand.* Extra fcap. 8vo, 5s.

Books I and II, separately, each 1s. 6d.

Books VI and VII. Extra fcap. 8vo, 1s. 6d.

Homer (*continued*).

Odyssey, Books VII–XII. By the same Editor. Extra fcap. 8vo, 3*s*.

Odyssey, Books XIII–XXIV. By the same Editor. *Thirteenth Thousand.* Extra fcap. 8vo, 5*s*.

Odyssey, Books XIII–XVIII. By the same Editor. Extra fcap. 8vo, 3*s*.

Lucian. Vera Historia. By C. S. JERRAM, M.A. *Second Edition.* Extra fcap. 8vo, 1*s*. 6*d*.

Lysias. Epitaphios. Edited, with Introduction and Notes, by F. J. SNELL, B.A. Extra fcap. 8vo, 2*s*.

Plato. With Introduction and Notes. By ST. GEORGE STOCK, M.A. Extra fcap. 8vo.

The Apology. *Third Edition.* 2*s*. 6*d*.

Crito, 2*s*.

Meno. *Second Edition.* 2*s*. 6*d*.

—— Selections. With Introductions and Notes. By JOHN PURVES, M.A., and Preface by B. JOWETT, M.A. *Second Edition.* Extra fcap. 8vo, 5*s*.

—— A Selection of Passages from Plato for English Readers; from the Translation by B. JOWETT, M.A. Edited, with Introductions, by M. J. KNIGHT. 2 vols. Crown 8vo, gilt top, 12*s*.

Plutarch. Lives of the Gracchi. Edited, with Introduction, Notes, and Indices, by G. E. UNDERHILL, M.A. Crown 8vo, 4*s*. 6*d*.

Sophocles. Edited, with Introductions and English Notes, by LEWIS CAMPBELL, M.A., and EVELYN ABBOTT, M.A. *New Edition.* 2 vols. Extra fcap. 8vo, 10*s*. 6*d*.

Sold separately: Vol. I, Text, 4*s*. 6*d*.; Vol. II, Notes, 6*s*.

Or in single Plays, 2s. each.

—— Oedipus Rex: Dindorf's Text, with Notes by the late Bishop of St. David's. Extra fcap. 8vo, limp, 1*s*. 6*d*.

Theocritus (for Schools). With English Notes. By H. KYNASTON, D.D. (late SNOW). *Fifth Edition.* Extra fcap. 8vo, 4*s*. 6*d*.

Thucydides. Book I. Edited, with Notes and Maps, by W. H. Forbes, M.A. 8vo, 8s. 6*d.*

Xenophon. Easy Selections (for Junior Classes). With a Vocabulary, Notes, and Map. By J. S. Phillpotts, B.C.L., and C. S. Jerram, M.A. *Third Edition.* Extra fcap. 8vo, 3s. 6*d.*

—— Selections (for Schools). With Notes and Maps. By J. S. Phillpotts, B.C.L. *Fourth Edition.* Extra fcap. 8vo, 3s. 6*d.*

*** A Key to Sections 1–3, *for Teachers only*, 2s. 6*d. net.*

—— Anabasis, Book I. Edited for the use of Junior Classes and Private Students. With Introduction, Notes, &c. By J. Marshall, M.A. Extra fcap. 8vo, 2s. 6*d.*

—— Anabasis, Book II. With Notes and Map. By C. S. Jerram, M.A. Extra fcap. 8vo, 2s.

—— Anabasis, Book III. With Introduction, Analysis, Notes, &c. By J. Marshall, M.A. Extra fcap. 8vo, 2s. 6*d.*

—— Anabasis, Book IV. By the same Editor. Extra fcap. 8vo, 2s.

—— Vocabulary to the Anabasis. By the same Editor. Extra fcap. 8vo, 1s. 6*d.*

—— Cyropaedia, Book I. With Introduction and Notes. By C. Bigg, D.D. Extra fcap. 8vo, 2s.

—— Cyropaedia, Books IV and V. With Introduction and Notes. By C. Bigg, D.D. Extra fcap. 8vo, 2s. 6*d.*

—— Hellenica, Books I, II. With Introduction and Notes, By G. E. Underhill, M.A. Extra fcap. 8vo, 3s.

—— Memorabilia. Edited, with Introduction and Notes, &c. by J. Marshall, M.A. Extra fcap. 8vo, 4s. 6*d.*

SECTION V.

ORIENTAL LANGUAGES*.

THE SACRED BOOKS OF THE EAST.

TRANSLATED BY VARIOUS ORIENTAL SCHOLARS, AND EDITED BY THE RIGHT HON. F. MAX MÜLLER.

First Series, Vols. I—XXIV. Demy 8vo, cloth.

Vol. I. The Upanishads. Translated by F. MAX MÜLLER. Part I. 10s. 6d.

Vol. II. The Sacred Laws of the Âryas, as taught in the Schools of Âpastamba, Gautama, Vâsish*th*a, and Baudhâyana. Translated by GEORG BÜHLER. Part I. 10s. 6d.

Vol. III. The Sacred Books of China. The Texts of Confucianism. Translated by JAMES LEGGE. Part I. 12s. 6d.

Vol. IV. The Zend-Avesta. Part I. The Vendidâd. Translated by JAMES DARMESTETER. *Second Edition.* 14s.

Vol. V. The Pahlavi Texts. Translated by E. W. WEST. Part I. 12s. 6d.

Vols. VI and IX. The Qur'ân. Translated by E. H. PALMER. 21s.

Vol. VII. The Institutes of Vish*n*u. Translated by JULIUS JOLLY. 10s. 6d.

Vol. VIII. The Bhagavadgîtâ, with The Sanatsu*g*âtîya, and The Anugîtâ. Translated by KÂSHINÂTH TRIMBAK TELANG. 10s. 6d.

Vol. X. The Dhammapada, translated from Pâli by F. MAX MÜLLER; and The Sutta-Nipâta, translated from Pâli by V. FAUSBÖLL; being Canonical Books of the Buddhists. 10s. 6d.

---

* See also ANECDOTA OXON., Series II, III, pp. 51–53.

The Sacred Books of the East (*continued*).

Vol. XI. Buddhist Suttas. Translated from Pâli by T. W. Rhys Davids. 10*s*. 6*d*.

Vol. XII. The *S*atapatha-Brâhma*n*a, according to the Text of the Mâdhyandina School. Translated by Julius Eggeling. Part I. Books I and II. 12*s*. 6*d*.

Vol. XIII. Vinaya Texts. Translated from the Pâli by T. W. Rhys Davids and Hermann Oldenberg. Part I. 10*s*. 6*d*.

Vol. XIV. The Sacred Laws of the Âryas, as taught in the Schools of Âpastamba, Gautama, Vâsish*th*a, and Baudhâyana. Translated by Georg Bühler. Part II. 10*s*. 6*d*.

Vol. XV. The Upanishads. Translated by F. Max Müller. Part II. 10*s*. 6*d*.

Vol. XVI. The Sacred Books of China. The Texts of Confucianism. Translated by James Legge. Part II. 10*s*. 6*d*.

Vol. XVII. Vinaya Texts. Translated from the Pâli by T. W. Rhys Davids and Hermann Oldenberg. Part II. 10*s*. 6*d*.

Vol. XVIII. Pahlavi Texts. Translated by E. W. West. Part II. 12*s*. 6*d*.

Vol. XIX. The Fo-sho-hing-tsan-king. A Life of Buddha by A*s*vaghosha Bodhisattva, translated from Sanskrit into Chinese by Dharmaraksha, A.D. 420, and from Chinese into English by Samuel Beal. 10*s*. 6*d*.

Vol. XX. Vinaya Texts. Translated from the Pâli by T. W. Rhys Davids and Hermann Oldenberg. Part III. 10*s*. 6*d*.

Vol. XXI. The Saddharma-pu*nd*arîka; or, the Lotus of the True Law. Translated by H. Kern. 12*s*. 6*d*.

Vol. XXII. *G*aina-Sûtras. Translated from Prâkrit by Hermann Jacobi. Part I. 10*s*. 6*d*.

Vol. XXIII. The Zend-Avesta. Part II. Translated by James Darmesteter. 10*s*. 6*d*.

Vol. XXIV. Pahlavi Texts. Translated by E. W. West. Part III. 10*s*. 6*d*.

London: Henry Frowde, Amen Corner, E.C.

The Sacred Books of the East (*continued*).

Second Series.

Vol. XXV. Manu. Translated by GEORG BÜHLER. 21*s.*

Vol. XXVI. The *S*atapatha-Brâhma*n*a. Translated by JULIUS EGGELING. Part II. 12*s.* 6*d.*

Vols. XXVII and XXVIII. The Sacred Books of China. The Texts of Confucianism. Translated by JAMES LEGGE. Parts III and IV. 25*s.*

Vols. XXIX and XXX. The G*r*ihya-Sûtras, Rules of Vedic Domestic Ceremonies. Translated by HERMANN OLDENBERG.

Part I (Vol. XXIX). 12*s.* 6*d.*

Part II (Vol. XXX). 12*s.* 6*d.*

Vol. XXXI. The Zend-Avesta. Part III. Translated by L. H. MILLS. 12*s.* 6*d.*

Vol. XXXII. Vedic Hymns. Part I. Translated by F. MAX MÜLLER. 18*s.* 6*d.*

Vol. XXXIII. The Minor Law-books. Translated by JULIUS JOLLY. Part I. Nârada, B*r*ihaspati. 10*s.* 6*d.*

Vol. XXXIV. The Vedânta-Sûtras, with *S*aṅkara's Commentary. Translated by G. THIBAUT. Part I. 12*s.* 6*d.*

Vol. XXXV. The Questions of King Milinda. Part I. Translated from the Pâli by T. W. RHYS DAVIDS. 10*s.* 6*d.*

Vol. XXXVI. The Questions of King Milinda. Part II. 12*s.* 6*d.*

Vol. XXXVII. The Contents of the Nasks, as stated in the Eighth and Ninth Books of the Dinkard. Part I. Translated by E. W. WEST. 15*s.*

Vol. XXXVIII. The Vedânta-Sûtras. Translated by G. THIBAUT. Part II. With Index to Parts I and II. 12*s.* 6*d.*

Vols. XXXIX and XL. The Sacred Books of China. The Texts of Tâoism. Translated by JAMES LEGGE. 21*s.*

The Sacred Books of the East (*continued*).

Vol. XLI. *S*atapatha-Brâhma*n*a. Part III. Translated by JULIUS EGGELING. 12*s.* 6*d.*

Vol. XLII. Hymns of the Atharva-veda. Translated by M. BLOOMFIELD. 21*s.*

Vols. XLIII and XLIV. The *S*atapatha-Brâhma*n*a. Parts IV and V. [*In the Press.*]

Vol. XLV. The *G*aina-Sûtras. Translated from Prâkrit by HERMANN JACOBI. Part II. 12*s.* 6*d.*

Vol. XLVI. Vedic Hymns. Part II. Translated by HERMANN OLDENBERG. 14*s.*

Vol. XLVII. The Contents of the Nasks. Part II. [*In preparation.*]

Vol. XLVIII.

Vol. XLIX. Buddhist Mahâyâna Texts. Buddha-*k*arita, translated by E. B. COWELL. Sukhâvatî-vyûha, Va*g*ra*kk*hedikâ, &c., translated by F. MAX MÜLLER. Amitâyur-Dhyâna-Sûtra, translated by J. TAKAKUSU. 12*s.* 6*d.*

ARABIC. A Practical Arabic Grammar. Compiled by A. O. GREEN, Lieutenant-Colonel, R.E.

Part I. *Third Edition. Revised and Enlarged.* Crown 8vo, 7*s.* 6*d.*

Part II. *Third Edition. Revised and Enlarged.* 10*s.* 6*d.*

BENGALI. Grammar of the Bengali Language; Literary and Colloquial. By JOHN BEAMES. Crown 8vo, cloth, 7*s.* 6*d.*; cut flush, 6*s.*

BURMESE. A Burmese Reader. By R. F. ST. ANDREW ST. JOHN, Hon. M.A. Crown 8vo, 10*s.* 6*d.*

CHALDEE. Book of Tobit. A Chaldee Text, from a unique MS. in the Bodleian Library. Edited by AD. NEUBAUER, M.A. Crown 8vo, 6*s.*

CHINESE. The Chinese Classics: with a Translation, Critical and Exegetical Notes, Prolegomena, and Copious Indexes. By JAMES LEGGE, D.D., LL.D. In Eight Volumes. Royal 8vo.

Vol. I. Confucian Analects, &c. *New Edition.* 1*l.* 10*s.*

Vol. II. The Works of Mencius. *New Edition.* 1*l.* 16*s.*

Vol. III. The Shoo-King; or, The Book of Historical Documents. In two Parts. 1*l.* 10*s.* each.

Vol. IV. The She-King; or, The Book of Poetry. In two Parts. 1*l.* 10*s.* each.

Vol. V. The Ch'un Ts'ew, with the Tso Chuen. In two Parts. 1*l.* 10*s.* each.

CHINESE. The Nestorian Monument of Hsî-an Fû in Shen-hsî, China, relating to the Diffusion of Christianity in China in the Seventh and Eighth Centuries. By JAMES LEGGE, D.D. 2*s.* 6*d.*

CHINESE. Record of Buddhistic Kingdoms; being an Account by the Chinese Monk FÂ-HIEN of his travels in India and Ceylon (A.D. 399-414). Translated and annotated, with a Corean recension of the Chinese Text, by JAMES LEGGE, D.D. Crown 4to, boards, 10*s.* 6*d.*

—— A Record of the Buddhist Religion, as practised in India and the Malay Archipelago (A.D. 671-695). By I-TSING. Translated by J. TAKAKUSU, B.A., Ph.D. With a Letter from the Right Hon. F. MAX MÜLLER. Crown 4to, boards, with Map, 14*s.* net.

—— Catalogue of the Chinese Translation of the Buddhist Tripiṭaka, the Sacred Canon of the Buddhists in China and Japan. Compiled by BUNYIU NANJIO. 4to, 1*l.* 12*s.* 6*d.*

—— Handbook of the Chinese Language. Parts I and II. Grammar and Chrestomathy. By JAMES SUMMERS. 8vo, 1*l.* 8*s.*

COPTIC. Libri Prophetarum Majorum, cum Lamentationibus Jeremiae, in Dialecto Linguae Aegyptiacae Memphitica seu Coptica. Edidit cum Versione Latina H. TATTAM, S.T.P. Tomi II. 8vo, 17*s.*

—— Libri duodecim Prophetarum Minorum in Ling. Aegypt. vulgo Coptica. Edidit H. TATTAM, A.M. 8vo, 8*s.* 6*d.*

—— Novum Testamentum Coptice, cura D. WILKINS. 12*s.* 6*d.*

HEBREW. Psalms in Hebrew (without points). Cr. 8vo, 2*s.*

Driver. Notes on the Hebrew Text of the Books of Samuel. By S. R. DRIVER, D.D. 8vo, 14*s.*

Hebrew (*continued*).

Driver. Treatise on the use of the Tenses in Hebrew. By S. R. Driver, D.D. *Third Edition.* Crown 8vo, 7s. 6d.

—— Commentary on the Book of Proverbs. Attributed to Abraham Ibn Ezra. Edited from a Manuscript in the Bodleian Library by S. R. Driver, D.D. Crown 8vo, paper covers, 3s. 6d.

A Hebrew and English Lexicon of the Old Testament, with an Appendix containing the Biblical Aramaic, based on the Thesaurus and Lexicon of Gesenius, by Francis Brown, D.D., S. R. Driver, D.D., and C. A. Briggs, D.D. Parts I—V. Small 4to, each 2s. 6d. Part VI. [*In the Press.*]

Neubauer. Book of Hebrew Roots, by Abu 'l-Walîd Marwân ibn Janâh, otherwise called Rabbi Yônâh. Now first edited, with an Appendix, by Ad. Neubauer. 4to, 2l. 7s. 6d.

Spurrell. Notes on the Text of the Book of Genesis. By G. J. Spurrell, M.A. *Second Edition.* Crown 8vo, 12s. 6d.

Wickes. Hebrew Accentuation of Psalms, Proverbs, and Job. By William Wickes, D.D. 8vo, 5s.

—— Hebrew Prose Accentuation. 8vo, 10s. 6d.

HINDŪSTĀNĪ. A Hindūstānī Grammar. By A. O. Green, Lieut.-Colonel, R.E. In two Parts. Crown 8vo.

Part I, 8s. 6d. Part II, 7s. 6d.

SANSKRIT. Sanskrit-English Dictionary, Etymologically and Philologically arranged. By Sir M. Monier-Williams, D.C.L. 4to, 4l. 14s. 6d.

—— Practical Grammar of the Sanskrit Language. By Sir M. Monier-Williams, D.C.L. *Fourth Edition.* 8vo, 15s.

—— Nalopákhyánam. Story of Nala, an Episode of the Mahá-bhárata: Sanskrit Text, with a copious Vocabulary, &c. By Sir M Monier-Williams, D.C.L. *Second Edition*, 8vo, 15s.

—— Sakuntalā. A Sanskrit Drama, in seven Acts. Edited by Sir M. Monier-Williams, D.C.L. *Second Edition.* 8vo, 1l. 1s.

SYRIAC. Thesaurus Syriacus: collegerunt Quatremère, Bernstein, Lorsbach, Arnoldi, Agrell, Field, Roediger: edidit R. PAYNE SMITH, S.T.P. Vol. I, containing Fasc. I–V. Sm. fol. 5*l*. 5*s*.

Fasc. VI, 1*l*. 1*s*.; VII, 1*l*. 11*s*. 6*d*.; VIII, 1*l*. 16*s*.; IX, 1*l*. 5*s*.

The First Five Fasciculi may also be had separately.

—— Compendious Syriac Dictionary. Founded on the above, and edited by J. PAYNE SMITH (Mrs. MARGOLIOUTH). Part I, 8*s*. 6*d*, *net*.

—— **The Book of Kalīlah and Dimnah.** Translated from Arabic into Syriac. Edited by W. WRIGHT, LL.D. 8vo, 1*l*. 1*s*.

—— **Cyrilli** Archiepiscopi Alexandrini Commentarii in Lucae Evangelium quae supersunt Syriace. E MSS. apud Mus. Britan. edidit R. PAYNE SMITH, D.D. 4to, 1*l*. 2*s*.

—— —— Translated by the late R. PAYNE SMITH, D.D. 2 vols. 8vo, 14*s*.

—— **Ephraemi Syri, Rabulae** Episcopi Edesseni, **Balaei,** &c., Opera Selecta. E Codd. Syriacis MSS. in Musco Britannico et Bibliotheca Bodleiana asservatis primus edidit J. J. OVERBECK. 8vo, 1*l*. 1*s*.

—— **John,** Bishop of Ephesus. The Third Part of his Ecclesiastical History. [In Syriac.] Now first edited by WILLIAM CURETON, M.A. 4to, 1*l*. 12*s*.

—— —— Translated by the late R. PAYNE SMITH, D.D. 8vo, 10*s*.

TAMIL. First Lessons in Tamil. By G. U. POPE, D.D. *Fifth Edition.* Crown 8vo, 7*s*. 6*d*.

—— The First Catechism of Tamil Grammar. By G. U. POPE, D.D., with an English Translation by D. S. HERRICK, B.A. Crown 8vo, 3*s*.

—— The Nālaḍiyār, or Four Hundred Quatrains in Tamil. Edited by G. U. POPE, D.D. 8vo, 18*s*. *Large Paper*, 2*l*. *half Roxburgh.*

Also issued as follows, in paper covers:—

Part I (Quatrains 1–130) price 3*s*. 6*d*.

Part II (Quatrains 131–320) price 4*s*. 6*d*.

ZEND. The Ancient MS. of the Yasna, with its Pahlavi Translation (A.D. 1323), generally quoted as J2, and now in the possession of the Bodleian Library. Reproduced in Facsimile, and Edited with an Introductory Note by L. H. MILLS, D.D. Half-bound, Imperial 4to, 10*l*. 10*s*. *net*.

SECTION VI.

ANECDOTA OXONIENSIA.

(Crown 4to, stiff covers.)

I. CLASSICAL SERIES.

I. The English Manuscripts of the Nicomachean Ethics. By J. A. Stewart, M.A. 3s. 6d.

II. Nonius Marcellus, de Compendiosa Doctrina, Harleian MS. 2719. Collated by J. H. Onions, M.A. 3s. 6d.

III. Aristotle's Physics. Book VII. With Introduction by R. Shute, M.A. 2s.

IV. Bentley's Plautine Emendations. From his copy of Gronovius. By E. A. Sonnenschein, M.A. 2s. 6d.

V. Harleian MS. 2610; Ovid's Metamorphoses I, II, III. 1–622; XXIV Latin Epigrams from Bodleian or other MSS.; Latin Glosses on Apollinaris Sidonius from MS. Digby 172. Collated and Edited by Robinson Ellis, M.A., LL.D. 4s.

VI. A Collation with the Ancient Armenian Versions of the Greek Text of Aristotle's Categories, De Interpretatione, De Mundo, De Virtutibus et Vitiis, and of Porphyry's Introduction. By F. C. Conybeare, M.A. 14s.

VII. Collations from the Harleian MS. of Cicero 2682. By Albert C. Clark, M.A. 7s. 6d.

II. SEMITIC SERIES.

I. Commentary on Ezra and Nehemiah. By Rabbi Saadiah. Edited by H. J. Mathews, M.A. 3s. 6d.

II. The Book of the Bee. Edited by Ernest A. Wallis Budge, M.A. 21s.

III. A Commentary on the Book of Daniel. By Japhet Ibn Ali. Edited and Translated by D. S. Margoliouth, M.A. 21s.

ANECDOTA OXONIENSIA (*continued*).

IV, VI. Mediaeval Jewish Chronicles and Chronological Notes. Edited by AD. NEUBAUER, M.A.

Part I, 14*s*. Part II, 18*s*. 6*d*.

V. The Palestinian Version of the Holy Scriptures. Five more Fragments recently acquired by the Bodleian Library. Edited by G. H. GWILLIAM, B.D. 6*s*.

VII. Churches and Monasteries of Egypt; attributed to Abû Ṣâliḥ, the Armenian. Edited and translated by B. T. A. EVETTS, M.A., with Notes by A. J. BUTLER, M.A., F.S.A. 1*l*. 11*s*. 6*d*.

*** Translation from the Original Arabic. With Map, buckram, 21*s*.

VIII. The Ethiopic Version of the Hebrew Book of Jubilees. Edited by R. H. CHARLES, M.A. 12*s*. 6*d*.

IX. Biblical and Patristic Relics of the Palestinian Syriac Literature. Edited by G. H. GWILLIAM, F. C. BURKITT, and J. F. STENNING. 12*s*. 6*d*.

III. ARYAN SERIES.

I. Buddhist Texts from Japan. 1. Va*g*ra*kkh*edikâ. Edited by F. MAX MÜLLER. 3*s*. 6*d*.

II. Buddhist Texts from Japan. 2. Sukhâvatî Vyûha. Edited by F. MAX MÜLLER, M.A., and BUNYIU NANJIO. 7*s*. 6*d*.

III. Buddhist Texts from Japan. 3. The Ancient Palm-leaves containing the Pra*gñ*â-Pâramitâ-H*ri*daya-Sûtra and the Ushnîsha-Vigaya-Dhâra*n*î, edited by F. MAX MÜLLER, M.A., and BUNYIU NANJIO, M.A. With an Appendix by G. BÜHLER. 10*s*.

IV. Kâtyâyana's Sarvânukrama*n*î of the *Ri*gveda. With Extracts from Sha*d*guru*s*ishya's Commentary entitled Vedârthadîpikâ. Edited by A. A. MACDONELL, M.A., Ph.D. 16*s*.

V. The Dharma Sa*m*graha. Edited by KENJIU KASAWARA, F. MAX MÜLLER, and H. WENZEL. 7*s*. 6*d*.

VII. The Buddha-*K*arita of A*s*vaghosha. Edited, from three MSS., by E. B. COWELL, M.A. 12*s*. 6*d*.

IV. MEDIAEVAL AND MODERN SERIES.

I. Sinonoma Bartholomei. Edited by J. L. G. MOWAT, M.A. 3*s*. 6*d*.

II. Alphita. Edited by J. L. G. MOWAT, M.A. 12*s*. 6*d*.

III. The Saltair Na Rann. Edited from a MS. in the Bodleian Library, by WHITLEY STOKES, D.C.L. 7*s*. 6*d*.

IV. The Cath Finntrága, or Battle of Ventry. Edited by KUNO MEYER, Ph.D., M.A. 6*s*.

V. Lives of Saints, from the Book of Lismore. Edited, with Translation, by WHITLEY STOKES, D.C.L. 1*l*. 11*s*. 6*d*.

VI. The Elucidarium and other Tracts in Welsh, from Llyvyr Agkyr Llandewivrevi, A.D. 1346. Edited by J. MORRIS JONES, M.A., and JOHN RHŶS, M.A. 21*s*.

VII. The Crawford Collection of Early Charters and Documents, now in the Bodleian Library. Edited by A. S. NAPIER and W. H. STEVENSON. Price 10*s*. 6*d*., or in cloth, 12*s*.

VIII. Hibernica Minora. Being a fragment of an Old-Irish Treatise on the Psalter. With Translation, Notes and Glossary, Edited by KUNO MEYER. 7*s*. 6*d*.

X. The earliest Translation of the Old Testament into the Basque Language (a Fragment). Edited, with Facsimile, by LLEWELYN THOMAS, M.A. 18*s*. 6*d*.

London: HENRY FROWDE, Amen Corner, E.C.

II. THEOLOGY.

A. THE HOLY SCRIPTURES, APOCRYPHA, &c.

COPTIC. Libri Prophetarum Majorum, cum Lamentationibus Jeremiae, in Dialecto Linguae Aegyptiacae Memphitica seu Coptica. Edidit cum Versione Latina H. TATTAM, S.T.P. Tomi II. 8vo, 17*s*.

—— Libri duodecim Prophetarum Minorum in Ling. Aegypt. vulgo Coptica. Edidit H. TATTAM, A.M. 8vo, 8*s*. 6*d*.

—— Novum Testamentum Coptice, cura D. WILKINS. 1716. 4to, 12*s*. 6*d*.

ENGLISH. The Holy Bible in the **Earliest English Versions,** made from the Latin Vulgate by JOHN WYCLIFFE and his followers: edited by FORSHALL and MADDEN. 4 vols. Royal 4to, 3*l*. 3*s*.

Also reprinted from the above, with Introduction and Glossary by W. W. SKEAT, Litt.D.

I. The Books of Job, Psalms, Proverbs, Ecclesiastes, and the Song of Solomon. Extra fcap. 8vo, 3*s*. 6*d*.

II. The New Testament. Extra fcap. 8vo, 6*s*.

—— **The Holy Bible: an exact reprint, page for page, of the Authorized Version published in the year 1611.** Demy 4to, half-bound. 1*l*. 1*s*.

—— **The Holy Bible, Revised Version*.**

Cheap editions for School Use.

Revised Bible. Pearl 16mo, cloth boards, 1*s*. 6*d*.

Revised New Testament. Nonpareil 32mo, 6*d*.; Brevier 16mo, 1*s*. Long Primer 8vo, 1*s*. 6*d*.

—— **The Oxford Bible for Teachers,** containing the Holy Scriptures, together with a new, enlarged, and illustrated edition of the OXFORD HELPS TO THE STUDY OF THE BIBLE, comprising Introductions to the several Books, the History and Antiquities of the Jews, the results of Modern Discoveries, and the Natural History of Palestine, with copious Tables, Concordance and Indices, and a series of Maps. Prices in various sizes and bindings from 3*s*. to 50*s*.

*** *The Revised Version is the joint property of the Universities of Oxford and Cambridge.*

ENGLISH (*continued*).

—— **Helps to the Study of the Bible**, taken from the OXFORD BIBLE FOR TEACHERS. *New, Enlarged, and Illustrated Edition.*

Pearl 16mo, stiff covers, 1*s. net.*
Nonpareil 8vo, cloth boards, 2*s.* 6*d. net.*
Large Type edition, long primer 8vo, cloth boards, 4*s.* 6*d. net.*

—— **Old Testament History for Schools.** By T. H. STOKOE, D.D. Part I. From the Creation to the Settlement in Palestine. Part II. From the Settlement to the Disruption of the Kingdom. Extra fcap. 8vo, 2*s.* 6*d.* each, with maps. Part III. [*In the Press.*]

—— **Notes on the Gospel of St. Luke,** for Junior Classes. By E. J. MOORE SMITH, Lady Principal of the Ladies' College, Durban, Natal. Extra fcap. 8vo, stiff covers, 1*s.* 6*d.*

—— **The Psalter,** or Psalms of David, and certain Canticles, with a Translation and Exposition in English, by RICHARD ROLLE of Hampole. Edited by H. R. BRAMLEY, M.A., Fellow of S. M. Magdalen College, Oxford. With an Introduction and Glossary. Demy 8vo, 1*l.* 1*s.*

—— **Studia Biblica et Ecclesiastica.** Essays in Biblical and Patristic Criticism, and kindred subjects. By Members of the University of Oxford. 8vo.
Vol. I, 10*s.* 6*d.* Vol. II, 12*s.* 6*d.* Vol. III, 16*s.* Vol. IV, 12*s.* 6*d.*

—— **Deuterographs.** Duplicate passages in the Old Testament. Arranged and Annotated by R. B. GIRDLESTONE, M.A. 8vo, 7*s.* 6*d.*

—— **Lectures on the Book of Job.** Delivered in Westminster Abbey by the Very Rev. G. G. BRADLEY, D.D. *Second Edition.* Crown 8vo, 7*s.* 6*d.*

—— **Lectures on Ecclesiastes.** By the same Author. Cr. 8vo, 4*s.* 6*d.*

—— **The Book of Wisdom:** the Greek Text, the Latin Vulgate, and the Authorised English Version; with an Introduction, Critical Apparatus, and a Commentary. By W. J. DEANE, M.A. 4to, 12*s.* 6*d.*

—— **The Five Books of Maccabees,** in English, with Notes and Illustrations by HENRY COTTON, D.C.L. 8vo, 10*s.* 6*d.*

—— **The Book of Enoch.** Translated from Dillmann's Ethiopic Text (emended and revised), and Edited by R. H. CHARLES, M.A. 8vo, 16*s.*

—— **The Book of the Secrets of Enoch.** Translated from the Slavonic by W. R. MORFILL, M.A., and Edited, with Introduction, Notes, &c., by R. H. CHARLES, M.A. 8vo, 7*s.* 6*d.*

—— **List of Editions of the Bible in English.** By HENRY COTTON, D.C.L. *Second Edition.* 8vo, 8*s.* 6*d.*

ENGLISH (*continued*).

—— **Rhemes and Doway.** An attempt to show what has been done by Roman Catholics for the diffusion of the Holy Scriptures in English. By HENRY COTTON, D.C.L. 8vo, 9*s.*

GOTHIC. Evangeliorum Versio Gothica, cum Interpr. et Annott. E. BENZELII. Edidit E. LYE, A.M. 4to, 12*s.* 6*d.*

—— **The Gospel of St. Mark in Gothic,** according to the translation made by WULFILA in the Fourth Century. Edited by W. W. SKEAT, Litt.D. Extra fcap. 8vo, 4*s.*

GREEK. Old Testament. Vetus Testamentum ex Versione Septuaginta Interpretum secundum exemplar Vaticanum Romae editum. Accedit potior varietas Codicis Alexandrini. Tomi III. 18mo, 18*s.*

—— Vetus Testamentum Graece cum Variis Lectionibus. Editionem a R. HOLMES, S.T.P. inchoatam continuavit J. PARSONS, S.T.B. Tomi V. folio, 7*l.*

—— **A Concordance to the Septuagint** and the other Greek Versions of the Old Testament (including the Apocryphal Books). By the late EDWIN HATCH, M.A., and H. A. REDPATH, M.A. In six Parts. Imperial 4to, *each* 21*s.*

—— Origenis Hexaplorum quae supersunt; sive, Veterum Interpretum Graecorum in totum Vetus Testamentum Fragmenta. Edidit FREDERICUS FIELD, A.M. 2 vols. 1875. 4to, 5*l.* 5*s.*

—— Essays in Biblical Greek. By EDWIN HATCH, M.A., D.D. 8vo, 10*s.* 6*d.*

—— An Essay on the Place of Ecclesiasticus in Semitic Literature. By D. S. MARGOLIOUTH, M.A. Small 4to, 2*s.* 6*d.*

—— **New Testament.** Novum Testamentum Graece. Antiquissimorum Codicum Textus in ordine parallelo dispositi. Edidit E. H. HANSELL, S.T.B. Tomi III. 8vo, 24*s.*

—— Novum Testamentum Graece. Accedunt parallela S. Scripturae loca, &c. Edidit CAROLUS LLOYD, S.T.P.R. 18mo, 3*s.*

On writing paper, with wide margin, 7*s.* 6*d.*

Critical Appendices to the above, by W. SANDAY, D.D. Extra fcap. 8vo, cloth, 3*s.* 6*d.*

—— Novum Testamentum Graece. Accedunt parallela S. Scripturae loca, &c. Ed. C. LLOYD, with SANDAY'S Appendices. Cloth, 6*s.*; paste grain, 7*s.* 6*d.*; morocco, 10*s.* 6*d.*

GREEK (*continued*).

—— Novum Testamentum Graece juxta Exemplar Millianum. 18mo, 2*s*. 6*d*. *On writing paper, with wide margin*, 7*s*. 6*d*.

—— Evangelia Sacra Graece. Fcap. 8vo, limp, 1*s*. 6*d*.

—— The Greek Testament, with the Readings adopted by the Revisers of the Authorised Version:—

(1) Pica type, with Marginal References. Demy 8vo, 10*s*. 6*d*.

(2) Long Primer type. Fcap. 8vo, 4*s*. 6*d*.

(3) *The same, on writing paper, with wide margin*, 15*s*.

—— The New Testament in Greek and English. Edited by E. Cardwell, D.D. 2 vols. 1837. Crown 8vo, 6*s*.

—— The Parallel New Testament, Greek and English; being the Authorised Version, 1611; the Revised Version, 1881; and the Greek Text followed in the Revised Version. 8vo, 12*s*. 6*d*.

—— Diatessaron; sive Historia Jesu Christi ex ipsis Evangelistarum verbis apte dispositis confecta. Ed. J. White. 3*s*. 6*d*.

—— Outlines of Textual Criticism applied to the New Testament. By C. E. Hammond, M.A. *Fifth Edition*. Crown 8vo, 4*s*. 6*d*.

—— A Greek Testament Primer. An Easy Grammar and Reading Book for the use of Students beginning Greek. By E. Miller, M.A. *Second Edition*. Extra fcap. 8vo, paper, 2*s*.; cloth, 3*s*. 6*d*.

—— Canon Muratorianus. Edited, with Notes and Facsimile, by S. P. Tregelles, LL.D. 4to, 10*s*. 6*d*.

HEBREW, &c. A Hebrew and English Lexicon of the Old Testament, with an Appendix containing the Biblical Aramaic, based on the Thesaurus and Lexicon of Gesenius, by Francis Brown, D.D., S. R. Driver, D.D., and C. A. Briggs, D.D. Parts I—V. Small 4to, each 2*s*. 6*d*.

—— Notes on the Text of the Book of Genesis. By G. J. Spurrell, M.A. *Second Edition*. Crown 8vo, 12*s*. 6*d*.

—— Notes on the Hebrew Text of the Books of Samuel. By S. R. Driver, D.D. 8vo, 14*s*.

—— The Psalms in Hebrew without points. Stiff covers, 2*s*.

—— A Commentary on the Book of Proverbs. Attributed to Abraham Ibn Ezra. Edited from a MS. in the Bodleian Library by S. R. Driver, D.D. Crown 8vo, paper covers, 3*s*. 6*d*.

HEBREW, &c. (*continued*).

—— The Book of Tobit. A Chaldee Text, from a unique MS. in the Bodleian Library; with other Rabbinical Texts, English Translations, and the Itala. Edited by AD. NEUBAUER, M.A. Crown 8vo, 6*s*.

—— Ecclesiasticus (xxxix. 15—xlix. 11). The Original Hebrew, with Early Versions and English Translation, &c. Edited by A. E. COWLEY, M.A., and AD. NEUBAUER, M.A. 4to, 10*s*. 6*d*. *net*.

—— Hebrew Accentuation of Psalms, Proverbs, and Job. By WILLIAM WICKES, D.D. 8vo, 5*s*.

—— Hebrew Prose Accentuation. By the same. 8vo, 10*s*. 6*d*.

—— Horae Hebraicae et Talmudicae, a J. LIGHTFOOT. A new Edition, by R. GANDELL, M.A. 4 vols. 8vo, 1*l*. 1*s*.

LATIN. Libri Psalmorum Versio antiqua Latina, cum Paraphrasi Anglo-Saxonica. Edidit B. THORPE, F.A.S. 8vo, 10*s*. 6*d*.

—— Nouum Testamentum Domini Nostri Iesu Christi Latine, secundum Editionem Sancti Hieronymi. Ad Codicum Manuscriptorum fidem recensuit IOHANNES WORDSWORTH, S.T.P., Episcopus Sarisburiensis; in operis societatem adsumto HENRICO IULIANO WHITE, A.M. 4to.

Fasc. I. 12*s*. 6*d*.; *Fasc. II.* 7*s*. 6*d*.; *Fasc. III.* 12*s*. 6*d*.; *Fasc. IV.* 10*s*. 6*d*.

—— Old-Latin Biblical Texts: No. I. The Gospel according to St. Matthew, from the St. Germain MS. (g_1). Edited by JOHN WORDSWORTH, D.D. Small 4to, stiff covers, 6*s*.

—— Old-Latin Biblical Texts: No. II. Portions of the Gospels according to St. Mark and St. Matthew, from the Bobbio MS. (k), &c. Edited by JOHN WORDSWORTH, D.D., W. SANDAY, D.D., and H. J. WHITE, M.A. Small 4to, stiff covers, 21*s*.

—— Old-Latin Biblical Texts: No. III. The Four Gospels, from the Munich MS. (q), now numbered Lat. 6224 in the Royal Library at Munich. With a Fragment from St. John in the Hof-Bibliothek at Vienna (Cod. Lat. 502). Edited, with the aid of Tischendorf's transcript (under the direction of the Bishop of Salisbury), by H. J. WHITE, M.A. Small 4to, stiff covers, 12*s*. 6*d*.

OLD-FRENCH. Libri Psalmorum Versio antiqua Gallica e Cod. MS. in Bibl. Bodleiana adservato, una cum Versione Metrica aliisque Monumentis pervetustis. Nunc primum descripsit et edidit FRANCISCUS MICHEL, Phil. Doc. 8vo, 10*s*. 6*d*.

SYRIAC. Collatio Cod. Lewisiani Evangeliorum Syriacorum cum Cod. Curetoniano, auctore A. BONUS, A.M. Demy 4to, 8*s*. 6*d*. *net*.

B. FATHERS OF THE CHURCH, &c.

St. Athanasius: Orations against the Arians. With an Account of his Life by WILLIAM BRIGHT, D.D. Crown 8vo, 9*s*.

—— Historical Writings, according to the Benedictine Text. With an Introduction by W. BRIGHT, D.D. Crown 8vo, 10*s*. 6*d*.

St. Augustine: Select Anti-Pelagian Treatises, and the Acts of the Second Council of Orange. With an Introduction by WILLIAM BRIGHT, D.D. Crown 8vo, 9*s*.

St. Basil: The Book of St. Basil on the Holy Spirit. A Revised Text, with Notes and Introduction by C. F. H. JOHNSTON, M.A. Crown 8vo, 7*s*. 6*d*.

Barnabas, The Editio Princeps of the Epistle of, by Archbishop Ussher, as printed at Oxford, A.D. 1642, and preserved in an imperfect form in the Bodleian Library. With a Dissertation by J. H. BACKHOUSE, M.A. Small 4to, 3*s*. 6*d*.

Canons of the First Four General Councils of Nicaea, Constantinople, Ephesus, and Chalcedon. With Notes, by W. BRIGHT, D.D. *Second Edition.* Crown 8vo, 7*s*. 6*d*.

Catenae Graecorum Patrum in Novum Testamentum. Edidit J. A. CRAMER, S.T.P. Tomi VIII. 8vo, 2*l*. 4*s*.

Clementis Alexandrini Opera, ex recensione Guil. Dindorfii. Tomi IV. 8vo, 3*l*.

Cyrilli Archiepiscopi Alexandrini in XII Prophetas. Edidit P. E. PUSEY, A.M. Tomi II. 8vo, 2*l*. 2*s*.

—— in D. Joannis Evangelium. Accedunt Fragmenta Varia necnon Tractatus ad Tiberium Diaconum Duo. Edidit post Aubertum P. E. PUSEY, A.M. Tomi III. 8vo, 2*l*. 5*s*.

—— Commentarii in Lucae Evangelium quae supersunt Syriace. E MSS. apud Mus. Britan. edidit R. PAYNE SMITH, D.D. 4to, 1*l*. 2*s*.

—— —— Translated by R. PAYNE SMITH, D.D. 2 vols. 14*s*.

Ephraemi Syri, Rabulae Episcopi Edesseni, Balaei, aliorumque Opera Selecta. E Codd. Syriacis MSS. in Museo Britannico et Bibliotheca Bodleiana asservatis primus edidit J. J. OVERBECK. 8vo, 1*l*. 1*s*.

Eusebii Pamphili Evangelicae Praeparationis Libri XV. Ad Codd. MSS. recensuit T. GAISFORD, S.T.P. Tomi IV. 8vo, 1*l*. 10*s*.

—— Evangelicae Demonstrationis Libri X. Recensuit T. GAISFORD, S.T.P. Tomi II. 8vo, 15*s*.

—— contra Hieroclem et Marcellum Libri. Recensuit T. GAISFORD, S.T.P. 8vo, 7*s*.

Eusebius' Ecclesiastical History, according to the text of BURTON, with an Introduction by W. BRIGHT, D.D. *Second Edition.* Crown 8vo, 8*s*. 6*d*.

—— —— Annotationes Variorum. Tomi II. 8vo, 17*s*.

Evagrii Historia Ecclesiastica, ex recensione H. VALESII. 1844. 8vo, 4*s*.

Irenaeus: The Third Book of St. Irenaeus, Bishop of Lyons, against Heresies. With short Notes and a Glossary by H. DEANE, B.D. Crown 8vo, 5*s*. 6*d*.

Origenis Philosophumena; sive omnium Haeresium Refutatio. E Codice Parisino nunc primum edidit EMMANUEL MILLER. 8vo, 10*s*.

Patrum Apostolicorum, S. Clementis Romani, S. Ignatii, S. Polycarpi, quae supersunt. Edidit GUIL. JACOBSON, S.T.P.R. Tomi II. *Fourth Edition.* 8vo, 1*l*. 1*s*.

Philo. About the Contemplative Life; or, the Fourth Book of the Treatise concerning Virtues. Critically edited, with a defence of its genuineness. By FRED. C. CONYBEARE, M.A. With a Facsimile. 8vo, 14*s*.

Reliquiae Sacrae secundi tertiique saeculi. Recensuit M. J. ROUTH, S.T.P. Tomi V. *Second Edition.* 8vo, 1*l*. 5*s*.

Scriptorum Ecclesiasticorum Opuscula. Recensuit M. J. ROUTH, S.T.P. Tomi II. *Third Edition.* 8vo, 10*s*.

Socratis Scholastici Historia Ecclesiastica. Gr. et Lat. Edidit R. HUSSEY, S.T.B. Tomi III. 1853. 8vo, 15*s*.

Socrates' Ecclesiastical History, according to the Text of HUSSEY, with an Introduction by WILLIAM BRIGHT, D.D. *Second Edition.* Crown 8vo, 7*s*. 6*d*.

Sozomeni Historia Ecclesiastica. Edidit R. HUSSEY, S.T.B. Tomi III. 8vo, 15*s*.

Tertulliani Apologeticus adversus Gentes pro Christianis. Edited, with Introduction and Notes, by T. HERBERT BINDLEY, B.D. Crown 8vo, 6*s*.

Tertulliani De Praescriptione Haereticorum: ad Martyras: ad Scapulam. With Introductions and Notes. By T. HERBERT BINDLEY, B.D. Crown 8vo, 6*s*.

Theodoreti Ecclesiasticae Historiae Libri V. Recensuit T. GAISFORD, S.T.P. 8vo, 7*s*. 6*d*.

—— Graecarum Affectionum Curatio. Ad Codices MSS. recensuit T. GAISFORD, S.T.P. 8vo, 7*s*. 6*d*.

C. ECCLESIASTICAL HISTORY, &c.

Adamnani Vita S. Columbae. Edited, with Introduction, Notes, and Glossary, by J. T. FOWLER, M.A., D.C.L. Crown 8vo, half-bound, 8*s*. 6*d*. net.

—— The same, together with Translation. 9*s*. 6*d*. *net*.

Baedae Historia Ecclesiastica. *A New Edition, in Two Volumes.* Edited by C. PLUMMER, M.A. Crown 8vo, 21*s*. *net*.

Bigg. The Christian Platonists of Alexandria; being the Bampton Lectures for 1886. By CHARLES BIGG, D.D. 8vo, 10*s*. 6*d*.

Bingham's Antiquities of the Christian Church, and other Works. 10 vols. 8vo, 3*l*. 3*s*.

Bright. Chapters of Early English Church History. By W. BRIGHT, D.D. *Second Edition.* 8vo, 12*s*.

Burnet's History of the Reformation of the Church of England. *A new Edition.* Carefully revised, and the Records collated with the originals, by N. POCOCK, M.A. 7 vols. 8vo, 1*l*. 10*s*.

Cardwell's Documentary Annals of the Reformed Church of England; being a Collection of Injunctions, Declarations, Orders, Articles of Inquiry, &c., from 1546 to 1716. 2 vols. 8vo, 18*s*.

Councils and Ecclesiastical Documents relating to Great Britain and Ireland. Edited, after SPELMAN and WILKINS, by A. W. HADDAN, B.D., and W. STUBBS, D.D. Vols. I and III. Medium 8vo, each 1*l*. 1*s*.

Vol. II, Part I. Medium 8vo, 10*s*. 6*d*.

Vol. II, Part II. Church of Ireland; Memorials of St. Patrick. Stiff covers, 3*s*. 6*d*.

Formularies of Faith set forth by the King's authority during the Reign of Henry VIII. 8vo, 7*s*.

Fuller's Church History of Britain. Edited by J. S. BREWER, M.A. 6 vols. 8vo, 1*l*. 19*s*.

Gibson's Synodus Anglicana. Edited by E. CARDWELL, D.D. 8vo, 6*s*.

Hamilton's (Archbishop John) Catechism, 1552. Edited, with Introduction and Glossary, by THOMAS GRAVES LAW. With a Preface by the Right Hon. W. E. GLADSTONE. Demy 8vo, 12*s*. 6*d*.

Inett's Origines Anglicanae (in continuation of Stillingfleet). Edited by J. GRIFFITHS, M.A. 3 vols. 8vo, 15*s*.

John, Bishop of Ephesus. The Third Part of his Ecclesiastical History. [In Syriac.] Now first edited by WILLIAM CURETON, M.A. 4to, 1*l*. 12*s*.

—— The same, translated by R. PAYNE SMITH, D.D. 8vo, 10*s*.

Le Neve's Fasti Ecclesiae Anglicanae. Corrected and continued from 1715 to 1853 by T. DUFFUS HARDY. 3 vols. 8vo, 1*l*. 1*s*.

Noelli (A.) Catechismus sive prima institutio disciplinaque Pietatis Christianae Latine explicata. Editio nova cura GUIL. JACOBSON, A.M. 8vo, 5*s*. 6*d*.

Prideaux's Connection of Sacred and Profane History. 2 vols. 8vo, 10*s*.

Primers put forth in the Reign of Henry VIII. 8vo, 5*s*.

Records of the Reformation. The Divorce, 1527–1533. Mostly now for the first time printed from MSS. in the British Museum and other Libraries. Collected and arranged by N. POCOCK, M.A. 2 vols. 8vo, 1*l*. 16*s*.

Reformatio Legum Ecclesiasticarum. The Reformation of Ecclesiastical Laws, as attempted in the reigns of Henry VIII, Edward VI, and Elizabeth. Edited by E. CARDWELL, D.D. 8vo, 6*s*. 6*d*.

Shirley. Some Account of the Church in the Apostolic Age. By W. W. SHIRLEY, D.D. *Second Edition.* Fcap. 8vo, 3*s*. 6*d*.

Shuckford's Sacred and Profane History connected (in continuation of Prideaux). 2 vols. 8vo, 10*s*.

Stillingfleet's Origines Britannicae, with LLOYD'S Historical Account of Church Government. Edited by T. P. PANTIN, M.A. 2 vols. 8vo, 10*s*.

Stubbs. Registrum Sacrum Anglicanum. An attempt to exhibit the course of Episcopal Succession in England. By W. STUBBS, D.D. Small 4to, 8*s*. 6*d*.

Strype's Memorials of Cranmer. 2 vols. 8vo, 11*s*.
Life of Aylmer. 8vo, 5*s*. 6*d*.
Life of Whitgift. 3 vols. 8vo, 16*s*. 6*d*.
General Index. 2 vols. 8vo, 11*s*.

Sylloge Confessionum sub tempus Reformandae Ecclesiae editarum. Subjiciuntur Catechismus Heidelbergensis et Canones Synodi Dordrechtanae. 8vo, 8*s*.

D. LITURGIOLOGY.

Brightman. Liturgies, Eastern and Western. Vol. I. *Eastern Liturgies.* Edited, with Introductions and Appendices, by F. E. Brightman, M.A., on the Basis of a former work by C. E. Hammond, M.A. 8vo, 21*s*.

Cardwell's Two Books of Common Prayer, set forth by authority in the Reign of King Edward VI, compared with each other. *Third Edition.* 8vo, 7*s*.

—— History of Conferences on the Book of Common Prayer from 1551 to 1690. *Third Edition.* 8vo, 7*s*. 6*d*.

Gelasian Sacramentary. Liber Sacramentorum Romanae Ecclesiae. Edited, with Introduction, Critical Notes, and Appendix, by H. A. Wilson, M.A. Medium 8vo, 18*s*.

Helps to the Study of the Book of Common Prayer. Being a Companion to Church Worship. Crown 8vo, 3*s*. 6*d*.

Leofric Missal, The; together with some Account of the Red Book of Derby, the Missal of Robert of Jumièges, &c. Edited, with Introduction and Notes, by F. E. Warren, B.D., F.S.A. 4to, half-morocco, 1*l*. 15*s*.

Maskell. Ancient Liturgy of the Church of England, according to the uses of Sarum, York, Hereford, and Bangor, and the Roman Liturgy arranged in parallel columns, with preface and notes. By W. Maskell, M.A. *Third Edition.* 8vo, 15*s*.

—— Monumenta Ritualia Ecclesiae Anglicanae. The occasional Offices of the Church of England according to the old use of Salisbury, the Prymer in English, and other prayers and forms, with dissertations and notes. *Second Edition.* 3 vols. 8vo, 2*l*. 10*s*.

Warren. The Liturgy and Ritual of the Celtic Church. By F. E. Warren, B.D. 8vo, 14*s*.

E. ENGLISH THEOLOGY.

Bradley. Lectures on the Book of Job. By GEORGE GRANVILLE BRADLEY, D.D., Dean of Westminster. *Second Edition.* Crown 8vo, 7*s*. 6*d*.

—— Lectures on Ecclesiastes. By G. G. BRADLEY, D.D. Crown 8vo, 4*s*. 6*d*.

Bull's Works, with NELSON'S Life. Edited by E. BURTON, D.D. 8 vols. 8vo, 2*l*. 9*s*.

Burnet's Exposition of the XXXIX Articles. 8vo, 7*s*.

Burton's (Edward) Testimonies of the Ante-Nicene Fathers to the Divinity of Christ. 1829. 8vo, 7*s*.

—— Testimonies of the Ante-Nicene Fathers to the Doctrine of the Trinity and of the Divinity of the Holy Ghost. 1831. 8vo, 3*s*. 6*d*.

Butler. The Works of Bishop Butler. Edited by the Right Hon. W. E. GLADSTONE. 2 vols. Medium 8vo, 1*l*. 8*s*.

—— Works. 2 vols. 8vo, 11*s*.

—— Sermons. 5*s*. 6*d*. Analogy of Religion. 5*s*. 6*d*.

Chillingworth's Works. 3 vols. 8vo, 1*l*. 1*s*. 6*d*.

Clergyman's Instructor. *Sixth Edition.* 8vo, 6*s*. 6*d*.

Cranmer's Works. Collected and arranged by H. JENKYNS. 4 vols. 8vo, 1*l*. 10*s*.

Du Buisson. Origin and Peculiar Characteristics of the Gospel of S. Mark. By J. C. DU BUISSON, B.A. 8vo, paper covers, 1*s*. 6*d*. net.

Enchiridion Theologicum Anti-Romanum.

Vol. I. JEREMY TAYLOR'S Dissuasive from Popery, and Treatise on the Real Presence. 8vo, 8*s*.

Vol. II. BARROW on the Supremacy of the Pope, with his Discourse on the Unity of the Church. 8vo, 7*s*. 6*d*.

Vol. III. Tracts selected from WAKE, PATRICK, STILLINGFLEET, CLAGETT, and others. 8vo, 11*s*.

Greswell's Harmonia Evangelica. *Fifth Edition.* 8vo, 9*s*. 6*d*.

Hall's Works. Edited by P. WYNTER, D.D. 10 vols. 8vo, 3*l*. 3*s*.

Heurtley. Harmonia Symbolica: Creeds of the Western Church. By C. HEURTLEY, D.D. 8vo, 6*s*. 6*d*.

Homilies appointed to be read in Churches. Edited by J. GRIFFITHS, M.A. 8vo, 7*s*. 6*d*.

HOOKER'S WORKS, with his Life by WALTON, arranged by JOHN KEBLE, M.A. *Seventh Edition.* Revised by R. W. CHURCH, M.A., and F. PAGET, D.D. 3 vols. Medium 8vo, 1*l*. 16*s*.

—— the Text as arranged by J. KEBLE, M.A. 2 vols. 8vo, 11*s*.

Hooper's Works. 2 vols. 8vo, 8*s*.

Jackson's (Dr. Thomas) Works. 12 vols. 8vo, 3*l*. 6*s*.

Jewel's Works. Edited by R. W. JELF, D.D. 8 vols. 8vo, 1*l*. 10*s*.

Ommanney. A Critical Dissertation on the Athanasian Creed. By G. D. W. OMMANNEY, M.A. 8vo, 16*s*.

Patrick's Theological Works. 9 vols. 8vo, 1*l*. 1*s*.

Pearson's Exposition of the Creed. Revised and corrected by E. BURTON, D.D. *Sixth Edition.* 8vo, 10*s*. 6*d*.

—— Minor Theological Works. Edited with a Memoir, by EDWARD CHURTON, M.A. 2 vols. 8vo, 10*s*.

Sanderson's Works. Edited by W. JACOBSON, D.D. 6 vols. 8vo, 1*l*. 10*s*.

Stillingfleet's Origines Sacrae. 2 vols. 8vo, 9*s*.

—— Rational Account of the Grounds of Protestant Religion. 2 vols. 8vo, 10*s*.

Wall's History of Infant Baptism. Edited by HENRY COTTON, D.C.L. 2 vols. 8vo, 1*l*. 1*s*.

Waterland's Works, with Life, by Bp. VAN MILDERT. *A new Edition*, with copious Indexes. 6 vols. 8vo, 2*l*. 11*s*.

—— Review of the Doctrine of the Eucharist, with a Preface by the late Bishop of London. *Third Edition.* Crown 8vo, 6*s*. 6*d*.

Wheatly's Illustration of the Book of Common Prayer. 8vo, 5*s*.

Wyclif. A Catalogue of the Original Works of John Wyclif. By W. W. SHIRLEY, D.D. 8vo, 3*s*. 6*d*.

—— Select English Works. By T. ARNOLD, M.A. 3 vols. 8vo, 1*l*. 1*s*.

—— Trialogus. With the Supplement now first edited. By GOTTHARD LECHLER. 8vo, 7*s*.

III. HISTORY, BIOGRAPHY, POLITICAL ECONOMY, &c.

Arbuthnot. The Life and Works of John Arbuthnot. By GEORGE A. AITKEN. 8vo, cloth extra, with Portrait, 16*s*.

Baker's Chronicle. Chronicon Galfridi le Baker de Swynebroke. Edited with Notes by Sir E. MAUNDE THOMPSON, K.C.B., D.C.L., F.S.A. Small 4to, stiff covers, 18*s*.; cloth, gilt top, 21*s*.

Bentham. A Fragment on Government. By JEREMY BENTHAM. Edited by F. C. MONTAGUE, M.A. 8vo, 7*s*. 6*d*.

Bluntschli. The Theory of the State. By J. K. BLUNTSCHLI. Translated from the Sixth German Edition. Second Edition, Revised. Crown 8vo, half-bound, 8*s*. 6*d*.

Boswell's Life of Samuel Johnson, LL.D.; including BOSWELL'S Journal of a Tour to the Hebrides, and JOHNSON'S Diary of a Journey into North Wales. Edited by G. BIRKBECK HILL, D.C.L. In six vols., 8vo. With Portraits and Facsimiles. Half-bound, 3*l*. 3*s*.

Burnet's History of James II. 8vo, 9*s*. 6*d*.

—— History of My Own Time. Vol. I. *A New Edition.* Edited by OSMUND AIRY, M.A. 12*s*. 6*d*.

—— Life of Sir M. Hale, and **Fell's** Life of Dr. Hammond. Small 8vo, 2*s*. 6*d*.

Calendar of the Clarendon State Papers, preserved in the Bodleian Library. In three volumes. 1869–76.

Vol. I. From 1523 to January 1649. 8vo, 18*s*.
Vol. II. From 1649 to 1654. 8vo, 16*s*.
Vol. III. From 1655 to 1657. 8vo, 14*s*.

Calendar of Charters and Rolls preserved in the Bodleian Library. 8vo, 1*l*. 11*s*. 6*d*.

Carte's Life of James Duke of Ormond. A new Edition, carefully compared with the original MSS. 6 vols. 8vo, 1*l*. 5*s*.

Casaubon (Isaac), Life of, by MARK PATTISON, B.D. *Second Edition.* 8vo, 16*s*.

Casauboni Ephemerides, cum praefatione et notis J. RUSSELL, S.T.P. Tomi II. 8vo, 15*s*.

Chesterfield. Letters of Philip Dormer Fourth Earl of Chesterfield, to his Godson and Successor. Edited from the Originals, with a Memoir of Lord Chesterfield, by the late EARL OF CARNARVON. *Second Edition.* With Appendix of Additional Correspondence. Royal 8vo, cloth extra, 21*s.*

Clarendon's History of the Rebellion and Civil Wars in England. Re-edited from a fresh collation of the original MS. in the Bodleian Library, with marginal dates and occasional notes, by W. DUNN MACRAY, M.A., F.S.A. 6 vols. Crown 8vo, 2*l.* 5*s.*

—— History of the Rebellion and Civil Wars in England. To which are subjoined the Notes of BISHOP WARBURTON. 1849. 7 vols. Medium 8vo, 2*l.* 10*s.*

—— History of the Rebellion and Civil Wars in England. Also his Life, written by himself, in which is included a Continuation of his History of the Grand Rebellion. Royal 8vo, 1*l.* 2*s.*

Clarendon's Life, including a Continuation of his History. 2 vols. 1857. Medium 8vo, 1*l.* 2*s.*

Clinton's Fasti Hellenici. The Civil and Literary Chronology of Greece, from the LVIth to the CXXIIIrd Olympiad. *Third Edition.* 4to, 1*l.* 14*s.* 6*d.*

—— Fasti Hellenici. The Civil and Literary Chronology of Greece, from the CXXIVth Olympiad to the Death of Augustus. *Second Edition.* 4to, 1*l.* 12*s.*

—— Epitome of the Fasti Hellenici. 8vo, 6*s.* 6*d.*

—— Fasti Romani. The Civil and Literary Chronology of Rome and Constantinople, from the Death of Augustus to the Death of Heraclius. 2 vols. 4to, 2*l.* 2*s.*

—— Epitome of the Fasti Romani. 8vo, 7*s.*

Codrington. The Melanesians. Studies in their Anthropology and Folk-Lore. By R. H. CODRINGTON, D.D. 8vo, 16*s.*

Cramer's Geographical and Historical Description of Asia Minor. 2 vols. 8vo, 11*s.*

—— Description of Ancient Greece. 3 vols. 8vo, 16*s.* 6*d.*

Earle. Handbook to the Land-Charters, and other Saxonic Documents. By JOHN EARLE, M.A. Crown 8vo, 16*s.*

Elizabethan Seamen, Voyages of, to America. Edited by E. J. PAYNE, M.A. *First Series.* HAWKINS. FROBISHER. DRAKE. *Second Edition.* Crown 8vo, 5*s.*

Finlay. A History of Greece from its Conquest by the Romans to the present time, B.C. 146 to A.D. 1864. By GEORGE FINLAY, LL.D. A new Edition, revised throughout, and in part re-written, with considerable additions, by the Author, and edited by H. F. TOZER, M.A. 7 vols. 8vo, 3*l.* 10*s.*

Fortescue. The Governance of England: otherwise called The Difference between an Absolute and a Limited Monarchy. By Sir JOHN FORTESCUE, Kt. A Revised Text. Edited, with Introduction, Notes, &c., by CHARLES PLUMMER, M.A. 8vo, half-bound, 12*s.* 6*d.*

Freeman. The History of Sicily from the Earliest Times. By E. A. FREEMAN, M.A., D.C.L.

Vols. I and II. 8vo, 2*l.* 2*s.*

Vol. III. The Athenian and Carthaginian Invasions. 1*l.* 4*s.*

Vol. IV. From the Tyranny of Dionysios to the Death of Agathoklês. Edited from Posthumous MSS., by ARTHUR J. EVANS, M.A. 1*l.* 1*s.*

—— History of the Norman Conquest of England; its Causes and Results. By E. A. FREEMAN, D.C.L. In Six Volumes, 8vo, 5*l.* 9*s.* 6*d.*

—— The Reign of William Rufus and the Accession of Henry the First. 2 vols. 8vo, 1*l.* 16*s.*

—— A Short History of the Norman Conquest of England. *Third Edition.* Extra fcap. 8vo, 2*s.* 6*d.*

French Revolutionary Speeches. See STEPHENS, H. Morse.

Gardiner. The Constitutional Documents of the Puritan Revolution. 1628–1660. Selected and Edited by SAMUEL RAWSON GARDINER, D.C.L. Crown 8vo, 9*s.*

Gascoigne's Theological Dictionary ('Liber Veritatum'): Selected Passages, illustrating the Condition of Church and State, 1403–1458. With an Introduction by JAMES E. THOROLD ROGERS, M.A. Small 4to, 10*s.* 6*d.*

George. Genealogical Tables illustrative of Modern History. By H. B. GEORGE, M.A. *Third Edition.* Small 4to, 12*s.*

Greswell's Fasti Temporis Catholici. 4 vols. 8vo, 2*l.* 10*s.*

—— Tables to Fasti, 4to, and Introduction to Tables, 8vo, 15*s.*

—— Origines Kalendariæ Italicæ. 4 vols. 8vo, 2*l.* 2*s.*

—— Origines Kalendariæ Hellenicæ. 6 vols. 8vo, 4*l.* 4*s.*

Greswell (W. Parr). History of the Dominion of Canada. By W. PARR GRESWELL, M.A., under the Auspices of the Royal Colonial Institute. With Eleven Maps. Crown 8vo, 7*s*. 6*d*.

—— Geography of the Dominion of Canada and Newfoundland. By the same Author. With Ten Maps. Crown 8vo, 6*s*.

—— Geography of Africa South of the Zambesi. With Maps. Crown 8vo, 7*s*. 6*d*.

Gross. The Gild Merchant: a Contribution to British Municipal History. By C. GROSS, Ph.D. 2 vols. 8vo, half-bound, 24*s*.

Hastings. Hastings and The Rohilla War. By Sir JOHN STRACHEY, G.C.S.I. 8vo, cloth, 10*s*. 6*d*.

Hodgkin. Italy and her Invaders. With Plates and Maps. By THOMAS HODGKIN, D.C.L. (A.D. 376–553).

Vols. I–II. The Visigothic Invasions. The Hunnish Invasion. The Vandal Invasion, and the Herulian Mutiny. *Second Edition*, 2*l*. 2*s*.

Vols. III–IV. The Ostrogothic Invasion. The Imperial Restoration. *Second Edition*, 36*s*.

Vols. V–VI. The Lombard Invasion, and the Lombard Kingdom. 36*s*.

—— The Dynasty of Theodosius; or, Seventy Years' Struggle with the Barbarians. By the same Author. Crown 8vo, 6*s*.

Hume. Letters of David Hume to William Strahan. Edited with Notes, Index, &c., by G. BIRKBECK HILL, D.C.L. 8vo, 12*s*. 6*d*.

Hunter. A Brief History of the Indian Peoples. By Sir W. W. HUNTER, K.C.S.I. *Eighty-Second Thousand*. Crown 8vo, 3*s*. 6*d*.

Jackson. Dalmatia, the Quarnero, and Istria; with Cettigne in Montenegro and the Island of Grado. By T. G. JACKSON, M.A. 3 vols. With many Plates and Illustrations. 8vo, half-bound, 2*l*. 2*s*.

Johnson. Letters of Samuel Johnson, LL.D. Collected and Edited by G. BIRKBECK HILL, D.C.L. In two volumes. Medium 8vo, half-roan (uniform with Boswell's Life of Johnson), 28*s*.

—— Johnsonian Miscellanies. Arranged and Edited by G. BIRKBECK HILL, D.C.L., LL.D. 2 vols. Medium 8vo, 28*s*.

Jones (Benj.). Co-operative Production. By BENJAMIN JONES. With Preface by the Rt. Hon. A. H. DYKE ACLAND, M.P. 2 vols. Crown 8vo, 15*s*.

Kitchin. A History of France. With numerous Maps, Plans, and Tables. By G. W. KITCHIN, D.D. *Third Edition*. In three Volumes. Crown 8vo, each 10*s*. 6*d*.

Vol. I, to 1453. Vol. II, 1453–1624. Vol. III, 1624–1793.

Knight's Life of Dean Colet. 1823. 8vo, *7s. 6d.*

Lewes, The Song of. Edited, with Introduction and Notes, by C. L. KINGSFORD, M.A. Extra fcap. 8vo, 5*s.*

Lewis (Sir G. Cornewall). An Essay on the Government of Dependencies. Edited by C. P. LUCAS, B.A. 8vo, half-roan, 14*s.*

Lloyd's Prices of Corn in Oxford, 1583–1830. 8vo, 1*s.*

Lucas. Historical Geography of the British Colonies. By C. P. LUCAS, B.A.

Introduction. With Eight Maps. Crown 8vo, 4*s.* 6*d.*

Vol. I. The Mediterranean and Eastern Colonies (exclusive of India). With Eleven Maps. 5*s.*

Vol. II. The West Indian Colonies. With Twelve Maps. 7*s.* 6*d.*

Vol. III. West Africa. With Five Maps. 7*s.* 6*d.*

Vol. IV. South and East Africa. Historical and Geographical. With Ten Maps. 9*s.* 6*d.*

Also in two Parts:—

Part I. Historical, 6*s.* 6*d.* Part II. Geographical, 3*s.* 6*d.*

Ludlow. The Memoirs of Edmund Ludlow, 1625–1672. Edited, with Appendices of Letters and Illustrative Documents, by C. H. FIRTH, M.A. 2 vols. 8vo, 1*l.* 16*s.*

Luttrell's (Narcissus) Diary. A Brief Historical Relation of State Affairs, 1678–1714. 6 vols. 8vo, 1*l.* 4*s.*

Machiavelli (Niccolò). Il Principe. Edited by L. ARTHUR BURD. With an Introduction by LORD ACTON. 8vo, 14*s.*

—— The Prince. Translated by NINIAN HILL THOMSON, M.A. Extra fcap. 8vo, 3*s.* 6*d.* net.

Macray. Annals of the Bodleian Library, Oxford, with a Notice of the Earlier Library of the University. By W. DUNN MACRAY, M.A., F.S.A. *Second Edition, enlarged and continued from* 1868 to 1880. Medium 8vo, half-bound, 25*s.*

Madan. Manuscript Materials relating to the History of Oxford; contained in the Printed Catalogues of the Bodleian and College Libraries. By F. MADAN, M.A. 8vo, 7*s.* 6*d.*

—— The Early Oxford Press. A Bibliography of Printing and Publishing at Oxford, '1468'–1640. With Notes, Appendices, and Illustrations. By FALCONER MADAN, M.A. 8vo, cloth, 18*s.*

Magna Carta, a careful Reprint. Edited by W. STUBBS, D.D., Lord Bishop of Oxford. 4to, stitched, 1*s*.

Metcalfe. Passio et Miracula Beati Olaui. Edited from a Twelfth-Century MS. by F. METCALFE, M.A. Small 4to, 6*s*.

More. The Utopia of SIR THOMAS MORE. Edited by J. H. LUPTON, B.D. 8vo, half-bound, 10*s*. 6*d*. *net*.

Napier and Stevenson. The Crawford Collection of Early Charters and Documents, now in the Bodleian Library. Small 4to, cloth, 12*s*.

OXFORD, University of. For Official Publications, see back of cover.

Pattison. Essays by the late MARK PATTISON, sometime Rector of Lincoln College. Collected and arranged by HENRY NETTLESHIP, M.A. 2 vols. 8vo, 24*s*.

—— Life of Isaac Casaubon (1559–1614). By the same Author. *Second Edition*. 8vo, 16*s*.

Payne. History of the New World called America. By E. J. PAYNE, M.A. Vol. I, 8vo, 18*s*. Vol. II. [*In the Press*.]

—— Voyages of the Elizabethan Seamen to America. Edited by E. J. PAYNE, M.A. *First Series*. HAWKINS. FROBISHER. DRAKE. *Second Edition*. Crown 8vo, 5*s*.

Poole. Historical Atlas of Modern Europe, from the decline of the Roman Empire. Comprising also Maps of parts of Asia and of the New World connected with European history. Edited by R. L. POOLE, M.A. Imperial 4to. Parts I–VI. To be completed in thirty Monthly Parts, each 3*s*. 6*d*. net.

Prothero. Select Statutes and other Constitutional Documents, illustrative of the Reigns of Elizabeth and James I. Edited by G. W. PROTHERO, M.A. Crown 8vo, 10*s*. 6*d*.

—— Select Statutes and other Documents bearing on the Constitutional History of England, from A.D. 1307 to 1558. By the same Editor. [*In Preparation*.]

Ralegh. Sir Walter Ralegh. A Biography. By W. STEBBING, M.A. 8vo, 10*s*. 6*d*.

Ramsay (Sir James H.). **Lancaster and York.** A Century of English History (A.D. 1399–1485). 2 vols. 8vo, with Index, 1*l*. 17*s*. 6*d*.

Index to the above, separately, paper cover, 1*s*. 6*d*.

Ramsay (W. M.). The Cities and Bishoprics of Phrygia. By W. M. Ramsay, D.C.L., LL.D. Royal 8vo.

Vol. I. Part I. The Lycos Valley and South-Western Phrygia. 18s. *net.*

Vol. I. Part II. West and West Central Africa. 21s. *net.*

Ranke. A History of England, principally in the Seventeenth Century. By L. von Ranke. Translated under the superintendence of G. W. Kitchin, D.D., and C. W. Boase, M.A. 6 vols. 8vo, 3*l.* 3*s.*

*** *Revised Index separately*, paper cover, 1*s.*

Rashdall. The Universities of Europe in the Middle Ages. By Hastings Rashdall, M.A. 2 vols. 8vo, with Maps and Illustrations. 2*l.* 5*s.* *net cash.*

Rawlinson. A Manual of Ancient History. By George Rawlinson, M.A. *Second Edition.* Demy 8vo, 14*s.*

Rhŷs. Studies in the Arthurian Legend. By John Rhŷs, M.A., Principal of Jesus College, Oxford. 8vo, 12*s.* 6*d.*

Ricardo. Letters of David Ricardo to T. R. Malthus (1810–1823). Edited by James Bonar, M.A. 8vo, 10*s.* 6*d.*

Rogers. History of Agriculture and Prices in England, A.D. 1259–1793. By James E. Thorold Rogers, M.A.

Vols. I and II (1259–1400). 8vo, 2*l.* 2*s.*

Vols. III and IV (1401–1582). 8vo, 2*l.* 10*s.*

Vols. V and VI (1583–1702). 8vo, 2*l.* 10*s.*

Vols. VII and VIII. [*In the Press.*]

—— First Nine Years of the Bank of England. 8vo, 8*s.* 6*d.*

—— Protests of the Lords, including those which have been expunged, from 1624 to 1874; with Historical Introductions. In three volumes. 8vo, 2*l.* 2*s.*

RULERS OF INDIA: The History of the Indian Empire in a carefully planned succession of Political Biographies. Edited by Sir William Wilson Hunter, K.C.S.I. In crown 8vo. Half-crown volumes.

Akbar. By Colonel Malleson, C.S.I.
Albuquerque. By H. Morse Stephens.
Aurangzíb. By Stanley Lane-Poole, B.A.
Mádhava Ráo Sindhia. By H. G. Keene, M.A., C.I.E.
Lord Clive. By Colonel Malleson, C.S.I.
Dupleix. By Colonel Malleson, C.S.I.
Warren Hastings. By Captain L. J. Trotter.

RULERS OF INDIA (*continued*).

The Marquess of Cornwallis. By W. S. SETON-KARR.
Haidar Alí and Tipú Sultán. By L. B. BOWRING, C.S.I.
The Marquess Wellesley, K.G. By W. H. HUTTON, M.A.
Marquess of Hastings. By Major ROSS-OF-BLADENSBURG, C.B.
Mountstuart Elphinstone. By J. S. COTTON, M.A.
Sir Thomas Munro. By JOHN BRADSHAW, M.A., LL.D.
Earl Amherst. By ANNE THACKERAY RITCHIE and RICHARDSON EVANS.
Lord William Bentinck. By DEMETRIUS C. BOULGER.
The Earl of Auckland. By Captain L. J. TROTTER.
Viscount Hardinge. By his son, VISCOUNT HARDINGE.
Ranjit Singh. By Sir LEPEL GRIFFIN, K.C.S.I.
The Marquess of Dalhousie. By Sir W. W. HUNTER.
John Russell Colvin. By Sir AUCKLAND COLVIN, K.C.S.I., &c.
Clyde and Strathnairn. By Major-General Sir OWEN TUDOR BURNE, K.C.S.I.
Earl Canning. By Sir H. S. CUNNINGHAM, K.C.I.E.
Lord Lawrence. By Sir C. AITCHISON, K.C.S.I., LL.D.
The Earl of Mayo. By Sir W. W. HUNTER, K.C.S.I.

SUPPLEMENTARY VOLUMES.

A Brief History of the Indian Peoples. By Sir W. W. HUNTER, K.C.S.I. *Eighty-Second Thousand.* 3*s.* 6*d.*

James Thomason. By Sir RICHARD TEMPLE, Bart. 3*s.* 6*d.*

Selden. The Table Talk of JOHN SELDEN. Edited, with an Introduction and Notes, by S. H. REYNOLDS, M.A. 8vo, half-roan, 8*s.* 6*d.*

Smith (Adam). Lectures on Justice, Police, Revenue, and Arms. Edited, with Introduction and Notes, by EDWIN CANNAN. 8vo, cloth, 10*s.* 6*d.* *net.*

—— Wealth of Nations. A new Edition, with Notes, by J. E. THOROLD ROGERS, M.A. 2 vols. 8vo, 21*s.*

Sprigg's England's Recovery; being the History of the Army under Sir Thomas Fairfax. 8vo, 6*s.*

Stephens. The Principal Speeches of the Statesmen and Orators of the French Revolution, 1789–1795. With Introductions, Notes, &c. By H. MORSE STEPHENS, M.A. 2 vols. Crown 8vo, 21*s.*

Stubbs. Select Charters and other Illustrations of English Constitutional History, from the Earliest Times to the Reign of Edward I. Arranged and edited by W. STUBBS, D.D., Lord Bishop of Oxford. *Eighth Edition.* Crown 8vo, 8*s.* 6*d.*

—— The Constitutional History of England, in its Origin and Development. *Library Edition.* 3 vols. Demy 8vo, 2*l.* 8*s.*

Also in 3 vols. crown 8vo, price 12*s.* each.

—— Seventeen Lectures on the Study of Mediaeval and Modern History. *Second Edition.* Crown 8vo, 8*s.* 6*d.*

Swift (F. D.). The Life and Times of James the First of Aragon. By F. DARWIN SWIFT, B.A. 8vo, 12*s.* 6*d.*

Tozer. The Islands of the Aegean. By H. FANSHAWE TOZER, M.A., F.R.G.S. Crown 8vo, 8*s.* 6*d.*

Vinogradoff. Villainage in England. Essays in English Mediaeval History. By PAUL VINOGRADOFF, Professor in the University of Moscow. 8vo, half-bound, 16*s.*

Wellesley. A Selection from the Despatches, Treaties, and other Papers of the MARQUESS WELLESLEY, K.G., during his Government of India. Edited by S. J. OWEN, M.A. 8vo, 1*l.* 4*s.*

Wellington. A Selection from the Despatches, Treaties, and other Papers relating to India of Field-Marshal the DUKE OF WELLINGTON, K.G. Edited by S. J. OWEN, M.A. 8vo, 1*l.* 4*s.*

Whitelock's Memorials of English Affairs from 1625 to 1660. 4 vols. 8vo, 1*l.* 10*s.*

Cannan. Elementary Political Economy. By EDWIN CANNAN, M.A. Extra fcap. 8vo, stiff covers, 1*s.*

Raleigh. Elementary Politics. By THOMAS RALEIGH, M.A. *Sixth Edition.* Extra fcap. 8vo, stiff covers, 1*s.*

IV. LAW.

Anson. Principles of the English Law of Contract, and of Agency in its Relation to Contract. By SIR W. R. ANSON, D.C.L. *Eighth Edition.* 8vo, 10*s.* 6*d.*

—— Law and Custom of the Constitution. In two Parts.
Part I. Parliament. *Second Edition.* 8vo, 12*s.* 6*d.*
Part II. The Crown. *Second Edition.* 8vo, 14*s.*

Baden-Powell. Land-Systems of British India; being a Manual of the Land-Tenures, and of the Systems of Land-Revenue Administration prevalent in the several Provinces. By B. H. BADEN-POWELL, C.I.E., F.R.S.E., M.R.A.S. 3 vols. 8vo, with Maps, 3*l.* 3*s.*

—— Land-Revenue and Tenure in British India. By the same Author. With Map. Crown 8vo, 5*s.*

Bentham. An Introduction to the Principles of Morals and Legislation. By JEREMY BENTHAM. Crown 8vo, 6*s.* 6*d.*

Digby. An Introduction to the History of the Law of Real Property. By KENELM E. DIGBY, M.A. *Fourth Edition.* 8vo, 12*s.* 6*d.*

Greenidge. Infamia; its place in Roman Public and Private Law. By A. H. J. GREENIDGE, M.A. 8vo, 10*s.* 6*d.*

Grueber. Lex Aquilia. The Roman Law of Damage to Property: being a Commentary on the Title of the Digest 'Ad Legem Aquiliam' (ix. 2). With an Introduction to the Study of the Corpus Iuris Civilis. By ERWIN GRUEBER, Dr. Jur., M.A. 8vo, 10*s.* 6*d.*

Hall. International Law. By W. E. HALL, M.A. *Fourth Edition.* 8vo, 22*s.* 6*d.*

—— A Treatise on the Foreign Powers and Jurisdiction of the British Crown. By the same Author. 8vo, 10*s.* 6*d.*

Holland. The Elements of Jurisprudence. By T. E. HOLLAND, D.C.L. *Eighth Edition.* 8vo, 10*s.* 6*d.*

—— The European Concert in the Eastern Question, a Collection of Treaties and other Public Acts. Edited, with Introductions and Notes, by T. E. HOLLAND, D.C.L. 8vo, 12*s.* 6*d.*

—— Gentilis, Alberici, I.C.D., I.C.P.R., de Iure Belli Libri Tres. Edidit T. E. HOLLAND, I.C.D. Small 4to, half-morocco, 21*s.*

—— The Institutes of Justinian, edited as a recension of the Institutes of GAIUS, by T. E. HOLLAND, D.C.L. *Second Edition.* Extra fcap. 8vo, 5*s.*

Holland and **Shadwell.** Select Titles from the Digest of Justinian. By T. E. Holland, D.C.L., and C. L. Shadwell, B.C.L. 8vo, 14*s.*

Also sold in Parts, in paper covers, as follows:—

Part I. Introductory Titles. 2*s.* 6*d.*
Part II. Family Law. 1*s.*
Part III. Property Law. 2*s.* 6*d.*
Part IV. Law of Obligations (No. 1). 3*s.* 6*d.*
Part IV. Law of Obligations (No. 2). 4*s.* 6*d.*

Markby. Elements of Law considered with reference to Principles of General Jurisprudence. By Sir William Markby, D.C.L. *Fifth Edition.* 8vo, 12*s.* 6*d.*

Moyle. Imperatoris Iustiniani Institutionum Libri Quattuor; with Introductions, Commentary, Excursus, and Translation. By J. B. Moyle, D.C.L. *Third Edition.* 2 vols. 8vo, 22*s.*

*** Also sold separately:
Vol. I, Introduction, Text, Notes, 16*s.*; Vol. II, Translation, 6*s.*

—— Contract of Sale in the Civil Law. By J. B. Moyle, D.C.L. 8vo, 10*s.* 6*d.*

Pollock and **Wright.** An Essay on Possession in the Common Law. By Sir F. Pollock, Bart., M.A., and Sir R. S. Wright, B.C.L. 8vo, 8*s.* 6*d.*

Poste. Gaii Institutionum Juris Civilis Commentarii Quattuor; or, Elements of Roman Law by Gaius. With a Translation and Commentary by Edward Poste, M.A. *Third Edition.* 8vo, 18*s.*

Raleigh. An Outline of the Law of Property. By Thomas Raleigh, M.A. 8vo, cloth, 7*s.* 6*d.*

Sohm. Institutes of Roman Law. By Rudolph Sohm, Professor in the University of Leipzig. Translated (from the Fourth Edition of the German) by J. C. Ledlie, B.C.L., M.A. With an Introductory Essay by Erwin Grueber, Dr. Jur., M.A. 8vo, 18*s.*

Stokes. Anglo-Indian Codes. By Whitley Stokes, LL.D. Vol. I. Substantive Law. 8vo, 30*s.* Vol. II. Adjective Law. 8vo, 35*s.*

—— First Supplement to the above, 1887, 1888. 2*s.* 6*d.*

—— Second Supplement, to May 31, 1891. 4*s.* 6*d.*

—— First and Second Supplements in one volume, price 6*s.* 6*d.*

Twiss. The Law of Nations considered as Independent Political Communities. By Sir Travers Twiss, D.C.L.

Part I. On the rights and Duties of Nations in time of Peace. New Edition, Revised and Enlarged. 8vo, 15*s.*

V. PHILOSOPHY, LOGIC, &c.

Bacon. Novum Organum. Edited, with Introduction, Notes, &c., by T. FOWLER, D.D. *Second Edition.* 8vo, 15*s*.

—— Novum Organum. Edited, with English Notes, by G. W. KITCHIN, D.D. 8vo, 9*s*. 6*d*.

—— The Essays. Edited, with Introduction and Illustrative Notes, by S. H. REYNOLDS, M.A. Demy 8vo, half-bound, 12*s*. 6*d*.

Berkeley. The works of GEORGE BERKELEY, D.D., formerly Bishop of Cloyne; including many of his writings hitherto unpublished. With Prefaces, Annotations, and an Account of his Life and Philosophy, by A. CAMPBELL FRASER, Hon. D.C.L. and LL.D. 4 vols. 8vo, 2*l*. 18*s*.

The Life, Letters, &c., separately, 16*s*.

—— Selections. With Introduction and Notes. For the use of Students in the Universities. By the same Editor. *Fourth Edition.* Crown 8vo, 8*s*. 6*d*.

Bosanquet. Logic; or, The Morphology of Knowledge. By B. BOSANQUET, M.A. 8vo, 21*s*.

British Moralists. Selections from Writers principally of the Eighteenth Century. Edited by L. A. SELBY-BIGGE, M.A. 2 vols. Crown 8vo, 18*s*.

Butler. The Works of Bishop Butler. Edited by the Right Hon. W. E. GLADSTONE. 2 vols. Medium 8vo, 1*l*. 8*s*.

—— Works, with Index to the Analogy. 2 vols. 8vo, 11*s*.

Fowler. The Elements of Deductive Logic, designed mainly for the use of Junior Students in the Universities. By T. FOWLER, D.D. *Tenth Edition*, with a Collection of Examples. Extra fcap. 8vo, 3*s*. 6*d*.

—— The Elements of Inductive Logic, designed mainly for the use of Students in the Universities. *Sixth Edition.* Extra fcap. 8vo, 6*s*.

—— Logic; Deductive and Inductive, combined in a single volume. Extra fcap. 8vo, 7*s*. 6*d*.

Fowler and Wilson. The Principles of Morals. By T. FOWLER, D.D., and J. M. WILSON, B.D. 8vo, 14*s*.

Also, separately—

Part I. Introductory Chapters. By T. FOWLER, D.D., and J. M. WILSON, B.D. 8vo, 3*s*. 6*d*.

Part II. The Principles of Morals. By T. FOWLER, D.D. 8vo, 10*s*. 6*d*.

Green. Prolegomena to Ethics. By T. H. GREEN, M.A. Edited by A. C. BRADLEY, M.A. *Third Edition.* 8vo, 12s. 6d.

Hegel. The Logic of Hegel; translated from the Encyclopaedia of the Philosophical Sciences. With Prolegomena to the Study of Hegel's Logic and Philosophy. By WILLIAM WALLACE, M.A., LL.D. *Second Edition, Revised and Augmented.* 2 vols. Crown 8vo, 10s. 6d. each.

Hegel's Philosophy of Mind. Translated from the Encyclopaedia of the Philosophical Sciences. With Five Introductory Essays. By WILLIAM WALLACE, M.A., LL.D. Crown 8vo, 10s. 6d.

Hume's Treatise of Human Nature. Reprinted from the Original Edition in Three Volumes, and Edited by L. A. SELBY-BIGGE, M.A. *Second Edition.* Crown 8vo, 8s.

—— Enquiry concerning the Human Understanding, and an Enquiry concerning the Principles of Morals. Edited by L. A. SELBY-BIGGE, M.A. Crown 8vo, 7s. 6d.

Locke. An Essay concerning Human Understanding. By JOHN LOCKE. Collated and Annotated with Prolegomena, Biographical, Critical, and Historical, by A. CAMPBELL FRASER, Hon. D.C.L. and LL.D. 2 vols. 8vo, 1*l.* 12s.

Locke's Conduct of the Understanding. Edited by T. FOWLER, D.D. *Third Edition.* Extra fcap. 8vo, 2s. 6d.

Lotze's Logic, in Three Books; of Thought, of Investigation, and of Knowledge. English Translation; Edited by B. BOSANQUET, M.A. *Second Edition.* 2 vols. Crown 8vo, 12s.

—— Metaphysic, in Three Books; Ontology, Cosmology, and Psychology. English Translation; Edited by B. BOSANQUET, M.A. *Second Edition.* 2 vols. Crown 8vo, 12s.

Martineau. Types of Ethical Theory. By JAMES MARTINEAU, D.D. *Third Edition.* 2 vols. Crown 8vo, 15s.

—— A Study of Religion: its Sources and Contents. *Second Edition.* 2 vols. Crown 8vo, 15s.

Plato. A Selection of Passages from Plato for English Readers; from the Translation by B. JOWETT, M.A. Edited, with Introductions, by M. J. KNIGHT. 2 vols. Crown 8vo, gilt top, 12s.

VI. PHYSICAL SCIENCE AND MATHEMATICS, &c.

Acland. Synopsis of the Pathological Series in the Oxford Museum. By Sir H. W. ACLAND, M.D., F.R.S. 8vo, 2s. 6d.

Adler. Alternating Generations; a Biological Study of Oak Galls and Gall Flies. By HERMANN ADLER, M.D. Translated and Edited by C. R. STRATON, F.R.C.S. Ed., F.E.S. With coloured Illustrations of forty-two Species. Crown 8vo, cloth extra, 10s. 6d. *net.*

Aldis. A Text-Book of Algebra: with Answers to the Examples. By W. S. ALDIS, M.A. Crown 8vo, 7s. 6d.

Aplin. The Birds of Oxfordshire. By O. V. APLIN. 8vo. with a Map and one coloured Plate, 10s. 6d.

Baynes. Lessons on Thermodynamics. By R. E. BAYNES, M.A. Crown 8vo, 7s. 6d.

Beddard. A Monograph, Structural and Systematic, of the Order Oligochaeta. By FRANK EVERS BEDDARD, M.A., F.R.S. 4to. *With Plates and Illustrations.* Demy 4to, 2l. 2s. *net.*

BIOLOGICAL SERIES. (Translations of Foreign Memoirs.)

I. Memoirs on the Physiology of Nerve, of Muscle, and of the Electrical Organ. Edited by J. BURDON-SANDERSON, M.D., F.R.SS.L. & E. Medium 8vo, 1l. 1s.

II. The Anatomy of the Frog. By Dr. ALEXANDER ECKER, Professor in the University of Freiburg. Translated, with numerous Annotations and Additions, by GEORGE HASLAM, M.D. Medium 8vo, 21s.

IV. Essays upon Heredity and kindred Biological Problems. By Dr. AUGUST WEISMANN. Authorized Translation. Crown 8vo.

Vol. I. Edited by E. B. POULTON, S. SCHÖNLAND, and A. E. SHIPLEY. *Second Edition.* 7s. 6d.

Vol. II. Edited by E. B. POULTON and A. E. SHIPLEY. 5s.

BOTANICAL SERIES.

History of Botany (1530–1860). By JULIUS VON SACHS. Authorized Translation, by H. E. F. GARNSEY, M.A. Revised by ISAAC BAYLEY BALFOUR, M.A., M.D., F.R.S. Crown 8vo, 10*s.*

Comparative Anatomy of the Vegetative Organs of the Phanerogams and Ferns. By Dr. A. DE BARY. Translated and Annotated by F. O. BOWER, M.A., F.L.S., and D. H. SCOTT, M.A., Ph.D., F.L.S. Royal 8vo, half-morocco, 1*l.* 2*s.* 6*d.*

Outlines of Classification and Special Morphology of Plants. By Dr. K. GOEBEL. Translated by H. E. F. GARNSEY, M.A., and Revised by ISAAC BAYLEY BALFOUR, M.A., M.D., F.R.S. Royal 8vo, half-morocco, 1*l.* 1*s.*

Lectures on the Physiology of Plants. By JULIUS VON SACHS. Translated by H. MARSHALL WARD, M.A., F.L.S. Royal 8vo, half-morocco, 1*l.* 11*s.* 6*d.*

Comparative Morphology and Biology of Fungi, Mycetozoa and Bacteria. By Dr. A. DE BARY. Translated by H. E. F. GARNSEY, M.A. Revised by ISAAC BAYLEY BALFOUR, M.A., M.D., F.R.S. Royal 8vo, half-morocco, 1*l.* 2*s.* 6*d.*

Lectures on Bacteria. By Dr. A. DE BARY. *Second Improved Edition.* Translated by H. E. F. GARNSEY, M.A. Revised by ISAAC BAYLEY BALFOUR, M.A., M.D., F.R.S. Crown 8vo, 6*s.*

Introduction to Fossil Botany. By Count H. ZU SOLMS-LAUBACH. Translated by H. E. F. GARNSEY, M.A. Revised by ISAAC BAYLEY BALFOUR, M.A., M.D., F.R.S. Royal 8vo, half-morocco, 18*s.*

Index Kewensis; an enumeration of the Genera and Species of Flowering Plants from the time of Linnaeus to the year 1885 inclusive. Edited by Sir J. D. HOOKER and B. D. JACKSON. 2 vols. 4to, half-morocco, 10*l.* 10*s. net.*

Annals of Botany. Edited by ISAAC BAYLEY BALFOUR, M.A., M.D., F.R.S., SYDNEY H. VINES, D.Sc., F.R.S., D. H. SCOTT, M.A., Ph.D., F.L.S., and W. G. FARLOW, M.D.; assisted by other Botanists. Royal 8vo, half-morocco, gilt top.

Already published—

Vol. I, Parts I–IV, consisting of pp. 415, and pp. cix, Record of Current Literature and Necrology, with eighteen Plates, in part coloured, and six Woodcuts. 1*l.* 16*s.*

Vol. II, Parts V–VIII, consisting of pp. 436, and pp. cxxxviii, Record of Current Literature and Necrology, with twenty-four Plates, in part coloured, and twenty-three Woodcuts. 2*l.* 2*s.*

Annals of Botany (*continued*).

Vol. III, Parts IX–XII, consisting of pp. 495, and pp. cxviii, Record of Current Literature and Necrology, with twenty-six Plates, in part coloured, and eight Woodcuts. *2l. 12s. 6d.*

Vol. IV, Parts XIII–XVI, consisting of pp. 385, and pp. cxviii, Record of Current Literature, with twenty-two Plates, in part coloured, and thirteen Woodcuts. *2l. 5s.*

Vol. V, Parts XVII–XX, consisting of pp. 526, with twenty-seven Plates, in part coloured, and four Woodcuts. *2l. 10s.*

Vol. VI, Parts XXI–XXIV, consisting of pp. 383, with twenty-four Plates, in part coloured, and sixteen Woodcuts. *2l. 4s.*

Vol. VII, Parts XXV–XXVIII, consisting of pp. 532, with twenty-seven Plates, in part coloured, and five Woodcuts. *2l. 10s.*

Vol. VIII, Parts XXIX–XXXII, consisting of pp. 470, with twenty-four Plates, in part coloured, and five Woodcuts. *2l. 10s.*

Vol. IX, Parts XXXIII–XXXVI, consisting of pp. 668, with twenty-five Plates, in part coloured, and thirteen Woodcuts. *2l. 15s.*

Vol. X, Parts XXXVII–XL, consisting of pp. 661, with twenty-eight Plates, in part coloured, and three Woodcuts. *2l. 16s.*

Vol. XI, Part XLI, with nine Plates. *14s.*

Reprints from the 'Annals of Botany.'

Holmes and Batters. Revised List of British Marine Algae (with Appendix). Price *2s. 6d. net.*

Baker (J. G.). A Summary of New Ferns (1874–90). Price *5s. net.* This forms a supplement to the Synopsis Filicum.

—— A Synopsis of the Genera and Species of Museae. Price *1s. 6d. net.*

—— New Ferns of 1892–3. Price *1s. net.*

Bradley's Miscellaneous Works and Correspondence. With an Account of Harriot's Astronomical Papers. 4to, *17s.*

Chambers. A Handbook of Descriptive Astronomy. By G. F. CHAMBERS, F.R.A.S. *Fourth Edition.*

Vol. I. The Sun, Planets, and Comets. 8vo, *21s.*

Vol. II. Instruments and Practical Astronomy. 8vo, *21s.*

Vol. III. The Starry Heavens. 8vo, *14s.*

Cremona. Elements of Projective Geometry. By LUIGI CREMONA. Translated by C. LEUDESDORF, M.A. *Second Edition.* 8vo, 12*s.* 6*d.*

—— Graphical Statics. Two Treatises on the Graphical Calculus and Reciprocal Figures in Graphical Statics. By the same Author. Translated by T. HUDSON BEARE. Demy 8vo, 8*s.* 6*d.*

Daubeny's Introduction to the Atomic Theory. 16mo, 6*s.*

Dixey. Epidemic Influenza, a Study in Comparative Statistics. By F. A. DIXEY, M.A., D.M. Medium 8vo, 7*s.* 6*d.*

Donkin. Acoustics. By W. F. DONKIN, M.A., F.R.S. *Second Edition.* Crown 8vo, 7*s.* 6*d.*

Elliott. An Introduction to the Algebra of Quantics. By E. B. ELLIOTT, M.A. Demy 8vo, 15*s.*

Emtage. An Introduction to the Mathematical Theory of Electricity and Magnetism. By W. T. A. EMTAGE, M.A. *Second Edition.* Crown 8vo, 7*s.* 6*d.*

Etheridge. Fossils of the British Islands, Stratigraphically and Zoologically arranged. Part I. PALAEOZOIC. By R. ETHERIDGE, F.R.SS.L. & E., F.G.S. 4to, 1*l.* 10*s.*

Euclid Revised. Containing the Essentials of the Elements of Plane Geometry as given by Euclid in his first Six Books. Edited by R. C. J. NIXON, M.A. *Third Edition.* Crown 8vo, 6*s.*

Sold separately as follows:—

Book I. 1*s.*	Books I, II. 1*s.* 6*d.*
Books I–IV. 3*s.*	Books V, VI. 3*s.* 6*d.*

Euclid. Geometry in Space. Containing parts of Euclid's Eleventh and Twelfth Books. By R. C. J. NIXON, M.A. Cr. 8vo, 3*s.* 6*d.*

Fisher. Class-Book of Chemistry. By W. W. FISHER, M.A., F.C.S. Fourth Edition. Crown 8vo, 4*s.* 6*d.*

Fock (Andreas). An Introduction to Chemical Crystallography. By ANDREAS FOCK, Ph.D. Translated and Edited by W. J. POPE; with a Preface by N. STORY-MASKELYNE, M.A. Crown 8vo, 5*s.*

Galton. The Construction of Healthy Dwellings. By Sir DOUGLAS GALTON, K.C.B., F.R.S. *Second Edition.* 8vo, 10*s.* 6*d.*

—— Healthy Hospitals. Observations on some points connected with Hospital Construction. By the same Author. With Illustrations. *Second Edition.* 8vo, 10*s.* 6*d.*

Greenwell. British Barrows, a Record of the Examination of Sepulchral Mounds in various parts of England. By W. GREENWELL, M.A., F.S.A. Together with Description of Figures of Skulls, General Remarks on Prehistoric Crania, and an Appendix by GEORGE ROLLESTON, M.D., F.R.S. Medium 8vo, 25*s.*

Gresswell. A Contribution to the Natural History of Scarlatina, derived from Observations on the London Epidemic of 1887–1888. By D. ASTLEY GRESSWELL, M.D. Medium 8vo, 10*s.* 6*d.*

Hamilton and **Ball.** Book-keeping. New and enlarged Edition. By Sir R. G. C. HAMILTON and JOHN BALL. Cloth, 2*s.*

Ruled Exercise books adapted to the above may be had, price 1s. 6d.; also, adapted to the Preliminary Course only, price 4d.

Harcourt and **Madan.** Exercises in Practical Chemistry. By A. G. VERNON HARCOURT, M.A., and H. G. MADAN, M.A. *Fifth Edition.* Crown 8vo, 10*s.* 6*d.*

Madan. Tables of Qualitative Analysis. By H. G. MADAN, M.A. Large 4to, paper covers, 4*s.* 6*d.*

Hensley. Figures made Easy. A first Arithmetic Book. By LEWIS HENSLEY, M.A. Crown 8vo, 6*d.* Answers, 1*s.*

—— The Scholar's Arithmetic. 2*s.* 6*d.* Answers, 1*s.* 6*d.*

—— The Scholar's Algebra. Crown 8vo, 2*s.* 6*d.*

Hughes. Geography for Schools. By ALFRED HUGHES, M.A. Part I. Practical Geography. With Diagrams. Crown 8vo, 2*s.* 6*d.*

Johnston. An Elementary Treatise on Analytical Geometry. By W. J. JOHNSTON, M.A. Crown 8vo, 10*s.* 6*d.*

Kelvin. The Molecular Tactics of a Crystal. By LORD KELVIN, P.R.S. With Twenty Illustrations. 8vo, 3*s.* 6*d.*

Maclaren. A System of Physical Education: Theoretical and Practical. By ARCHIBALD MACLAREN. *New Edition,* re-edited and enlarged by WALLACE MACLAREN, M.A., Ph.D. Crown 8vo, 8*s.* 6*d.* *net.*

Maxwell. A Treatise on Electricity and Magnetism. By J. CLERK MAXWELL, M.A. *Third Edition.* 2 vols. 8vo, 1*l.* 12*s.*

—— An Elementary Treatise on Electricity. Edited by WILLIAM GARNETT, M.A. 8vo, 7*s.* 6*d.*

Minchin. A Treatise on Statics with Applications to Physics. By G. M. MINCHIN, M.A.

Vol. I. Equilibrium of Coplanar Forces. *Fifth Edition.* 8vo, 10*s.* 6*d.*

Vol. II. Non-Coplanar Forces. *Fourth Edition.* 8vo, 16*s.*

—— Hydrostatics and Elementary Hydrokinetics. Crown 8vo, 10*s.* 6*d.*

Müller. On certain Variations in the Vocal Organs of the Passeres. By J. MÜLLER. Translated by F. J. BELL, B.A., and edited by A. H. GARROD, M.A., F.R.S. With Plates. 4to, 7*s.* 6*d.*

Nisbet. Studies in Forestry. Being a Short Course of Lectures on the Principles of Sylviculture, delivered at the Botanic Garden, Oxford. By JOHN NISBET, D.Oec. Crown 8vo, 6*s. net.*

Nixon. Elementary Plane Trigonometry. By R. C. J. NIXON, M.A. Crown 8vo, 7*s.* 6*d.* (See EUCLID REVISED.)

Phillips. Geology of Oxford and the Valley of the Thames. By JOHN PHILLIPS, M.A., F.R.S. 8vo, 21*s.*

—— Vesuvius. Crown 8vo, 10*s.* 6*d.*

Powell. The Surgical Aspect of Traumatic Insanity. By H. A. POWELL, M.A., M.D. 8vo, stiff cover, 2*s.* 6*d.*

Prestwich. Geology, Chemical, Physical, and Stratigraphical. By the late Sir JOSEPH PRESTWICH, D.C.L., F.R.S., F.G.S. In two Volumes.

Vol. I. Chemical and Physical. Royal 8vo, 1*l.* 5*s.*

Vol. II. Stratigraphical and Physical. With a new Geological Map of Europe. Royal 8vo, 1*l.* 16*s.*

Price. Treatise on Infinitesimal Calculus. By BARTHOLOMEW PRICE, D.D., F.R.S.

Vol. I. Differential Calculus. *Second Edition.* 8vo, 14*s.* 6*d.*

Vol. II. Integral Calculus, Calculus of Variations, and Differential Equations.

Vol. III. Statics, including Attractions; Dynamics of a Material Particle. *Second Edition.* 8vo, 16*s.*

Vol. IV. Dynamics of Material Systems. *Second Edition.* 8vo, 18*s.*

Price (W. A.). A Treatise on the Measurement of Electrical Resistance. By W. A. PRICE, M.A., A.M.I.C.E. 8vo, 14*s.*

Pritchard. Astronomical Observations made at the University Observatory, Oxford, under the direction of C. PRITCHARD, D.D. No. 1. Royal 8vo, paper covers, 3*s*. 6*d*.

—— No. II. Uranometria Nova Oxoniensis. A Photometric determination of the magnitudes of all Stars visible to the naked eye, from the Pole to ten degrees south of the Equator. Royal 8vo, 8*s*. 6*d*.

—— No. III. Researches in Stellar Parallax by the aid of Photography. Royal 8vo, 7*s*. 6*d*.

—— No. IV. Researches in Stellar Parallax by the aid of Photography. Part II. Royal 8vo, 4*s*. 6*d*.

Rigaud's Correspondence of Scientific Men of the 17th Century, with Table of Contents by A. de MORGAN, and Index by J. RIGAUD, M.A. 2 vols. 8vo, 18*s*. 6*d*.

Rolleston. Scientific Papers and Addresses. By GEORGE ROLLESTON, M.D., F.R.S. Arranged and edited by WILLIAM TURNER, M.B., F.R.S. With a Biographical Sketch by EDWARD TYLOR, F.R.S. 2 vols. 8vo, 1*l*. 4*s*.

Rolleston and Jackson. Forms of Animal Life. A Manual of Comparative Anatomy, with descriptions of selected types. By GEORGE ROLLESTON, M.D., F.R.S. *Second Edition.* Revised and enlarged by W. HATCHETT JACKSON, M.A. Medium 8vo, 1*l*. 16*s*.

Russell. An Elementary Treatise on Pure Geometry. With numerous Examples. By J. WELLESLEY RUSSELL, M.A. Cr. 8vo, 10*s*. 6*d*.

Selby. Elementary Mechanics of Solids and Fluids. By A. L. SELBY, M.A. Crown 8vo, 7*s*. 6*d*.

Smith. The Collected Mathematical Papers of Henry John Stephen Smith, M.A., F.R.S., late Savilian Professor of Geometry in the University of Oxford. Edited by J. W. L. GLAISHER, Sc.D., F.R.S. 2 vols. 4to, 3*l*. 3*s*.

Smyth. A Cycle of Celestial Objects. Observed, Reduced, and Discussed by Admiral W. H. SMYTH, R.N. Revised, condensed, and greatly enlarged by G. F. CHAMBERS, F.R.A.S. 8vo, 12*s*.

Stewart. An Elementary Treatise on Heat, with numerous Woodcuts and Diagrams. By BALFOUR STEWART, LL.D., F.R.S. *Sixth Edition*, Revised with Additions, by R. E. BAYNES, M.A. Crown 8vo, 8*s*. 6*d*.

Story-Maskelyne. Crystallography. A Treatise on the Morphology of Crystals. By N. STORY-MASKELYNE, M.A., F.R.S., Professor of Mineralogy, Oxford. Crown 8vo, 12*s*. 6*d*.

Swinhoe. Catalogue of Eastern and Australian Lepidoptera Heterocera in the Collection of the Oxford University Museum. By Colonel C. Swinhoe, F.L.S., F.Z.S., &c. Part I. Sphinges and Bombyces. 8vo, with eight Plates, 21*s*.

Thompson. A Glossary of Greek Birds. By D'ARCY W. THOMPSON. 8vo. Buckram, 10*s*. *net*.

Thomson. Notes on Recent Researches in Electricity and Magnetism, intended as a sequel to Professor CLERK MAXWELL'S 'Treatise on Electricity and Magnetism.' By J. J. THOMSON, M.A., F.R.S. 8vo, 18*s*. 6*d*.

Van 't Hoff. Chemistry in Space. Translated and Edited by J. E. MARSH, B.A. Crown 8vo, 4*s*. 6*d*.

Vernon-Harcourt. Rivers and Canals. The Flow, Control and Improvement of Rivers, and the Design, Construction, and Development of Canals. By L. F. VERNON-HARCOURT, M.A. *New Edition.* 2 vols. 8vo. 1*l*. 11*s*. 6*d*.

—— Harbours and Docks; their Physical Features, History, Construction, Equipment, and Maintenance. 2 vols. 8vo, 25*s*.

Walker. The Theory of a Physical Balance. By JAMES WALKER, M.A. 8vo, stiff cover, 3*s*. 6*d*.

Watson. A Treatise on the Kinetic Theory of Gases. By H. W. WATSON, D.Sc., F.R.S. *Second Edition.* Crown 8vo, 4*s*. 6*d*.

Watson and **Burbury.** A Treatise on the Application of Generalized Co-ordinates to the Kinetics of a Material System. By H. W. WATSON, D.Sc., and S. H. BURBURY, M.A. 8vo, 6*s*.

—— The Mathematical Theory of Electricity and Magnetism. Vol. I. Electrostatics. 8vo, 10*s*. 6*d*.
Vol. II. Magnetism and Electrodynamics. 8vo, 10*s*. 6*d*.

Westwood. Thesaurus Entomologicus Hopeianus. By J. O. WESTWOOD, M.A., F.R.S. With 40 Plates. Small folio, 7*l*. 10*s*.

Williamson. Chemistry for Students. With Solutions. By A. W. WILLIAMSON, Phil. Doc., F.R.S. Extra fcap. 8vo, 8*s*. 6*d*.

Woollcombe. Practical Work in General Physics. By W. G. WOOLLCOMBE, M.A., B.Sc. Crown 8vo, 3*s*.

—— Practical Work in Heat. By the same Author. Crown 8vo, 3*s*.

—— Practical Work in Light and Sound. By the same Author. Crown 8vo, 3*s*.

—— Practical Work in Electricity and Magnetism. By the same Author. [*In preparation.*]

VII. ART AND ARCHAEOLOGY.

Butler. Ancient Coptic Churches of Egypt. By A. J. BUTLER, M.A., F.S.A. 2 vols. 8vo, 30*s*.

Farnell. The Cults of the Greek States. By L. R. FARNELL, M.A. 8vo. Vols. I and II, with 61 Plates and over 100 Illustrations, *cloth*, 1*l*. 12*s*. *net*. [Vol. III, completing the work, *in preparation*.]

Fortnum. Maiolica; A Historical Treatise on the Glazed and Enamelled Earthenwares of Italy, &c., with Plates, Marks, &c. By C. DRURY E. FORTNUM, D.C.L. Small quarto, 2*l*. 2*s*. *net*.

—— A Descriptive Catalogue of the Maiolica and Kindred Wares in the Ashmolean Museum, Oxford. With Introductory Notice and Illustrations. By C. DRURY E. FORTNUM, D.C.L. Small quarto, 10*s*. 6*d*. *net*.

Gardner. Catalogue of the Greek Vases in the Ashmolean Museum. By PERCY GARDNER, M.A., Litt.D. Small folio, linen, with 26 Plates. Price 3*l*. 3*s*. *net*.
Three hundred and fifty copies only printed, all of which are numbered.

Head. Historia Numorum. A Manual of Greek Numismatics. By BARCLAY V. HEAD, D.C.L. Royal 8vo, half-morocco, 42*s*.

Jackson. Dalmatia, the Quarnero and Istria; with Cettigne in Montenegro and the Island of Grado. By T. G. JACKSON, M.A., R.A. 3 vols. 8vo. With many Illustrations. Half-bound, 42*s*.

—— Wadham College, Oxford; Its Foundation, Architecture and History. With an Account of the Family of Wadham, and their seats in Somerset and Devon. By T. G. JACKSON, M.A., R.A. 4to, half-persian, 2*l*. 2*s*. *net*.

MUSIC. Farmer. Hymns and Chorales for Schools and Colleges. Edited by JOHN FARMER, Organist of Balliol College. 5*s*.
☞ *The Hymns without the Tunes*, 2*s*.

Hullah. Cultivation of the Speaking Voice. By JOHN HULLAH. *Second Edition*. Extra fcap. 8vo, 2*s*. 6*d*.

Ouseley. Treatise on Harmony. By Sir F. A. GORE OUSELEY, Bart. *Third Edition*. 4to, 10*s*.

—— Treatise on Counterpoint, Canon, and Fugue, based upon that of Cherubini. *Second Edition*. 4to, 16*s*.

—— Treatise on Musical Form and General Composition. *Second Edition*. 4to, 10*s*.

MUSIC (*continued*).

Troutbeck and Dale. Music Primer. By J. TROUTBECK, D.D., and F. DALE, M.A. *Second Edition.* Crown 8vo, 1*s*. 6*d*.

Raffaelle, Drawings by, in the University Galleries, Oxford. Drawn on Stone by JOSEPH FISHER. In an ornamental box, 21*s*.

Robinson. A Critical Account of the Drawings by Michel Angelo and Raffaelle in the University Galleries, Oxford. By SIR J. C. ROBINSON, F.S.A. Crown 8vo, 4*s*.

Thomson. A Handbook of Anatomy for Art Students. With many Illustrations. By Prof. ARTHUR THOMSON, M.A. 8vo, buckram, 16*s*. *net*.

Tyrwhitt. Handbook of Pictorial Art. With Illustrations, and a chapter on Perspective by A. Macdonald. By R. St. J. TYRWHITT, M.A. *Second Edition.* 8vo, half-morocco, 18*s*.

Upcott. Introduction to Greek Sculpture. By L. E. UPCOTT, M.A. Crown 8vo, 4*s*. 6*d*.

Vaux. Catalogue of the Castellani Collection in the University Galleries, Oxford. By W. S. W. VAUX, M.A. Crown 8vo, 1*s*.

VIII. PALAEOGRAPHY.

Allen. Notes on Abbreviations in Greek Manuscripts. By T. W. ALLEN, M.A. Royal 8vo, 5*s*.

Fragmenta Herculanensia. A Descriptive Catalogue of the Oxford copies of the Herculanean Rolls, together with the texts of several papyri. Edited by WALTER SCOTT, M.A. Royal 8vo, 21*s*.

—— Thirty-six Engravings of Texts and Alphabets from the Herculanean Fragments, taken from the original Copper-plates executed under the direction of the Rev. JOHN HAYTER, M.A., and now in the Bodleian Library. With an Introductory Note by BODLEY'S LIBRARIAN. Folio, *small paper*, 10*s*. 6*d*.; *large paper*, 21*s*.

Gardthausen. Catalogus Codicum Graecorum Sinaiticorum. Scripsit V. GARDTHAUSEN Lipsiensis. With Facsimiles. 8vo, *linen*, 25*s*.

Herculanensium Voluminum Partes II. 1824. 8vo, 10*s*.